SPEAKING OF CARDINALS

Speaking
of Cardinals

BY THOMAS B. MORGAN

Essay Index Reprint Series

BOOKS FOR LIBRARIES PRESS
FREEPORT, NEW YORK

INTERNATIONAL STANDARD BOOK NUMBER:
0-8369-2002-3

LIBRARY OF CONGRESS CATALOG CARD NUMBER:
70-134119

PRINTED IN THE UNITED STATES OF AMERICA

CONTENTS

SPEAKING OF CARDINALS

1. Cardinals Are Easy—in Rome

THE first time I saw a cardinal was in Holy Week of 1919. The event and the cardinal are colorfully though delicately sketched and safely preserved in my memory plasm. I like splashing pageantry and ravishing splendor, especially when the men who officiate awe me with their authority and dignity, to say nothing of the purple and gold and precious stones all around them.

Young and imperious, I had arrived in Rome as the new staff correspondent for the Associated Press, just the week before. The highest Roman ecclesiastics I had ever seen previously were one lone archbishop, the late Archbishop Elder of Cincinnati, and three bishops, all of whom had come to Steubenville, Ohio, in 1903, when I was in high school. They had come to consecrate Father James J. Hartley, parish priest of Holy Name Church, as the bishop of Columbus. I saw that ceremony. Of it, I have written before.

But I had never seen a cardinal until this Holy Week in Rome. The new assignment had made it mandatory if the Vatican ceremonies were to be covered with any pride to the A.P. and glory to me, albeit reflected, that I see a great deal of cardinals. I realized that though the United States had had sometimes three cardinals at a time, I had never even got near one. I had seen every President of the

United States since Theodore Roosevelt, either on their trips about the country or on their campaign jaunts. Certainly it was easier to see a President in the United States than it was to see a cardinal.

We all know how a President is in election-duty bound to get out and get around if he is to win the hearts and, more desirably for him, the votes of the people. A cardinal, on the other hand, can stay at home as much as he wishes and can make his trips as private and be as choosy as he wishes. He is answerable to no one. Though there were cardinals in Baltimore, New York, and Boston, and later in Philadelphia, Chicago, and Detroit, they stayed at home most of the time to tend their considerable flocks. They did not have to put in an appearance anywhere else, unless they liked to get around and show themselves, which as age crept on and thrill wore off turned out to be more of a chore than a frolic.

Christian Rome breathes the Passion during Holy Week. Of the scores of sacred devotions, on Holy Thursday I chose to attend St. Peter's. There, an arresting symbolism on the eve of Gethsemane stirred the emotions. During the afternoon, the ritual of washing the papal altar emblematized the purging for the resurrection. All the canons and priests in purple cassocks and ermine capes filled the apse. Scores of bishops and monsignors prayed and silently meditated. The Gregorian chant by the Julian choir and prelates poured sonorously through the echoing arches of the overpowering basilica. The massive papal altar, its top an imposing slab of white marble situated right under the dome, had been cleared of all ornaments in acccordance with Holy Week ritual.

Two priests in stole and chasuble amid the incantations and the multitudes approached the altar, the one bearing a crystal flask of water, the other a silver *flacon* of wine.

They poured the water and wine over the bare marble and then descended. Then, slowly and solemnly, the stately figure of Cardinal Merry del Val, archpriest of St. Peter's, ascended the steps and approached the altar. His lofty bearing set the focus for the vast and breathless crowd. Tall and erect, seemingly predestined for the high and solemn role, he bestowed an overawing presence on the function. His reverent face, chiseled to grace the sublime rite, signalized the solemn depth of the sacred re-enactments. He was the first cardinal I ever saw.

He held in his right hand a slender reed with a round sponge at the end. While the liturgical tones of the choir filled the edifice, he ceremoniously applied the sponge to the marble and then slowly descended.

The priests then came forward a second time and poured the water and wine. Six canons in purple and ermine approached the altar, each bearing a reed and sponge. They in turn performed the same ceremony as the archpriest. More water and wine were poured and still more canons engaged in the rite. When all the water and wine were used and the last wave of canons had applied the sponges, the ceremony ended with the Litany of the Saints, and . . . I had seen a cardinal.

From then on, I was to see cardinals quite regularly. They had just started to use the Villa Borghese, the exotic public park of Rome, as a promenading retreat. Several of them in black cassocks for street wear would stroll through the gardens just to get the air and stretch the limbs. One could almost set a watch by the hours they kept. I often saw Cardinal Gasquet, the English Benedictine, Billot, the French royalist, Van Rossum, the Dutch prefect of Propaganda Fide, and Pompili, the cardinal-vicar. They all had a slow and even pace, and just as their time was personally clocked when they entered the gardens, it was just as intimately precise when they left. Then each to his own choice dropped into some church at the moment of the Angelus.

As I saw them in their daily adherence to an established personal regime, I reflected on their ancient addictions. Through time, many hundreds of them had trodden the same hills and wandered through the same gardens in Rome. Though the dignity of cardinal was not of apostolic origin, yet the lofty rank possessed its very deep recesses in the early centuries of the Christian faith. The word is derived from the Latin *cardo,* meaning hinge, and was applied to those important priests who held administrative functions about the bishop of Rome. In modern times we would probably call them pivot men or, as is so often used, key men. We can see how the Pope, when the Church had extended to foreign lands, would call the key men to be his chief advisers. Nowadays, this is the Sacred College of Cardinals.

They were not invested with the "red hat" until 1245, when Pope Innocent IV first designated this elaborate adornment as their symbol of office. In its most ceremonial form, it is a low-crowned hat with a broad brim. Cords of red and gold embellished with tassels drape from the base of the crown down over the shoulders. Today, while this lavish headpiece is the badge of rank, it is never worn but remains in the cardinal's possession to be placed on his casket and then hung in his cathedral at his death. There it is allowed to disintegrate into the air. Quite probably to his complete satisfaction, less elaborate headgear suffices during the cardinal's lifetime.

Along with the hat, Innocent IV accorded the red robes of watered silk as a token of a cardinal's pledge to shed, if necessary, his blood for the faith. On days of mourning and during the penitential season, the red robes must be laid aside. Then purple is substituted. In fact, the Italians ascribe to the purple a greater importance than the red. Purple is the emblem of royalty. In Rome they often refer to a cardinal as the *porporato,* "the purpled one." They rank above bishops, archbishops, and patriarchs. In Europe, only a king can precede a cardinal.

But most interesting of all in these times was the dean of the Sacred College, Cardinal Vincenzo Vannutelli, six feet three and nobly born. He was eighty-four and lived to be ninety-six. With his secretary he would walk a mile out and a mile back in a leisurely gait, taking sixty minutes, no more, no less. His route varied from day to day, but whatever route he took, there was no variation in his gait nor in his timing. When he became a nonagenarian, no change was noticeable in his bearing. Of tough physical fiber, he could eat a six- or seven-course dinner of galantines, lobster, game, or beef. He continued to take wine until the last. Though his face did not disguise the ravages of age, his movements were brisk, his conversation lively, and his wit ready.

He was cardinal-bishop of the ancient see of Ostia, on the Roman coast. Ostia had remained but a scattering of fishermen's huts for centuries until Mussolini built it up as a seaside resort for Rome. The ancient cathedral was, by either vandal, wind, or wave, destroyed. This meant that at ninety, Vannutelli had to get to work. With the zeal of a youthful pastor in a promising parish, he built a new cathedral.

Getting money out of the little resort was a trying task. Its hundreds of thousands of summer patrons sought lightness of heart rather than loftiness of spirit. In winter it counted only three thousand inhabitants, and none of them had money. To pay bills, the revered dean offered to lay aside cardinalatial lordliness and write articles for an American newspaper syndicate, for money. The syndicate, geared more for profit than charity, imposed an exacting condition. Its agents had sensed the priestly urge for solvency and exploited it. They offered to clear the debt if he would write a biography of the reigning pope, Pius XI. This was a tough assignment for a cardinal. Vannutelli said he would ask the Pontiff's permission.

In due course he approached the Pope. The Pope was seventy-five and active, too. Welcoming the youthful verve of so earnest a pastor, he rewarded it by granting the request to write of his life. Vannutelli was happy and retired to his residence in the Dataria Palace to prepare for this retarded show of talent in literary enterprise. In the meantime he informed the syndicate of his success. They in turn congratulated him and then set out to aggrandize their initiative and even stretch its glory by advertising in the papers, circus-like, that the Cardinal-Dean of the Sacred College was to write "the exclusive, intimate and only authorized life of the Pope."

The work was started. But the published ads began pouring back into the Vatican. The Pope was shown their gay and glorious claims. Pius XI was a decisive man. He did not like this garishness mixed with trade, even the newspaper trade. He immediately gave orders to announce publicly that the American syndicate had claimed too much in "the authorized life." He wanted no chances taken in dragging his person into a business transaction. He withdrew the permission.

When Vannutelli was told of it, he was downcast. Obediently, he bowed to the Pope's order.

"The Holy Father is right," said the aged though active cardinal, submitting to the higher word.

The articles were forgotten; but hearing of the incident, rich American businessmen came to Vannutelli's assistance. Though he was prepared to enter a new profession at ninety-two, he was spared the task. The money came in. When all was paid, he consecrated the cathedral with his own hands when he was ninety-five. He died the following year.

Cardinals aplenty appeared in Rome for the canonization of Joan of Arc in 1920. Then I was out of Rome tracking down a typhus epidemic in Yugoslavia, searching out a *comitagi* outbreak in Montenegro, and following the United States Adriatic fleet which was then stationed in Spalato, Dalmatia. But when I got back to Rome in 1921, I began to see cardinals in columns and even mass formations and to learn to know them in a somewhat cozy intimacy.

Cardinals always gathered for the annual anniversary celebration of the papal coronation. Then Benedict XV was reigning. This was the first time I ever saw the Sacred College in procession, at least that part of it which was resident in Rome. The ceremony is held in the Sistine Chapel, and the ritual consists in an abridged version of the actual coronation, which is always held in St. Peter's. Those who were so lucky as to get tickets congregated in two great halls, the Sala Regia and the Sala Ducale, and then in the Sistine Chapel itself. In another large room, the Hall of Vestments, the ritualistic robing of the cardinals and the Pope took place.

In the Hall of Vestments before the function, amid the cardinals in red and ermine, the papal master of ceremonies, Monsignor Respighi, placed the golden tiara, studded with precious gems, upon the Pope's head. The Pontiff in an enveloping mantle of silver and gold was lifted in his ceremonial throne. The procession began. The cardinals preceded him in twos according to their order of seniority, the junior ones coming first. The dazzling cortege passed first through the Sala Regia and then across the Sala Ducale to enter the Sistine Chapel. Swiss Guards and other Vatican soldiery wore uniforms of grand parade. Carried by purple-clad prelates, the huge ostrich-feather fans which accompany the Holy Father on occasions of high pomp enhanced the richness of the scene. Strange to the austere religious customs of the Nordic world, the Italian crowds burst out in vociferous shouts of *"Evviva il Papa,"* and clapped their hands with almost fanatic enthusiasm.

I sat with the diplomatic corps. The stunning variety of color is hardly ever equaled. The Sistine Chapel, rich in its magnificence of frescoes by many of the great masters, including Michelangelo, seemed warmly to welcome the moving procession. It was as colorful as the chapel. Red of watered silk, ermine, the red and gold of the Noble Guard, the red, yellow, and blue of the Swiss Guards, the purple of the papal prelates, and finally the rich gold and silver robe of the Pope surmounted by the bejeweled tiara found their places in the setting as if it were exactly what the great artists intended.

And the Sacred College was truly the senate of the Roman Church. Venerable and experienced, the cardinals seemed reposed in wisdom and so comfortably tucked into their ermine capes. A score of them were there. As they passed slowly down the aisles, they were impressive in their staid complacency. Except for the throne of Peter, they had all reached the highest post in the gift of the Church. It was as if life had been settled for them and they were now designated to bestow their talents and counsel wherever it should be required. Submissively, but not without a large measure of authority, they were accepting their world, and that world had accepted them conclusively, amid the clatter and bustle of the mass of mankind.

The procession was opened by an escort of Swiss Guards and the prelates of the papal court. The first of the cardinals to appear were Cardinal Bisleti and Cardinal Billot. Bisleti was of small and stocky stature while Billot was tall with a slight stoop. I was later to remember Bisleti because whenever a cardinal was ill, he invariably would go to see him, then leave his bedside saying, "I am next, I am next." He went for years to visit his indisposed brethren and always came away with the premonition of his own impending death. He lived fifteen years after that, to become an octogenarian, ominously seeing many pass on before him.

Cardinal Billot crowned Pius XI, with whom he quarreled violently over the French political situation. The strain became so great that he decided to resign the cardinalate and renounced all his rights and privileges in the Sacred College. He left Rome to retire to a Jesuit college in one of the suburbs. He was the first cardinal to resign in four hundred years.

Then the ascetic, tawny face of Cardinal Ascalesi seized attention. Tall and with marked Greek features, he was then but forty-eight, the youngest member in the Sacred College. Robes were draped about him as if he were a chosen prelatial subject for an artist of the Renaissance. His brown eyes, piercing and scintillating, lit up his olive-tan countenance. He was then assigned to Rome but later became the archbishop of Naples. Good looks as well as ecclesiastical authority stood him in good stead, for he was quite often chosen to officiate at royal weddings. The Fascists liked his presence, too, and woefully adopted him as a Fascist cardinal. Things got so hot for him two decades later when the Allies took Naples that he desired to withdraw to Rome to ease the situation. But he was asked to stay on in Naples, where the Neapolitans, just as magnanimous as they are excitable, were ready to forgive even though they would not forget.

I was present when he officiated at the miracle of St. Januarius, the patron saint of Naples. The miracle consists in the liquefaction of the saint's blood, which is kept in a highly engraved phial. The church was filled with howling Neapolitans. While the priests made their incantations, a band played. Finally Cardinal Ascalesi lifted up the phial, looked into its crystal cylinder, then waved it high in the air. The blood was liquid. The miracle had been performed. The crowds surged toward the altar in a mob. The phial is placed upon the forehead as a benediction. Seeing me in the sanctuary, the Cardinal called me to the altar.

"You see," he said, lifting up the phial before the assembled crowds, and to satisfy any doubt of mine, "it has liquefied."

He then placed it upon my forehead.

Many years ago, the late Archbishop Ryan of Philadelphia attended the miracle. He was amazed and not a little abashed at the blasting band and the wild scenes of the shouting Neapolitans, quite in contrast with the religious reverence in American churches.

"It is enough to make anybody's blood boil," he is reported to have mused in a strong Irish accent.

Then in the procession walked Cardinal Fruhwirth, an Austrian of the Dominican order in white robes rather than red. In contrast with the ascetic face of Ascalesi, his was of no ordered design and somewhat tilted forward. He was, besides, short and stumpy but with all his unhappy physique was reputed a power in the Pope's counsels. By pure chance he was paired with Cardinal Gasquet, the Englishman whose membership in the Benedictine order prescribed black robes. That morning they were remote from an exacting strain which had previously run through their earlier years.

Fruhwirth had been made a cardinal in 1915 while Gasquet was already a member of the Sacred College. World War I was on. No love was exacted between enemy and enemy. But they were cardinals and they met. Britain and France had just launched their great offensives to make the knockout of Germany and Austria.

"Well, my dear Eminence," greeted Fruhwirth in an apparent effort to clear the hostile air, "let's not talk of war."

"My dear Lord Cardinal," returned the stern and rigid Gasquet with British finality, "let's not talk of peace."

Others in the procession that day were Van Rossum, the Dutchman, reputed at that time to be the most profound scholar in the Roman Church; Giorgi, ruddy and of a suave mien; Ragonesi, mild and unobtrusive; Merry del Val, tempering the awe with a savoring affability; Pompili, large and cumbersome; and De Lai, measured and careful. Completing the ranks were the aged Granito di Belmonte and Vannutelli. Granito succeeded to the deanship on the death of Vannutelli.

After the ceremonies of the celebration of the coronation the procession was reformed and emerged, greeted by the shouts and applause of the unreserved Italians.

But while at this function there were but a score of cardinals, within a year Benedict XV died and the conclave to elect a new pope was convened. Cardinals began to arrive from everywhere. For nine days they attended funeral services for the deceased pontiff either in the Sistine Chapel or in St. Peter's. Every day brought new princes of the Church—Mercier of Belgium, Bourne of England, Logue of Ireland, Kakowski of Poland, Lucon of Rheims, Dubois of Paris, and others from Spain, Germany, and Austria. Besides, there were twenty-eight Italians. Non-Italians totaled twenty-five.

When the funeral rites were all concluded, preparations for the election of the new pope began. We all interviewed the various cardinals on any hints about the next Holy Father. None wished to give any indication of their choice. Seemingly, too, none appeared to be a candidate. Since it was generally accepted, then, that an Italian would succeed to the throne, certainly no Italian would ever commit himself. Italian cardinals would literally lapse into sealed silence. And why? This was it—there is a Roman proverb, *Entra Papa, esce cardinale,* which means, "He who enters as Pope comes out a cardinal." In other words, a favorite never wins. No cardinal wanted to be a favorite, and each feared lest his name be even mentioned.

The late James A. Mills, who had been sent down from Paris to assist me in covering the conclave and who later was assigned on stories all over the world, interviewed Cardinal Logue, archbishop of Armagh. This Irish prelate was well known in America on account of a visit he made in 1908. On his arrival in New York then, he was met by the usual array of ship news reporters. They told him that Irish Home Rule had been approved by the British parliament while he was on the ocean. Then they asked him if this meant peace for Ireland. The prelate, blessed with an uncommon sense of Irish wit and realizing the Irish propensity for combativeness, did not have to think long for an answer.

"Peace for Ireland?" he retorted. "God forbid."

Logue was eighty now. His wit was still with him.

"So you're from America?" he pleasantly inquired of Mills in a strong Irish flavor.

Mills replied that not only was he from America but he knew many there were curious to learn who would be the next pope.

But even that suggestion did not lead the Irish prelate to comment on the conclave.

"I was in America once," he mused, turning the subject and insisting on his own way about what he should say.

"How did you like it?" returned my A.P. colleague.

"They sent one of those ger-rl r-reporter-rs to inter-rview me," reminisced the Primate of Ireland. "And, do yoh knowh whhat? She asked me whhat I tho't was the gr-reatest thing in the wur-rld. I told her, 'That depends, miss,' I said. 'I suppose for a hungr-ry man,' I told her-r, 'it would be a foine meal. For-r you, miss,' I said, 'it may be a nice bonnet.' 'Then as for-r me,' I told her, 'I sup-pose sometimes that the gr-reatest thing in the wur-rld is a pinch of snuff.'"

On the sixth day after the last funeral service, the con-clave was to be sealed, "locked in" and isolated from the world. An air of heavy responsibility hovered over the entire Vatican. In a solemn cortege, fifty-three cardinals attended Mass in the Pauline Chapel. In the afternoon, their varying figures showing the seriousness with which they undertook their task, they all entered the Sistine Chapel to take the oath before the actual sealing of the doors and entrances.

At dusk they emerged from the Sistine Chapel each bearing a lighted candle. Cardinal Gasparri as the cam-erlengo of the Holy Roman Church was charged with inspecting each entrance personally to assure that it was unfailingly locked. Escorted by a squad of Swiss Guards, still in their multicolored uniforms and carrying their medieval halberds, he plodded slowly from entrance to entrance, his way lighted by torches carried by two purple-clad prelates. The memory of centuries was embodied in the quaint though solemn rite.

As the torchlit scene passed from entrance to entrance, the rest of the cardinals waited and watched in the Court-yard of St. Damasus. The softness of the candlelight in the Rome dusk cast a golden hue over their purple vestments. The falling darkness, the weird glow of torch and candle, the stony silence of the courtyard, men with halberds, and the cardinals gave mute witness that a centuries-old scene was re-enacted in all its unspoiled purity. It was a moving augury that great events were at hand. At the last entrance, Cardinal Gasparri gave orders for those having nothing to do with the election to leave. We emerged through the portals, but not without taking one last look at the stirring scene which was to herald the election of a new pope.

Three cardinals occupied the places of least importance in the array. They were the "babies" of the college and had been promoted only a few months previously. They were Tacci, Laurenti, and Ratti—all Italians. But what a difference the conclave made! Tacci only lacked one vote to be elected pope; Laurenti was elected but refused to accept; Ratti was elected and took the name of Pius XI.

2. *Go As Far As You Like*

We HAVE often glorified a righteous indignation. But this was more than that. While it may have been righteous it was more than indignation. It was even anger. It was wrath. Yes, we can affirm and in clear conscience say that in his robes of purple, purple because it was a period of mourning over the Pope's death, that His Eminence was mad.

With all due deference, custom and form dictate for the newspapers that they should never say that a cardinal was mad. In the case of the Pope they never say even that he was angry when things have gone wrong. They may say that he was displeased, which, though often an understatement, is stronger than "We are not amused."

Often popes have been very mad, and in recent times, too. Pope Pius X was actually in a frenzy when he drove the Austrian ambassador out of the Vatican in 1914 after being asked to impart the apostolic benediction to the Austrian Army.

"Get out of my sight! Get out of my sight!" he is officially reported to have said. "We grant blessings to no one who provokes the world to war."

And I have actually seen a pope who was in the throes of unreserved ire, righteous though it was. In the midst of the quarrel between Pope Pius XI and Mussolini

15

in 1931, I was received in audience. The quarrel arose because Mussolini had disbanded all Catholic clubs and had insisted on their being fascistized. The night before my audience he had broadcast a message to the world trying to discredit the Holy See for interfering in Italian politics. The Pope called this a distortion of the facts, to put it politely. As I entered his library, he assailed me with questions about the Mussolini message. One would have thought that it was I who was on the spot. He asked how it was transmitted, what countries had received it, and what newspapers had published the text. Rising, he clenched his fist. His lips quivered. His voice had a tremor. He vowed that he would find a way to shame the dictator before the world even though Mussolini controlled the telegraphs.

This was when he called in Monsignor Francis J. Spellman of Boston, now cardinal-archbishop of New York, to smuggle an encyclical to all the press of the world. There was drama in it—how the Pope had outwitted Mussolini.

But now we have a cardinal who was mad. The facts which led up to his emotional crisis and the events which followed have all been chronicled in detail. But that Cardinal O'Connell of Boston was mad has been veiled in the conventions of journalistic courtesy.

Some men cannot rise to a supreme expression of anger. They are the cold and perhaps supine ones. But it was not so with His Eminence of Boston. He had a superior talent for getting mad. Even in the very height of his rising wrath he had a most fortunate faculty of being able to emit the right epigram at the right moment. He dealt his blows to confound and terrorize the adversaries. Those who were fortunate enough to witness an encounter silently urged him on, for it was often a spectacle of delight. You wished that he would be the more provoked so that his retorts might be all the more poignant.

The cause of his anger resided in the fact that Cardinal Gasparri, who, as we said, was camerlengo, the one who ruled the conclave to elect a new pope, had rushed the balloting through so that the Boston archbishop did not arrive in time even to cast one vote. The story has often been told how the Italian government had placed a special train at his disposal to speed him to Rome from the steamer at Naples. But all this was of no avail. He arrived in Rome to be told that the new successor to St. Peter had been chosen even in the last moments of his journey and precisely when the special train was making its frantic efforts to get him there on time. It would seem to anyone that it was Gasparri's aim to beat the special train.

O'Connell and Gasparri had had a feud on anyway. He had not liked Gasparri in the position of secretary of state. Under a previous pope, Cardinal Merry del Val had been secretary of state. Not alone did he want Merry del Val as secretary of state, as a tried and intimate friend of long standing, he had wanted him pope. It was natural for him to conclude that it was Gasparri who was the undoing of all his designs.

In the long journey from Boston in the slow 10,000-ton steamer *President Wilson,* he had been hoping to get to the conclave to turn the tide for Merry del Val. He had thought that he could speak to some of the other cardinals in a general sort of way to show them how Merry del Val would make an excellent pope. But Gasparri had forestalled it. When he stepped from the platform of the train, a Vatican prelate greeted him with the news that Achille Ratti of Milan had been chosen pope that very morning.

The joy that he had shown when the Italian government had provided a special train changed in an instant to heated rage. He paced up and down the platform, his fists clenched, his teeth grit, and his jaw set. His combative face became redder and redder. All standing about wondered what had beset him. Going off to one side, he called a newsman to him.

"This is the work of Gasparri!" he exclaimed, biting his words. His lips were parched dry. "Gasparri only tolerates us for our dollars," he emitted as if he were ready then to come to grips with the cardinal who had ruined his cherished ambition.

"Go as far as you like on this story," he told the newsman in a parting command to convey his reproof.

He was driven to the Vatican and immediately entered the conclave, which was still in session even though the Pope had been elected. From what he afterward admitted to me, he was like a man hunting for his adversary among a crowd of mutual friends. The speed with which he got to his man was only impeded by the imposition of the ceremony of genuflecting before the new pope. But when the ceremony was over, he hunted out his rival.

"A nice thing you have done," he blurted in perfect Italian.

As hot as O'Connell was, just as cool was Gasparri. He was a shrewd and wily diplomat. He was one of those who never got mad. It had become a fight in which the suave adversary had refused to say something to give the other cause for abuse.

"How are you, my dear Eminence?" the Italian said in velvety and graceful tones.

"I'm all right, but why could you not have waited for

me?" impulsively demanded O'Connell with an imperious shake of the head.

"We simply followed the Apostolic Constitution," replied the perspicacious diplomat of the Holy See, quite content with his accomplishment and knowing that what was done could not be undone.

But the anger of O'Connell had not subsided.

"Yes, yes," he said in sarcastic voice and with curling lip, "you follow the constitution. You interpret the constitution your way when it suits your purpose. But America will not be denied. We Americans are not to be ignored."

But the calm and self-possessed camerlengo just shrugged his shoulders. That gesture only did more to increase Bostonian wrath. When O'Connell got to his hotel, he still was burning in his internal ire. That evening he paced up and down the sidewalk before his hotel. Rage as he would, there was nothing to be done. The new pope was reigning, but the feud with Gasparri had deepened.

The Pope was elected on a Tuesday, and according to rote the coronation of the Pope must occur the following Sunday. Great splendor ruled the event. And while five days had elapsed since O'Connell had set foot on the station platform in Rome, his ill humor increased. He was forced to watch the ceremony of crowning the new pope. He was compelled to comply with the ritual of genuflecting before him, kissing his slippered foot, his ring, and then of embracing him. It would have fulfilled a coddled dream to have done this for Merry del Val.

Great as was the rejoicing and lavish as was the pageant, O'Connell could see nothing that was right in it. Even during the sacred function he had remarked to Cardinal Bourne of England that a lot of it was quite unnecessary.

"Why do they have all this marching up and down with all these robes?" he told me he had said to the Archbishop of Westminster.

"It's ritual," replied the English prelate.

"It's unnecessary," retorted O'Connell.

When I met him after the ceremony, he asked me what I thought of it. I replied that it was a highly colorful function.

"All unnecessary," he growled. "Why didn't they say the Mass and put the crown on his head? That would have done it."

Edgar Ansell Mowrer, then Rome correspondent for the *Chicago Daily News,* reported that he told him that Belasco could have done a better job.

In harmony with his own virile and aggressive nature, O'Connell had taken seriously to heart the advice which had been given him by Pope Leo XIII when in 1901 the Holy Father had elected him bishop of Portland, Maine. The Pontiff had received his new bishop in audience before he was to leave his six-year rectorship of the North American College in Rome for the promotion and his see.

"As the head of a diocese," declared the venerable Supreme Pastor, then ninety-two, "there is no use today for a mere mystic. The bishop of today and especially in America must be a man of high and keen intellectual vision, thoroughly in touch with conditions that affect the public and spiritual welfare of his diocese and his nation. He must be a man of action. That is his particular duty as a bishop."

The personality of William O'Connell fitted the papal blueprint both by heredity and acquirement. Such an incisive design encompassed his dashing temperament and tenacious drive. And even beyond these exacting requisites, he possessed other talents which the next pope also discerned. For though it would appear that this prelate of dash and drive was not adapted for diplomacy, he was chosen by Pope Pius X to be his legate to Japan, a mission which was regarded as extremely high bracket in the hierarchical table.* His diplomacy not only satisfied the Pope but delighted him as well. He was immediately tabbed for heavier administrative duties. In this resides the reason why he in his turn became the archbishop of Boston.

On that pinnacle he manifested his talent for action and his gift of vision with such completeness that it is quite certain that Leo XIII would have rejoiced in the extemporaneous and informal advice he had given him as a youthful bishop. His zeal for getting things done penetrated all parts of the Boston area, though he did not find it an easy berth. Debts weighed on the activities of many parishes. Catholic education needed expansion. A more rigid organization was imperative. The ties between the parishes and the chancery were loose. Many pastors were deficient in the strict requirements of Catholic discipline.

O'Connell launched out to wipe out the debts of parishes in the red. He had been such a disciplinarian in this regard that when he died on April 22, 1944, all the old parishes were free of debt. The only parishes with heavy indebtedness were the more recent ones he had set up. Altogether in his thirty-seven years as archbishop he had erected more than two hundred new parishes. He appointed a commission to apply the provisions of the canon law all through the archdiocese. This especially was designed to tighten the relations between the priests and the chancery. He exercised stricter control over all parish priests and their assistants. He issued orders even fixing the hours they were to keep. Assistant pastors were not al-

* *The Listening Post,* G. P. Putnam's Sons, 1944.

lowed to own cars, and even full pastors were forbidden their use unless they could show good reason why a car was necessary.

His personality had so permeated the parishes that he was regarded as a living exemplification of firm episcopal authority. He was revered for all that he said and did. The ties which bound the large mass of the population to him took on the attributes of almost blind obedience. Since the population of Boston is four-fifths Roman Catholic, the position he held as a high priest was far greater in its influence than any political authority who ever administered the city or the state. He knew he possessed this latent power. He knew also when to use it.

No more opportune occasion came than when Governor James M. Curley, his oft spanked political *enfant terrible,* tried to railroad a bill to establish a lottery in the state of Massachusetts. All the Boston newspapers attacked the lottery. It was condemned on moral grounds as well as economic. It was decried as an escape from bona-fide taxing to hoodwink the public into thinking that it was paying the state debts while still having fun. The Protestant ministers were a unit in their opposition. But, despite such heavy phalanxes of public persuasion against the measure, the bill passed to its third reading by a majority of 108 to 101.

By this time the tiring opposition had despaired of being able to forestall defeat. The legislature itself was resigned to the acceptance of the bill because each legislator was now ready to jump on the bandwagon for its enactment. On the very evening before the measure was scheduled for its third and final vote, the newspapers received a telephone call from the archiepiscopal residence saying that Cardinal O'Connell had a statement to make. Newsmen were rushed to his home.

O'Connell, as we saw, had lived a number of years in Italy, where state lotteries are an established institution. He had seen at first hand how the citizenry had been led into squandering their meager pittances in a false hope. The state had served to make them poorer. The Cardinal's statement deplored the bill. It was called an "out-and-out gambling device." Calling on his Italian experience, he declared that everywhere that lotteries were operated they had become an instrument of corruption. The method by which the state administration hoped to replenish the depleted state treasury was only an excuse to endorse and legalize gambling not only among the people but by the state itself, he said.

This was front-page news in all the papers. The legislators had a whole morning to assimilate what the Cardinal had said. But what he had said had more or less been said before in the spirited though ineffective campaigns by press and pulpit. Now it was the Cardinal who had said it. That made the difference. On that basis, the politicians began to weigh their own electoral positions. That morning votes began to change sides. As the time for the third reading approached in the afternoon, more than enough evidence existed to show that the lottery would be defeated. When the vote was taken, 187 voted against the measure and only 40 for it. Sixty-eight representatives had changed their minds. Eighteen more who had not voted in the previous balloting now had also gone with the opposition. The unmistakable weight of O'Connell's influence had decided the issue. Curley was spanked again.

Curley's various political meanderings had drawn a permanent frown, if not always a slap, from the Cardinal. O'Connell had shown a marked predilection for men of high moral standards in public office and especially if they were Catholics. His reasoning as a churchman was simple.

If a Catholic official turned out badly or even unsatisfactorily, in certain Boston circles this would be interpreted as a reflection on the Church. Good men would always be a credit to the Church. Curley's political career did not measure up to his yardstick.

After the Presidential elections of 1932, Curley was waiting for a political reward from President Roosevelt. He had campaigned for the Democratic ticket in the Middle West and by virtue of his oratory had personally claimed a part in the victory. He had regarded this part as so impressive that he expected to rate a cabinet position. It was rumored that he wanted to be secretary of the treasury. But when the new cabinet was announced Curley's name was disappointingly missing.

In the fall of 1933 Cardinal O'Connell visited Rome. One evening I was his guest at dinner at the Grand Hotel. He always liked to be freshened up on Roman goings-on. A new United States ambassador to Rome, Breckinridge Long, had been installed. He knew something of the new ambassador, he said. Then I suggested that the Rome post had been sought by one of his own communicants. He was eating a chicken sandwich and not much else, since he always ate very lightly. He dropped his eyelids, betrayed a slight familiarity with this notion, but asked just the same who the Bostonian was who was self-proposed as United States ambassador. My answer was Curley.

"I heard that," he said quietly with a certain omniscience in the subject matter, which made me reluctant to go on.

There was a lull.

"I wonder what else you have heard," he elicited as if it were all in a pleasant spirit of reciprocal exchange.

He was interested, though I could not discern how much he had already known. I mentioned that Curley had been

quite intent on obtaining a cabinet position first of all.
It had been told to me that he wanted to be secretary of
the treasury, I said.

"Navy," he murmured in decisive correction without
looking up from the sandwich but still showing not only
political ubiquity but thoroughness as well.

I then related how Curley, after failing to receive a
cabinet position, had sought to be ambassador to Rome.
He frowned. He listened. The President had been em-
barrassed by this insistence of the former Boston mayor
for the Rome embassy, I said. At that time, it was not
thought good politics to send a Catholic to Rome.
Roosevelt eventually sent Catholics to London, Poland,
Ireland, Belgium, Spain, and elsewhere, but a Catholic in
Rome gave rise to unpleasant forebodings and innuendoes
in the political nip and tuck. There would be too much
hobnobbing with the papacy, though Catholics had been
ambassadors there before. A devout adherent of the faith
is our ambassador there now in James C. Dunn. Of all
men, Curley would be just the one who would make it
hard for the Democrats to explain what a Catholic was
doing in Rome.

O'Connell looked at me sidewise and smiled. He understood the political innuendo of it all. I continued:

Roosevelt called in James A. Farley, a devoted son of
Rome, too, who was then chairman of the Democratic
National Committee and in general charge of patronage.
They talked the Rome post over and both agreed that the
situation, being what it was, made it poor politics to send
a Catholic to Rome. Roosevelt instructed Farley to offer
Curley the ambassadorship to Poland, which was available.

When Curley called on Farley next day to press his case,
Farley did not think Rome was his best choice. Farley
was not one to send a loyal Democrat away empty-

handed. He told Curley that Poland was open. Why did he not take Poland? There were so many Poles in Boston. They would like it. Still, Curley wanted Rome. There were more Irish in Boston. Farley went into the political angles of the Rome embassy and tried to show Curley how it was not good national politics to send a Catholic to Rome. That reply did not satisfy Curley. He thought that it was the best politics in the world, meaning the world of James M. Curley. He could not accept Poland. He could not see that Rome was not good politics—for him. It was good for Boston—so why not? Curley was going to show Farley.

O'Connell was now greatly engrossed in what I had related. It was plain that he had not heard the ramifications of the story before.

Persistent Curley called on the Italian ambassador in Washington, Sig. Augusto Rosso. He asked the envoy if there would be any objection by the Italian government if a Catholic should become United States ambassador to Rome. Sig. Rosso replied that the Italian government certainly placed no objection whatever. It would instead be very pleased to have a Catholic if the United States so decided. Curley asked the Ambassador to write him a note saying there was no objection to a Catholic. The Ambassador complied. He went away with the nominal blessing and approval of the Italian embassy.

Pursuing his quest, he called on the Apostolic Delegate. Again the question was asked whether there was any objection on the part of the Holy See to the appointment of a Catholic as American ambassador to Rome. Affably and not at all disconcerted, the Apostolic Delegate replied that it would be a source of pleasure to the Holy See to know that a Catholic had been appointed to the Rome post. Curley begged the Delegate to jot it down—there was a green light for a Catholic appointee to Rome. The Pope's representative complied in a general way which, though quite innocuous, was wholly satisfactory to James M. Curley.

Meanwhile the persistence of the former Boston mayor, together with his local diplomatic incursions, had been reported to the President. He called Farley. He asked him to get Breckinridge Long, of St. Louis, on the telephone. Long had been assistant secretary of state under Wilson and had been a pal of the President's when he was undersecretary of the Navy in the same administration. The call was put through to the President. They exchanged old-time pleasantries, then the golden voice asked Long how he would like to go to Rome. Long replied as a loyal Democrat that he would do anything "the Boss" asked. Long accepted. The Rome post was filled.

Next morning, fortified with the unofficial *placet* of the Italian embassy and reinforced by the informal *nihil obstat* of the Apostolic Delegate, Curley paid his promised visit of the showdown to James A. Farley. He accused Farley or somebody of trying to give him the run-around. He had the documentary proof that it was not only legal but highly desirable to send a Catholic to Rome—the Italian embassy had said so and so had the Apostolic Delegate. Farley was consoling and evidently tried to tell him that he should see the situation in its right light. Curley could see it in the right light, only that light was his own.

"But I'm sorry, Jim," said Farley procrastinating before he was to deliver the death blow. "Rome is out. The Boss got Breckinridge Long to take Rome."

Long had arrived during the summer and was by this time well ensconced in the post.

O'Connell looked up. Then he looked down. Then he looked at me.

"Better this man," he said. "Better this man."

Never once did he utter the name Curley.

The O'Connell repudiation continued. Curley decided to run for mayor in 1937. The Boston mayor is elected on a nonpartisan ticket. There were a number of candidates but a new dark horse, one who had been a former secretary to Curley, popped up—handsome Maurice J. Tobin, thirty-six and reputedly honest. Curley spurned the newcomer in the Goliath-David tradition. He called his own chances of election "a soft touch" and even wagered $25,000 at five to four that he would be elected.

Up until the very eve of election, it looked like Curley. He went around Boston welcomed and cheered. He knew his political charm was bound to turn the tide.

But a skillful campaign ruse was perpetrated in this election by an editor of the *Boston Post*. Whether the tactics were ethical or unscrupulous was quite beside the point because up until now no punches were pulled or holds barred. Right across the front page on election morning, the civic-minded as well as the scornful could read in large black type above the masthead of the paper a warning, a friendly counsel, a means to save Boston itself from ignominy and degradation. It read:

"Cardinal O'Connell in speaking to the Alumni Association said: 'The walls are raised against honest men in civic life.' You can break down those walls by voting for an honest, clean, competent young man, MAURICE TOBIN today. He will redeem the city and take it out of the hands of those who have been responsible for graft and corruption."

The make-up of this paragraph made it appear as if the Cardinal had actually spoken for the election of Tobin.

What the clever editor had done was to use just ten words of a speech which O'Connell had delivered months previously. The exhortation to vote for Tobin was his own creation. Unless the civic-minded watched the punctuation closely, they could not decipher the catch. Many thousands did not watch the punctuation. Among the first to recognize the implication of it all were the Curley managers.

Voting had already begun. A Curley spokesman was sent to the Cardinal's house to ask audience. The spokesman was kept waiting in an antechamber. Every minute seemed to count a thousand votes going the wrong way. The Cardinal was not to be hurried. What was more important to the archdiocese, he was engaged on a highly intricate diocesan matter. Even after the hour's wait, he could not see the Curley spokesman. His ecclesiastical duties took marked precedence over political controversy.

The Curley managers wanted a repudiation of the *Post* and a denial that O'Connell had authorized the publication of the ten-word advice, especially since it had been trickily made to appear that he had endorsed Tobin and even urged the voters to support him. They wanted the Cardinal to denounce it as a deception. Curley's men intended to broadcast the denial throughout Boston, hoping thereby to stem the tide and turn it in their favor instead. But O'Connell was above their entreaties as if he could not descend to mingle in their not too sanctified traffic.

The *Post* was gobbled up by all the hundreds of thousands who held the Cardinal in worshipful reverence. For good or for bad, the subtle streamer fulfilled its electoral grand slam. Women carried a copy of the paper to their neighbors shouting, "His Eminence has come out for the lad." Groups went down to the polls in lively enthusiasm.

Certainly for those who were on the fence the stealthy streamer settled their doubts and aroused them from their civic inertia by firing them with a kind of awakened self-righteousness that they were doing the right thing electorally at least for this once.

Tobin was overwhelmingly swept into office that day. He had beaten the engaging and cocksure Curley by 25,520 votes. Losing, Curley did not turn and blame it on the trick streamer. He knew that was indeed ground where he was always careful about the way he trod. Instead, when he discovered that the women had turned to Tobin more than the men, he found words for public solace in the new mayor's youth and handsome frame. "Just a beauty contest," he said.

No one ever ventured to find out whether the editor of the *Post* had previously received any cardinalatial approval for his ingenuity and enterprise. Certain it is that whether he did or whether he did not, the demonstrative silence of His Eminence after the election confirmed an approval and left no doubt how he stood about Curley. Tobin was taken to his heart in the years which followed and was often invited into the sanctuary whenever the Cardinal said Mass. This was approval thrice blessed.

Cardinal O'Connell certainly had left his imprint on Boston, and on the whole state of Massachusetts. Power, latent and seldom unleashed, resided as much in his personality as in his office. He knew that that power was almost supreme and yet he only used it on those rare occasions when his word was necessary to enforce a principle where he discerned a moral issue. Speaking with him, anyone would feel his inherent but charily used authority. Whenever the call would come for a show of strength, he knew how to wield it. The manner in which he imposed his will was part of his own innate talent in sensing how to rule and yet make it appear as if it were by common consent. This strength of the resting lion was recognized in all social strata of Boston. It was certainly recognized by the politicians. They called him "Number One."

3. His Eminence Refuses to Be Pope

I T MAY be incredible but it is nevertheless true that not only one cardinal but at least two, to my knowledge, have refused to wear the white robes of supreme pontiff even after they have been elected by a two-thirds majority of the Sacred College of Cardinals. The first was Cardinal Serafini, who refused to assume the chair of St. Peter in the election which finally chose Pius X in 1903. He had begged his brother princes of the Church to excuse him because he felt he did not possess the strength to carry the burden of the high office.

I personally knew the second. He was Cardinal Laurenti. O'Connell had told me about him in the conclave of 1922 which finally elected Pius XI.

The bejeweled tiara was to be placed upon his head. Where he sat was to become the papal throne. Fifty-two cardinals in solemn and secret conclave had elected him pope, ruler of four hundred million Catholic souls. In the breathless silence and to the awed amazement of them all, he had said no.

He was known endearingly as "Piccolo" to his colleagues and intimates. American prelates and students in Rome had spoken of him as "Little Laurenti." Standing in all his cardinalatial dignity, he only reached five feet four, but what he lacked in height he made up in girth—and brains. In chunky build and low stature he resembled the late Senator Hiram Johnson, glasses and all; though unlike the stormy Californian's, his face was placid and benign. Formally he was Camillo Cardinal Laurenti. Now, at sixty, he had refused the foremost ecclesiastical office in the world. That chance would never come again.

He could wisecrack on occasions, smile nearly always, but his greatest qualities lay in his profound scholarship and in his knowing how to treat the exposed nerves of human nature. Every ounce of his energy had been given to his ecclesiastical mission. He had remained fastened to his work in the Propaganda Fide congregation for thirty-seven years. Many of these he had spent as a professor there. He had not traveled, though he had gained a rare insight into the personal deadlocks of mind and spirit, for while he was professor, students of all races and from all parts of the world came to him. He discovered the threads that made the whole world kin.

Born in the abject humbleness of the Italian rural village of Monte Porzio, which was hidden in the isolated recesses of the Alban Hills, twenty miles from Rome, he had passed his boyhood among the vineyards, the herds of sheep and goats, and the terraced gardens on the back-breaking slopes. It was an eleventh-century hill town, built for defense, and in its unspoiled entirety could offer the little Camillo at his birth in 1861 only what it had offered boys born when it was founded in 1078. As a child, therefore, he lived eight centuries ago.

Like many a medieval antecedent, he donned the cassock as a boy of twelve. Though the thought of the skirt would have proved a nightmare for a modern American boy trying to climb a fence or steal a base, it was not so bad even though regulations required that he keep it on.

American students in Rome today often play baseball in their cassocks, and while it seems a quaint, albeit nostalgic, performance, they do play. And in that same way Camillo played, but his sports were limited to long walks, with his classmates from the Frascati Seminary, over the hills where on every clear day they could look to the north and see the dome of St. Peter's. He had been to Rome on a primitive cart to see the sights. When he reached eighteen he went to live there as a student of the Capranica Theological College. He was indeed a country boy harassed by uncontrollable blushing and rural shyness, but he distinguished himself in all his scholastic studies and was graduated with the highest honors in theology and philosophy. At twenty-three he was ordained priest.

It was following his ordination that the College of Propaganda Fide congregation appointed him professor of philosophy. Little Camillo, as he was then known, became one of the monumental teachers whom the students year after year chiseled in their memories as one of the greatest scholars of the Roman Catholic Church. His prowess as a lecturer and preacher permeated the score or more of colleges in Rome, and he was often called to elaborate on theological or philosophical discussions.

He became a part of the world-wide administrative organization of Propaganda Fide and passed through every step to reach the post of secretary at forty-nine. Though this body is presided over by a cardinal, the secretary is really the effective executive. In this position he remained for eleven years. In all the long period since his ordination, he had known nothing but work and the daily plodding of the churchman completely surrendered to his task. Ambition for rank had not seared his brain. His career had remained above the jealousies which personal collisions create. He had labored on through nearly four decades, and only when Benedict XV called him to the cardinalate at the age of fifty-nine was he to accept an outward recognition of his learning and devotion.

Benedict created those three "baby" cardinals that day: Tacci, Achille Ratti, who became Pius XI, and Laurenti. Tacci and Ratti were made cardinal priests, while Laurenti was but a cardinal deacon, the lower grade. After they had donned their red robes, they appeared before the Holy Father in private audience and sat in a semicircle about him. This pope was endowed with a kind of prophetic vision, as he had often foretold the future as it related to things which revolved about his person.

"There has been a generous distribution of red during the past few days," he told them slowly and almost unconcernedly, "but soon there will be a distribution of white, and the white robes will surely fall upon one of you."

This meant that one of them would soon be pope. Seven months later Benedict contracted pneumonia. During his sickness he again foretold his death but now gave the day and hour. He fulfilled his prophecy to the minute on January 22, 1922, at six o'clock in the morning.

And it was in the conclave which had met to elect his successor that Laurenti had refused to be pope.

For days I had watched the preparations for this meeting of cardinals which, by the Apostolic Constitution, as we saw, is hermetically secret. A medley of riches and simplicity, of obsolete devices and modern gadgets, of priceless treasures of art and cooking utensils, gave the solemn and overpowering occasion of electing a pope a patch-quilt border of colorful incidentals.

A common potbelly stove, fifty feet of stovepipe, and half a dozen gunny sacks of damp straw were hauled into the Vatican's Sistine Chapel, the richest interior in works of art in all the world. These common farm and fireside chattels were set in the corner to the left of the entrance opposite what is famed as the greatest picture ever painted—Michelangelo's Last Judgment.

The stove, stovepipe, and sacks of straw took the show away from the priceless grandeur of the place. I watched the workmen begin setting up the stove. It was placed rather near the wall, for the long stovepipe was to go straight up to the high roof without an elbow and emerge six feet into the air. The projecting part was to be seen easily from St. Peter's Square, some sixty yards away, where crowds would gather daily to watch for a message in smoke.

I had kept the deathwatch over Benedict XV in the pope's antechamber for sixty continuous hours. When Cardinal Gasparri, papal secretary of state, lifting the veil from the deceased pontiff's face, had pronounced the formula, *"Vere papa mortuus est"* (The Pope is truly dead), the official pronouncement of death, I entered the bedroom and knelt at the *prie-dieu* at the foot of the bed. I then genuflected beside the lifeless form of Benedict and kissed his slippered foot. Genuflecting again, I kissed his hand and cheek.

I followed the body in its daily migration. First it was removed from the bedroom into the secret antechamber on the floor below. Daylong and nightlong it was surrounded with ceremony. Canons, members of religious orders, high-ranking and low-ranking prelates constantly intoned the prayers for the dead. That day, too, the robes of the still figure were changed from the white cassock and red mantle bordered with ermine to those of archbishop. The precious miter was placed upon his head.

On the second day, I accompanied the procession from the secret antechamber to St. Peter's. The remains were borne aloft by red-liveried *sediari,* servants of the papal household, and escorted by the cardinals in violet robes. There were scores of bishops and archbishops and hundreds of priests. These were all in black cassocks, as the transfer to St. Peter's, through an impressive procedure, was an informal and private function.

Official entombment occurred the fourth day. This, too, was private and limited to the Sacred College, the papal court, and the diplomatic court. I was privileged to be the only American present, I believe. The ceremony started at four o'clock in the afternoon and lasted until seven o'clock. The basilica was locked while the function was proceeding. I saw the remains first placed in a casket of cypress lined with red silk. This was then inserted in a casket of lead embossed with the papal arms. The whole was finally introduced into a third casket of oak. Cardinal Gasparri placed his seal upon it and it was lowered into the crypt.

Several days later I watched the workmen take sixty thrones into the Sistine Chapel for the cardinals. These thrones were papal election devices, used only in the conclave and provided with collapsible canopies. The canopy is a sign of sovereignty. Each cardinal entered the conclave a potential sovereign, since there was no pope. His canopy was therefore raised above him. The moment they would choose a pope, all the canopies would be lowered except the one above the cardinal elected.

Preparations were completed by the evening of the tenth day. Amid cardinals and thrones, the stove with its long pipe still domineered over the richness of the scene.

The projecting part had neither a veneer nor pretense of elegance. It brazenly stood erect in its rusty impropriety just off the façade of St. Peter's, the stupendous dome of which frowned down upon it in overpowering grandeur.

Its important role was that of communicating to the world the result of each ballot of the conclave. No news of the balloting would come in any other way than by this device. It was necessary for a candidate to receive a two-thirds majority before he could be elected Pope. Now, when no candidate obtained a two-thirds vote, the ballots were burned in the stove and mixed with damp straw so as to produce a large volume of smoke. The thick stream emerging from the projecting pipe signified that no pope was chosen. When some candidate received the necessary two-thirds majority, only the ballots, without straw, were burned. The decreased volume of smoke announced that the Church now had a pope.

Italians, both prelates and populace, indulge even avidly in picking the winner, much like our own "experts" in sports and politics. To them, the pontiff is no exception. The names are guessed around by priests and people alike. The cardinals, magnificent in their purple and patriarchal in dignity, resent being picked, because here the favorites never win, as we said. A crowd only chooses the big names. Gasparri, Merry del Val, and Maffi, all publicized and popular, on this occasion became the choices. The favorites could never muster the necessary two-thirds majority because big names, either from virulent jealousy or conflict, always had enemies among their own colleagues. Paradoxically, by picking the winners, the guessers realized they were picking the losers.

Little Laurenti entered without mention and so had a chance. Lowest in rank because he was a cardinal deacon and was the last one created by the late pontiff, he became the file closer of every procession. In all the ceremonies, he was last. After the cardinals were locked in, this circumstance gave genesis to omens. The last shall be first. From then on he became a favorite, and with the reassuring augury that when he had actually entered he had not been cited, Little Laurenti became a "popeable."

Crowds gathered early in St. Peter's Square the following morning to await the smoke. It was indeed an old Roman custom and somewhat defiant of explanation that ten or twelve thousand persons would gather just to see a burst of vapor issue from the unsightly though authoritative stovepipe. No one expected election on the first ballot, but the crowd stayed on. At noon, patience was rewarded in a thick though diminutive cloud silhouetted against the Italian sky. It was decisive. There was no pope. The crowd slowly turned away and soon the square was empty.

Similar groups gathered in the afternoon. Patience was again as necessary as curiosity. It was not until five o'clock that there was another abundant though short-lived belch, signifying that the cardinals were continuing to ballot.

They were solemn and orderly crowds. Only an occasional *"Niente papa"* (No pope) punctuated the twilight.

One day after another they came, and one day after another it was the same story, except that the smoke was never uniform. On two occasions its begrudging paucity provoked the false rumor that a pope had been elected. The multitude thought that the ballots had been burned without straw. Since there was not one sign of life from any of the Vatican windows, the slim hope for a great occasion vanished.

Inside the conclave, as I learned later from a cardinal who has since died, two strong tendencies appeared on the results of the first ballot. Cardinal Gasparri obtained twenty-four votes and Cardinal Merry del Val received twenty-three. The remainder was scattered among three or four candidates. These alignments followed a centuries-old tradition, as these two tendencies were always present in the choosing of a pontiff; namely, two strong parties with a small minority having no particular leaning. Traditionally, too, the one was called the "politicals" and the other the "zealots." To the scattered few without political alignment was assigned the name of "flying squadron" because they had the power, by uniting, to turn their support to either side and generally force a swing in favor of a candidate.

For four ballots the two parties kept in parallel lines without emerging from the Gasparri–Merry del Val deadlock. The second day, the conclave began to turn to Little Laurenti. On the third day he was nearing the necessary two-thirds vote. The conclave raised its emotional pitch. The Roman Catholic Church was approaching a moment when a new pope was about to be elected.

With heightened feelings Monsignor Sincero, secretary of the conclave, began his tabulations for the tenth ballot. He knew that the time was near. He checked the figures and found that Laurenti had received thirty-six votes, the necessary two-thirds. All the cardinals waited in restless anxiety for his announcement. With trembling voice he read out the results.

Everything stopped. Silence begot drama. The assemblage was now sitting in the presence of the new pope. Each wished to be the first to acclaim him. Following the ritual, the cardinal dean arose and, accompanied by two ceremoniers, approached the throne of Cardinal Laurenti. The dean halted a moment and then bowed.

"Acceptasne electionem de te canonice factam in Summum Pontificem?" (Dost thou accept the election which designates thee canonically to the Supreme Pontificate?) he recited with profound emotion.

There was a pause, a throbbing suspense. The moment Laurenti gave his acceptance, he would be pope and all present must bend the knee before him. He would be the supreme pastor of all Catholic Christendom. He lifted his head and looked toward the cardinal dean through his black-rimmed glasses.

"Esteem as I do the confidence you have shown in me," said the country boy from Monte Porzio on whose shoulders had fallen the mantle of pontiff and to whom all were gazing as the next successor of St. Peter, "I am humble and unworthy before the exalted throne of Peter. It is my wish that this lofty office pass into the hands of another, who is stronger and abler to carry the burden."

A unanimous and audible sigh coursed through the assemblage. He had refused to be pope. He preferred to obey rather than to command. Emotions accelerated again. Momentarily no one knew what to do. Laurenti, still the chief figure and still the focus of all, sat motionless. He alone could decide whether he wanted to be pope. Minutes elapsed. Slowly the cardinal dean turned to Monsignor Sincero and ordered the distribution of more ballots.

Voting continued all that day, and now the feeling-out by each successive ballot began to orient itself and to veer to other candidates. But Laurenti's words about another "stronger and abler" had had effect in that dramatic moment. Each subsequent ballot revealed that the conclave was turning to Achille Ratti, archbishop of Milan, who had been made a cardinal on the same day as Laurenti.

On the ballot which had elected Laurenti, Achille Ratti had received only fourteen votes. On the next ballot, the eleventh, he jumped to twenty-four, and this was decisive in making him a leading candidate. On the twelfth ballot, he gained three more, which gave him twenty-seven and put him still farther in the lead. Balloting closed for that day and the conclave retired for the night, with Ratti leading the whole field by a big margin. On the first ballot on the following day, he gained three more votes, which gave him thirty. He was now very far in the lead but had not yet reached the two-thirds majority. The fourteenth virtually swept everything toward him. He received forty-two votes.

Sincero again stood before the Sacred College. Another had been elected pope. Confidence in Ratti coursed through the conclave. The cardinals waited impatiently for Sincero's announcement. His voice was again tremulous as he proclaimed the designation of Achille Ratti as the choice.

Again there was silence. With dignified grace the cardinal dean arose, and flanked by the ceremoniers, approached the throne of the Milanese archbishop. Each one present riveted eyes and ears on the scene. Misty palms and humid foreheads registered the electric atmosphere and the anxious state of each participant. Addressing him by name, the cardinal dean repeated the formula in slow and almost chanting tones:

"Acceptasne electionem de te canonice factam in Summum Pontificem?"

Another pause quickened the beating hearts of cardinals and clerks. Eyes and ears strained to catch each movement and word. Were they sitting in the presence of the pope? On his response, Achille Ratti could be elevated from the pastor of an archdiocese to the ruler of four hundred million souls. He bowed his head in prayer. He lifted his eyes to the waiting dean. He began to speak.

"That it may not be said," he drawled in low liturgical and deliberate tones, "that I refuse to acquiesce in the Divine Will, that it may not be declared that I am recalcitrant toward the honor which must weigh heavily on my shoulders, and that no one can assert that I have not appreciated the votes of my colleagues—despite my unworthiness, whereof I have a profound cognizance—I accept."

Achille Ratti was pope.

The whole company rose. The canopies above the cardinals were lowered and only the one above Achille Ratti remained. He was sovereign pontiff now. All bowed him obeisance. All eyes were fastened upon the throne where the successor to St. Peter sat.

The new pontiff was then escorted into a small dressing room off the Sistine Chapel and there his robes of cardinal were divested for those of pope. Three sizes had been previously provided, and the medium size fitted Achille Ratti perfectly. A throne was placed on the steps of the altar of the chapel. The new pope re-entered and was assisted to the throne. All the cardinals performed the service of obedience by kissing his slippered foot, his hand, and his cheek.

Meanwhile, prelates burned the ballots without straw.

Outside, it was a misty day but this did not prevent about fifteen thousand people from gathering to see the smoke. Though the ballots were burned without straw, the smoke signal was so confused that the crowds could not tell whether the volume signified election or not. When the doors of the central loggia of St. Peter's were opened, it was definite that the new pope had been elected.

Cardinal Bisleti, who was designated to make the first announcement, emerged and with the papal ceremoniers came to the front of the balcony.

"Habemus Pontificem" (We have a Pontiff), he shouted, and then proclaimed that Achille Ratti had taken the name of Pius XI.

The crowd burst into wild acclamation of *"Evviva il*

Papa." Up until that moment no one knew whether the new pope would himself bestow his first blessing from the outside balcony or from the interior loggia. No pope had ever given the blessing from the outside since 1870—a protest against the taking of Rome by the Italians.

But it was just then that Pius XI was announcing to the Sacred College that he intended to bestow the blessing from the outside as a pledge of peace. Patiently the crowd waited and was finally rewarded when the papal cross appeared at the central balcony followed by the Pope. Here he bestowed the blessing *"Urbi et Orbi"* (To the City and to the World).

Months afterward, when Pius XI received Cardinal Laurenti with his collaborators of the Sacred Congregation of the Religious, of which he had newly been chosen prefect, he was moved in the thought that here was the man who might have been pontiff instead of himself.

"We are deeply conscious of the many great attributes of Cardinal Laurenti, of his travail without ceasing, of his sacrifice without stint," he told the little group. "And were it not for his humbleness of heart and soul, we would not be sitting on this throne nor wearing these robes today."

The little cardinal remained quite happy presiding over the Sacred Congregation, but in 1928 he was promoted to the more important post of prefect of the Sacred Congregation of Rites and made a cardinal priest.

Until the day of his death, in the summer of 1938, Little Laurenti lived in complacent satisfaction as he witnessed the pontifical stature of Pius XI, the man whom he had made pope, expand to historic proportions. He knew that it meant power and prestige for the Church. He revered and admired Pius XI. He knew that his decision to make him pope was right. He was satisfied.

4. Popes—Red, White, and Black

DEPENDING on viewpoint and not uncommonly on a streak of personal prejudice, certain critics and even apologists of the papacy either sibilate or shout that instead of one pope, there are three—the white, the red, and the black. The white pope wears the white cassock, donned at the conclave. His authority, derived from his prerogatives as successor to St. Peter, is ecclesiastically supreme. With a weak white pope, however, either through intrigue or persuasion, they say, certain influence is wielded by the cardinal secretary of state, administratively the highest prelate in the whole Roman hierarchy. Wearing red robes, he is characterized as the red pope. Forgetting robes, it is like saying that Secretary of State Byrnes is President when he tells Mr. Truman what to do.

Now the black pope is the general of the Jesuits. Though he is in an important position, his robes are always black, like those of a simple priest. He carries no mark of rank whatsoever. Jesuits take a vow to forego all dignities and distinction. They have nevertheless been variously accused of dark intrigue to overthrow governments, and of contriving to hand over whole nations to the Holy See. I have met and conversed with many Jesuits, such as Father Gannon, president of Fordham University, and even the recent general of the order, Father

Ledochowski, a Pole. Most Jesuits have full-time jobs, such as teaching, writing, publishing, preaching, and working in parishes with little time either for international intrigue or local mischief. The modesty by which Father Gannon and Father Ledochowski have fulfilled their highly directive tasks would dispel the notion of militarized intelligence or religious espionage. The influence of the black pope has been romantically overdone.

Here we can interject how a black-robed Jesuit was raised to the Sacred College and what he said.

Pope Pius XI wished to add a Jesuit on grounds of representing the order in the senate of the Church. He called Father Ledochowski and asked him to look over the field of hard-working Jesuits who occupied no great administrative positions but who exercised more the role of simple priests in laborious chores than those of management. Father Ledochowski reminded the Pope of the Jesuit vows of abstention from rank. In the face of the authority of the Pope, however, he was constrained to obey. In due time, he presented the name of Father Boetto, a hard-working Jesuit clerk in one of the administrative offices. The Pope approved the choice. Any Jesuit notified that he was going to be made a cardinal would be stunned. Boetto received his notification.

"I could not have had less surprise," breathlessly uttered the stupefied priest, "than if I had suddenly been ordered to become a Turk!"

Boetto was appointed archbishop of Genoa. He died in January 1946.

And now we return to red rather than Jesuits in black. We are to survey the landscape of our time to find a red pope. Every pope except one for the past hundred years has been trained in the Vatican school of diplomacy or had become well versed in international affairs through personal experience. There had been little hope for an ambitious secretary of state to twist the will of the pontiff without his knowing it, save for the one exception of the lone nondiplomatic pope.

He was Pius X, a mail carrier's son, modest though saintly, provincially minded though spiritually endowed, unworldly though humanly encompassing. He had chosen as his secretary of state the young and talented Monsignor Merry del Val. Fate had designated the monsignor to disrobe him as cardinal and to invest him in papal robes when he was elected pope. Showing his almost complete detachment from the diplomatic atmosphere of the Vatican, he had picked the lowly monsignor as his chief adviser, for no other reason than that he had made a captivating impression on him. Appointing him secretary of state on sight, he created him a cardinal, too, and at only thirty-six.

Merry del Val not alone had been trained in Vatican diplomacy but came of a family of diplomats. He was born in an embassy, when his father was Spanish ambassador to London. International currents and international upheavals had been his major study from childhood. When he went into the priesthood, Vatican diplomacy was his choice. He had already at this time surveyed the problems of the Holy See all over the world and more especially in Europe. Propitiously, he was secretary of state at the outbreak of World War I.

If the name of red pope can ever be applied, certainly here was an instance. The influence of this cardinal secretary of state was always decisive. A Spaniard, born in London, and educated in the Pontifical Academy of Noble Ecclesiastics in Rome, his policy took an Allied turn. We have seen how Pius X drove the Austrian ambassador out of his sight. And Merry del Val took up the favor of

France, which had been cold to the Holy See. Then France needed it, and France was thankful. And there were good relations with Protestant England, which established a legation with the Holy See. But it was later in 1914, too, that the Pope died, and the reign of his red pope went with him. The tenure of office of Merry del Val ended, and so did the veering toward an Allied orientation.

The young cardinal's father was a grandee of Spain, Marquis Merry del Val. While this Spanish nobleman was His Most Catholic Majesty's ambassador to the Court of St. James's, the son was sent to English schools. He learned all the sports and was quite good at cricket, soccer, and tennis. He could ride and often followed the hounds. Sometimes in England and sometimes on the ancestral estates in Spain, he went out on shooting excursions. His aim was sure. He was a skilled marksman.

When he became a priest, he had to forego most of the sports of his early schooling. But he did keep up his love of the rifle. This he could pursue without exposing his priestly station to the frown of his superiors, for in Italy during his early ecclesiastical career sports were under a ban as worldly and lighthearted. He would doubtless have liked to ride a great deal about Rome where the country is a horseman's paradise. As a recreation, horses were greatly enjoyed by the cardinals of the Renaissance and even by the popes. But in modern times, a cardinal on horseback was not alone a rarity, it was an indignity.

While he was secretary of state, he occupied a villa in summer on Lake Albano near the papal palace of Castel Gandolfo. Near by was the Villa Caternia, where the students of the North American College, retreating from the heat of Rome, continued their courses. Cardinal O'Connell, then a monsignor, was rector. The lifelong friendship of O'Connell and Merry del Val began there. The Secretary of State would invite students over for tea. They were enthralled by his nimble and athletic bearing and his knowledge of most of the sports.

It was a favorite pastime of his to pit his skill against them with the rifle. He would invite them to pick up a gun and see what they could do. Few of them knew how to shoot. Those who did were no match for him. He would line up a row of Italian pennies on the garden wall. Then at thirty paces, he would take aim and hit each penny one after the other, much as the expert rifle shots in the circus or a Wild West show. Outside of taking long walks, this was his only recreation. Though he missed the other sports, he always cherished a pride in his marksmanship, cardinalatial robes notwithstanding.

It was Cardinal O'Connell who presented me to Merry del Val. This was after the election of Pius XI as pope. Besides his conquering presence, Merry del Val dominated with voice and speech. While he spoke English with the finish of a professor of philology, yet he spoke it with an authoritative rhythm and in the hypnotic aura of a cosmopolitan. It had always been my impression that Cardinal O'Connell had tried to adopt this diction. The marked resemblance in the Bostonian's speech was compelling.

As archpriest of St. Peter's, Merry del Val lived in a palatial mansion at the rear of the basilica. He received anyone who wished to see him from ten to twelve o'clock in the morning. With this man of suavity, stiffness was easily softened, and he made it possible for the humblest to converse with him on their own terms. His knowledge outside of theology and philosophy was wide. Besides knowing sports, he had studied nature, loved birds, knew plants, horses, and some mechanics too. Doubtless Merry del Val would have liked to be pope. As we saw, O'Connell would have done anything within ecclesiastical propriety to have made him pope.

And it was not because he was a Spaniard that he lost. He had lived so long in Rome and become so much a part of the very landscape of the Vatican that Italians regarded him as one of them. He undoubtedly lost the election because he was a strong man. Strong men have strong rivals, and the rivals are their undoing. As it was, the conclave had elected an almost unknown man, a compromise candidate. His brother cardinals did not know whether he was weak or strong. Once in the papacy, they soon knew. He was mighty.

But Merry del Val had lost twice. On the morning of my visit, he did not show the slightest symptom of disappointment. He carried on, fulfilling the assignments which the new pope picked for him. I asked him whether he thought that the hostility which had arisen between France and Germany at that moment over reparations and the Ruhr would not lead to another war.

"The world has just concluded a peace," he said slowly with oracular assurance. "There can be no war until the wounds of the last war are healed. You have got to be healthy to make war. You have got to have food and material to fall back upon. At this moment, ¬o nation has recovered to be strong enough. It will take another generation before any nation could think of war."

And it did.

Pius XI gave him very important assignments in the administration of the Church. There had been little cause for differences between them, because Pius XI hardly knew him when he became pope. It was to Merry del Val that the new pope is reported to have made his historic retort when caution was counseled.

"Yesterday," he is said to have warned him, "I was a cardinal, but today I am Pope."

Nevertheless, he displayed intermittent admiration for his Spanish charm and chose him as his legate to preside over the septicentennial of St. Francis, a world-wide celebration. Arriving full-robed in the village of Assisi, the saint's birthplace, which constituted the heart of the devotions, the legate was received by the local population as if he had actually been pope. They genuflected before him, waved and cheered when his automobile moved through the narrow streets of the little Italian town. It was a gala day.

Besides, he was accorded royal honors by the Fascist government which then was in power. But this presented a problem. Would it mean that the representative of the Pope would recognize the Fascist government? The papacy was not friendly with Fascism, then.

Even Merry del Val himself was momentarily perplexed. But he made a quick decision. He decided to accept the guards of honor of full-dressed carabineers. But something else was to come. When he entered in state into the church of St. Francis, there to receive him was Pietro Fedele, Fascist minister of education. Would he ignore him or accept his bows? Here he was faced with the dilemma of either disturbing the sacred function or of recognizing the Fascist official. He decided not to disturb the function.

The Fascists made much of the occasion. It was widely published that the Pope's own legate had accepted the bows and handshakes of the Fascists. This was not for Fascist love of the Church but to win the faithful peasantry and hardy toilers to the Fascist emblem. In fact, an order went out from Mussolini's press office that the visit of the Cardinal Legate should be regarded as an important event.

Now, Merry del Val in compliance with rule and custom made a report to the Pope of what had happened. He was not a little apprehensive, even though Pius XI had already given some gentle signs for a settlement of the Italian quarrel. When he entered into the presence of the Pope he genuflected and then embraced the Holy Father. But the Pope was cold. Nothing is more paralyzing to a visitor to the pontiff than to be received with frigid eyes. In reality it is just how a cardinal gets spanked.

"He hardly said a word," reported Merry del Val after the audience. "He did not even utter one gratifying expression. I expected a warm welcome, but the Holy Father certainly put that aside."

The crestfallen legate then went to the office of Cardinal Gasparri, who was then secretary of state.

"Well, I have come to take my spanking from you, too," he said. "I suppose I went too far in Assisi."

"What spanking? What spanking?" returned Gasparri. "Everything you did was superb."

It was months later before Merry del Val understood the scowl of the Pope and the smile of Gasparri. On the same day that he had made his report, the Pope had personally started negotiations with Italy to settle their quarrel and did not want to let out the secret, even to a cardinal. Merry del Val took the spanking, and yet the Pope was pleased.

It was the colorless though firm-willed Benedict XV who had earlier rejected Merry del Val as secretary of state. They had been classmates in the diplomatic college and never liked each other. Both were nobly born, but Merry del Val was handsome while Giacomo della Chiesa, which was Benedict's name, was short, stoopish, and surly. They lived in a conflict in personality. Benedict called Gasparri to be his secretary of state. He became known as the papal secretary who was in office for the Lateran Treaty.

Gasparri was a scholar, Vatican jurist, diplomat, and radiated the atmosphere of Rome though he was born in the recesses of the Umbrian hills. This rustic character in his nature had elicited unpleasant epithets from his colleagues, as far as a churchman can go in uttering unpleasant epithets. He was born on what would correspond in the United States to a small sheep ranch. Never, in the very height of his position, did he try to make himself any other than the son of a sheep herder.

Around the pontifical throne and in many of the Vatican offices swarm many prelates of distinguished lineage. Quite often they resented the lack of finesse and grace which Gasparri showed. He would forget the "Eminencies," the "Excellencies." He would often not acknowledge obeisances made to him, more from the fact that he regarded them as so much social embroidery. A veritable little underground of nobly born prelates was formed, based on the resentment that the Cardinal Secretary of State did not know how to behave. As a mark of scorn, they secretly called him *"il pecoraro"*—the sheep-tender. They did not even honor him with the more dignified title of shepherd.

Eventually he found it out, but he passed it over without so much as a scowl. He waited his time. A high-ranking prelate wanted his instructions on how to receive the Belgian ambassador, and sent his messenger to ask for orders.

This was Gasparri's chance. He knew the prelate's liking for high pomp, and immediately instructed the messenger to tell his purple-robed superior that he should dress in a monk's habit and remain barefooted. This reduced him to the status of a beggar.

The monsignor resented it and sent the messenger back to ask if the Cardinal Secretary of State did not realize that it was an important diplomatic function.

"Tell your superior," commanded Gasparri in suave though unequivocal language, "that those are the orders. Tell him, too, that those are the orders of the sheep-tender to the sheep."

His simplicity was carried to extremes in his living. Though he resided in one of the most lavish apartments in the Vatican palaces, he gave up all the spacious, palatial rooms and used them only for his administrative work. His actual living quarters consisted in three very small rooms, a bedroom, a small dining room, and a sitting room. It was here that he trained his parrots, of which he kept a half dozen, to utter scriptural quotations and religious pronouncements in Latin.

Administrative system was not intended for Cardinal Gasparri. Though he was a tireless worker, he had his own system. Telephones, typewriters, interoffice communications would have discommoded him. In his correspondence he had a genial knack of separating the letters which he wanted personally to answer from those given to his subordinates. His own personal mail was not heavy, so that he would divide the great pile among the assistants and tell them to reply in any way they saw fit, as that would certainly meet the situation.

He received a check for 10,000 lire (about $500 in those days) and absent-mindedly threw it into the wastebasket. The donor, not receiving a word of thanks from him for some time, inquired whether it had reached him. There was a search high and low. The check could not be found.

The bank was asked to pay the check anyway and did so. Months later, looking through his desk, he discovered the check and wondered how it had been put there. His usher then volunteered that he had found it in the waste-basket and thought it looked important enough to keep. Then instead of sending it to the bank, Gasparri tore it up and murmured under his breath:

"Well, this has been paid."

This absent-mindedness led often to embarrassment if not concern. It was during the First World War that Count John de Salis was sent as minister of Great Britain to the Holy See. More than in the recent war, the various powers all tried to jockey for some favor or other from the Vatican, either to bolster world opinion or raise the confidence of their own citizens of Catholic faith. When the Germans bombed Paris in 1918 and struck the Church of St. Gervais on Good Friday, nearly two hundred worshiping French men and women lost their lives. Gasparri expected to get calls from the French and British envoys wanting an expression of papal condemnation. He also awaited a visit from the Germans and Austrians, who, he thought, would seek to deter the Holy See from saying anything at all.

Under the circumstances he decided to see no one. He gave orders to his subordinates and servants that if anyone called, he was confined to his room because of illness. De Salis arrived and asked to see him. He was told by the secretary that His Eminence was not well.

"I am very sorry," offered De Salis in sympathetic tone. "But then I would like to see him, if only to ask him how he is."

"He is quite all right," said the secretary. "There is nothing serious. It is just a little disturbance which has put him to bed."

"Then in that case," the count insisted, "there is all the more reason why I should see him. Since it is nothing serious, my little visit will not disturb him. It may make him feel better. I just want to tell him a friendly word."

De Salis had been so persistent that the secretary had to run back and forth three or four times to the Cardinal. Finally Gasparri decided to receive him. He had to take off his cassock and shoes and get into bed to produce the illusion of being ill. Then the envoy was shown in.

The conversation was stilted but courteous. No important international interests were brought up.

Rising to say good-by, De Salis with not a little subtlety in his eyes wished to give a word of counsel.

"Why, Eminence," he said, "you will find, I am sure, that when one is not feeling well and decides to get into bed, it is always a good thing to take off one's collar."

Gasparri in his haste had forgotten to take off his white Roman collar.

But the old Vatican diplomat was not undone even by the rapier thrust.

"That's right," he replied. "Except when the illness is diplomatic."

Aspiring to become secretary of state at the time Gasparri retired was Cardinal Buonaventura Cerretti. He had been undersecretary of state under Gasparri and had had a brilliant career as nuncio to Paris. At the same time another aspirant was in the running. He was Eugenio Pacelli, who had been nuncio to Berlin. The Pope picked Pacelli.

This detracted little from the diplomatic prowess of Cerretti, because his career had already been made in Paris. After his promotion to cardinal he received a letter from a young Frenchman who was seeking the hand of a French maiden of noble birth. The prospective bridegroom asked that he be recommended as a worthy eventual son-in-law to the family of his spouse-apparent. Cerretti complied. The family was so pleased with the lavish praise for the youth that they gladly gave the hand of their daughter. The wedding ensued.

Some months afterward, Cerretti received another letter from the now groom. This time it extolled the virtues of his family existence and gave all the credit for his happy condition to the Cardinal, through whose recommendation to his wife's parents the union was made possible. As a token of his gratitude, the young husband had ordered him a Rolls-Royce automobile; but before delivery, it would be better to have it upholstered in the color most desired by His Eminence. He begged the Cardinal to write him at his convenience on his choice of color.

The Cardinal confessed to me his embarrassment at being offered an automobile for so simple a favor, and pondered his action from day to day. He could not bring himself to think of accepting it. However, he finally wrote his answer. It told of his pain at being offered such a present and that he could not accept it, since all he did was his bounden duty in justly recommending a worthy character. After much explanation of the bounden duty, he added one lone paragraph which said:

"Since it embarrasses me to accept such a gift, I know how it embarrasses you that I reject it. You have already signed a contract for the car. Since I should prevent the greater embarrassment of embarrassing both of us at the same time, I am constrained to yield. The color I desire for the interior should be red."

Eugenio Pacelli became the next red pope. He had had a vivid and varied experience in World War I, in the vicissitudes of German national life between the wars, and finally in the advent of Hitler to power. It was he who drew up the concordat of the Vatican with the Nazi government. This document was declared a great achievement at the time. It turned out to be a great mistake, for it was never kept by the German dictator.

And when he was called to Rome to become secretary of state, diplomats freely predicted that Vatican affairs would take a distinctly German leaning. In the fullness of time, he became pope by unanimous consent of the Sacred College. Then, again, it was prophesied that a "German pope" had come to power. There were times when he was actually accused of siding with the Germans against the Allies.

As the red pope, he had obeyed the orders of his superior, Pius XI who, as we have seen, was a strong and decisive man. It almost inevitably follows that when a strong man is succeeded by one of his ablest lieutenants, the younger seldom achieves the greatness of the elder. It may well be that, great as was the pontificate of Pius XI, the reign of Pius XII will be even greater. He has caught the temper of the times. He has heard the cry of the world and has listened.

When he came to the throne of Peter, he appointed a classmate as his secretary of state, Cardinal Maglione, who was regarded as having a balanced diplomatic career. Maglione had been accused by the French of having German tendencies, yet when he was sent by the Holy See earlier as the nuncio to Paris, he so endeared himself to the ministers of France that they willingly accepted his realism and impartiality. So successful was his work in bringing France into the orbit of the Vatican that for this skillful diplomatic course Pius XI had promoted him to a cardinal. But he died three years after Pius XII had made him secretary of state.

Since that time, the White Pope has appointed no chief collaborator in red. He knows the world. He has traveled in both hemispheres. He knows the currents which move over the international fields. Few men in all the world have a grasp on international policies such as his. He needs no red pope.

5. *Little Old New York in Purple*

W<small>E WERE</small> all standing around waiting in the reception room of the North American College in Rome. Clerics in cassock and violet cape were there. A cluster of laymen, more or less in their better clothes, stalked about, some in morning coats and striped trousers and others in plain business suits. But the figure on whom everyone concentrated was the unpretentious prelate of medium height in cassock and purple mantle with a pectoral cross hung over his breast. Though he was unpretentious, he was impressively ascetic, spiritually lined, humble, and above all, a beckoning priest, drawing and impelling. He was Archbishop Patrick J. Hayes of New York. This was March 24, 1924.

He was standing before a throne. Presently a messenger from the Vatican was announced. The messenger, Monsignor Gervasi, approached the Archbishop and said:

"Your Excellency, His Eminence the Cardinal Secretary of State, on the command of the Holy Father, has charged me to deliver this *biglietto* to you."

I noticed specifically that this official Vatican messenger had addressed him as "Your Excellency." It is the address due an archbishop. And they never make mistakes in that.

The *biglietto* was the document of notification that Hayes had been created a cardinal that morning in the secret consistory the Pope was holding in the Vatican. This notification was read aloud for everyone to hear. Then the first to speak was Monsignor Gervasi again.

"Your Eminence," he said according to strict formula, "His Eminence, the Cardinal Secretary of State has instructed me to convey his hearty congratulations on the high honor which has been bestowed upon you."

From that moment, to all the world it was His Eminence, Patrick Cardinal Hayes, archbishop of New York. A lad from the depths of poverty and orphanhood had become a prince of the Church with the prerogatives of royalty.

The Roman Catholic Church in America provides one of the world's most outstanding phenomena, where the peasant becomes the prince. In no other domain of the Church of Rome is the rise from humbleness to regality so forcibly striking. The princes of the Church from Italy have nearly all descended in a genealogical table of noble pretensions. Rarely does an Italian cardinal come out from the simplicity of the humble folk. All the popes have been chosen from among men of aristocratic lineage, with the only recent exception, which we have so oft quoted—that of Pius X. In France, Spain, and Germany, cardinals emerge either from families of pedigree or homes of wealth. In England, Newman, Manning, Vaughan, and Bourne came from the upper middle class, while the one exception of Hinsley more than proves the rule.

But in America practically every cardinal called to wear the red robes and to be granted the royal privilege, at least when he is in Europe, comes from the humblest beginnings and often from a struggling mother and father in abject poverty. It was always a thrilling sight to me to witness the creation of American cardinals, for other reasons than the ceremony itself. It held that impressive significance that from the humble beginnings of a poor home, some outstanding intellect had effectively shown the world that though his birth was lowly, yet he held within himself the sterling worth to rise above birth and lineage and to present himself as being there among those of ancient genealogy in his own right, on his own and through the instrumentalities of his own inherent qualities and virtues—whether they were intellectual or spiritual.

Now, every cardinal allotted to the United States had been of Irish heritage, with the exception of Cardinal Mundelein, who came of German stock. Most of them were either the sons or grandsons of immigrants and thus a first- or second-generation American. Two had actually come from Ireland in their youth. Such men as McCloskey of New York, who was the first American created a cardinal, came of immigrant parents. O'Connell's parents had come from Ireland, too. The father and mother of Cardinal Gibbons were both of Irish antecedents. Cardinal Farley of New York was born in Ireland, and so was Cardinal Glennon of St. Louis. In them all, the strain of the strong and virile humble folk gave them the aggressiveness to take life on the assault. And that is why I always admired them whenever I saw them mingled with the cardinals of other lands. They were there in their own right.

And no cardinal in all the world came of a more humble origin than that of Patrick Cardinal Hayes. It was his gloomy fate to have lost his father before he was born, and then to have lost his mother soon after he was born. He was cared for, by a stroke of fortune, by his aunt and uncle, Mr. and Mrs. John Egan, in that quarter which we would call barely habitable as we know comfortable housing these days, near the site of the present Brooklyn

Bridge, New York. It is said that he had no recollection of his mother. He played in that cluster of streets on the East Side to the east of the City Hall. This was back in the 1870's. The street on which he came into the world is now known as Cardinal Place in his honor. New York barely extended beyond what is now Forty-second Street. Horse-drawn cars trundled down Broadway then.

Cardinal Hayes embodied in spirit and soul the story and transformation of the city of New York. The city has changed from a mere mediocre seaport to the most highly evolved aggregate in its metropolitan as well as its cosmopolitan character, in its commercial as well as cultural prowess. Little Paddy Hayes used to go and see the ships come in at the Battery with his uncle. While it is awe-inspiring to watch the huge liners of today ply up New York Bay, it was just as entrancing to young Hayes to see the puzzling variety of ships with the variegated crews along the wharves in the lower city. A great assemblage of sailing vessels congregated not only from the coastwise towns and the West Indies but also from all over the world. He had a chance to be impressed if not absorbed by the colorful strangeness of sail and hull, the contrasting aspect of humankind in white, red, yellow, brown, and black skins.

His frail physique did not permit him to engage much in the rugged games which the Irish boys of Cardinal Place played in those days much in the same way as the Irish boys do today in all the cities of the land. He played the lesser role of chasing the ball to bring it back for the others to play with. And in such a minor role in the gang, it was quite natural for him to find welcome in St. Andrew's Church, the church of the parish, where, even though his frame was not strong, the priest used him in the early Masses to assist him at the altar. Paddy Hayes

was regular at this, and it undoubtedly had determined
him for the Church, though he did not know how, because the poverty of his aunt and uncle was so great then
that he could not see his way clear to get much of an education. In time, however, that dark prospect of scholarship was cleared for brighter hopes. The Church became
richer. Education for the priesthood was much easier to
obtain.

When he was fourteen, he secured a job doing clerical
work and running errands in one of the merchants' offices
near the wharf. Brought up without much knowledge of
the play in which the young are usually encouraged to
give out their energy and exploit their strength, he developed not exactly a melancholy concept of life but at least
a serious one. He became a devoted employee, coming on
time to work and staying long after the hour of closing.
What he was going to be was not even now conceived as
being in the field of commerce. This forage into business
was to help his uncle and aunt and to show a certain gratitude for what they had bestowed on him by bringing him
up.

The merchant liked him and became so friendly that
he asked him to his house. What had captivated him more
than anything else was that while Paddy Hayes was never
lacking in his strict compliance with all the laborious demands of the little office, he found time to attend Mass
almost every day and to fulfill all the devotions required
in his faith. The merchant surely had a spiritual urge
himself. It turned out that so impressed was he by the
churchly attention of his youthful employee that he himself eventually became a convert to the faith.

And why Cardinal Hayes so personified New York is
richly set in his life, which was and could only be that of
New York itself. He knew the streets, the monuments,

the landmarks, and the churches as a boy from the provinces knows his own home town. In fact, while the village boy would be easily classified as provincial when he came to the big city, Cardinal Hayes, knowing only New York, could easily be designated a provincial in the larger sense should we take the larger world into our horizon. For though he lived in the most cosmopolitan of cities, he was not a cosmopolitan. He was New York with all the elements in feeling, change, social approach, and genuine growth which the city embodied and embodies today.

The influence of the course the city took in its swift but substantial rise made its impact upon him. Back in 1880, when he was thirteen, the construction of the Brooklyn Bridge was begun. The Manhattan anchor was situated right alongside the house where he was born. He played over the stones and the boxes of material which were gathered for the huge construction, the biggest bridge ever contemplated up until that time. He watched every proceeding step to its completion. The great excitement of the visit of President Arthur in 1883 to open the bridge created in him a memorable mental furrow. He was also a witness to the great catastrophe on the bridge. On its first Sunday after the opening, someone shouted that the bridge was falling down. Panic ensued and the thousands on the bridge rushed to the Brooklyn and Manhattan approaches. Their indiscriminate massing turned to desperation. More than a hundred persons were crushed to death.

He saw the birth of the skyscraper, the replacement of horse-drawn cars by electric trolleys, the construction of the elevateds, the opening of the subways, the tunneling of the Hudson and of the East River. He saw a new New York skyline rise with buildings like the Singer, the Woolworth, the Chrysler, and finally the Empire State. From the sailing vessels which were tied up along the battery wharves, the seagoing traffic had been transformed into steamers called floating palaces—even the great Cunarders of the turn of the century were to be surpassed by the *Rex,* the *Europa,* the *Normandie,* and the *Queen Mary.* The great Brooklyn Bridge was outmoded by the Queensboro, the George Washington, and the Triboro bridges. He saw air transport develop and then the great impact and change which the radio was to make on the life of America. This had been the span of his life and it was all in New York, which veritably, though the largest city in the world, was his own village—so much did he know of it, so much was he a part of it.

The great shopping center for his uncle and aunt was along Grand Street. Paddy Hayes enjoyed the treat of looking in the shop windows, but the greatest thrill of all his young days was to be given a dime to attend the so-called dime museum. Here was gathered a tawdry collection of curiosities picked up by the enterprising showmen to make them appear strange if not downright fantastic to the simple folk of even New York of those days. Then there was vaudeville in some of the tinseled palaces. This constituted a fiesta whenever the family could spare the dime and devote the time for the amusement of their ward. He was already a priest when the movies came. He was an archbishop when he heard his first radio program. He was a cardinal when Lindbergh flew from New York to Paris.

But one of the overpowering thrills which had advanced him toward an ecclesiastical career was the great ceremony of the opening of St. Patrick's Cathedral in 1879. It had enshrouded and possessed him. As a boy of twelve, he had walked from home the three miles to the new edifice. It was by far the most imposing structure, either civic or ecclesiastical, which New York could boast. The number of bishops and other prelates who had come for the function had surpassed his most lavish dreams when he thought of himself as a simple server in St. Andrew's. He succeeded in getting into the cathedral, but his short and limited frame could not tower over the standees scattered in every part of the building. He could only get glimpses of the elaborate scenes about the altar by an occasional peep from behind a pillar. And it is not without its touch of emotion to feel that the young lad who was not able to see the ceremony that day because of his low station and paucity of influence, would one day be able to call that same edifice the cathedral of his own see.

Good prospects were offered him for his steadiness in his clerical job. But he was spiritually minded. The inducements in business could not overcome the call. He was from infancy bound to the Church. It had been his overpowering passion. Life itself was inextricably involved in all that the Church contained. A joy and a contentment radiated from his soul when his course was combined with all that St. Andrew's and the faith encompassed. Life and the priesthood became one indivisible unit.

Eventually he was sent to De La Salle Institute and later to Manhattan College. His theological training was taken at St. Joseph's Seminary in Troy, New York. It was not his good fortune to study in Rome. He is one of the few hierarchs who were not trained in the shadow of St. Peter's basilica. And while he was more or less short-weighted in what he should have received as an education, he more than made up for it in the conformation of his life to a cozily homelike New York shepherd of souls.

Two or three years in Rome might conceivably have given him a more cosmopolitan outlook. From what his personality developed to be, this would have been less striking.

He passed through that discriminatory period when signs appeared in commercial houses saying, "Position vacant—No Irish Need Apply." He was part of the generation forced to read aspersions against his faith in the classified columns of the newspapers, where it often said, "Cook Wanted—No Catholics." Roman Catholics even until his early priesthood were regarded as worshipers of idols, and priest-ridden. They were shunned and scorned. Their places of residence were circumscribed. Not too pleasantly called the Irish neighborhood, their houses were sometimes depicted with even more picturesque language.

He had not reached twenty when he witnessed a pitched battle between an organization of Protestant diehards and Catholic zealots. The occasion was the St. Patrick's Day parade. The Protestants were composed mainly of Orangemen of northern Ireland, while the Catholics were quite inevitably the Hibernians of southern Ireland. Strict police precautions had been taken to keep the two sides apart. The parade started up Fifth Avenue, but around Madison Square the Orangemen broke loose and the battle was fought with or without police control. It swayed back and forth until both sides were exhausted and twenty of their number killed.

To have seen his people overcoming that period and then through toil and tenacity reaping the benefactions of the rising resources of the great city could not but fashion the character of Patrick Hayes in the mold of his experiences. It was in this supreme attachment to the turns which New York took, to the struggles of his own Irish groups, to the hardships which the Church encountered, to the gradual emergence of the Irish and the consolidation of their own strength in commerce, in civic affairs, and in their religion that produced his richness of spirit. It was his New Yorkism, coupled with the embodiment of his devotion and triumph as a priest, that bound him so inextricably to the hearts of all communicants.

As a young priest, he was assigned as assistant pastor to Monsignor James M. Farley, at St. Gabriel's parish in East 37th Street. Here a bond was forged which became stronger and stronger as the two men ran their earthly course. Farley was made vicar-general of the archdiocese. He made Hayes his secretary. Farley was elected auxiliary bishop in 1895 and then promoted to archbishop in 1902. On November 27, 1911, he was created a cardinal. All the time, Hayes was his secretary. Later he was promoted to vicar-general.

When the post of auxiliary bishop was vacant, it perhaps was not without the wish of Archbishop Farley that the Pope elected Hayes as his auxiliary. This was 1914. Another promotion came to him in 1917 on the entrance of the United States into World War I. Pope Benedict XV chose him as military ordinary and bishop to all the Catholics in the armed forces of the United States. In that post he increased the number of chaplains from 900 to 1,500.

Farley died on September 17, 1918. It was a troubled and confusing moment in the world-wide affairs of the Church. The armistice came in the following November. The Holy See was burdened with an avalanche of problems which involved a complete reorganization of many of the hierarchies. Poland was reconstructed. Germany and Hungary were contracted. Czechoslovakia and Yugoslavia were set up. The dioceses of Italy and of France were extended. In the midst of these engrossing problems, the Pontiff had the very onerous responsibility of choosing the new archbishop of New York. The archdiocese itself tingled with expectation. Finally, on March 10, 1919, the fulminating news was published in big streamers that Patrick Joseph Hayes had been chosen the next archbishop. For metropolitan yet so provincial New York communicants, the choice was a matter for jubilation.

And now, the step toward the next promotion was irresistibly beginning to open up. At that time the United States was honored by but two cardinals, though there had been three while Cardinal Farley lived. Inevitably the New York Archbishop was charted for cardinalatial dignity. But though the Pope held a consistory in 1921 and created Archbishop Dougherty of Philadelphia a cardinal, he did not so precipitously reward New York. In fact, it was too early; for just as in other fields of human endeavor, the superior wanted to see how his lesser brother in New York would fulfill his stewardship. McCloskey had served eleven years as archbishop, Farley had served nine, before their elevation as cardinals. In any case, though it could be not called precipitous, New York would eventually be recognized.

On Thursday morning, March 6, 1924, I received a dispatch from the New York office of the Associated Press which spirited the usually slow program of those days. It was to alert me. Archbishop Hayes and Archbishop Mundelein of Chicago, it read, had booked passage on the liner *Berengaria,* and were destined for Rome. This unusual occurrence, succinctly added the dispatch, had caused rumors that they were to be created cardinals. My job was to spike the rumor or confirm it. Neither Hayes nor Mundelein could talk, because it was a rigid custom that no American prelate could tell of a promotion until the Associated Press announced it from Rome. This has now been extended to include the United Press and the International News.

Other reporters had received the same alert. I went over to the Vatican and saw Monsignor Pizzardo, assistant secretary of state, and now a cardinal. He replied evasively, and not only evasively but in such a way as to imply a denial that the red robes were to be put on Hayes and Mundelein. I replied to the New York message and repeated what the Vatican chancery had said. Since it was an authoritative viewpoint, I thought that that would hold for a while until I got around to working the diverse approaches to Vatican news. Then came one of those newsmen's breaks out of which scoops are made. That noon, I was lunching at the Palace Hotel. It just plain coincided that Cardinal O'Connell was staying there on his way home from a pilgrimage to the Holy Land. Incidental to the lunch, I inquired if he were in, just to find out if he knew anything about the Hayes and Mundelein rumor. His Eminence was taking lunch outside.

But at about two-thirty Monsignor Richard Haberlin, the secretary to Cardinal O'Connell but now vicar-general of the Boston archdiocese, came through the dining room looking for me. He told me that the Cardinal wanted to see me. I left immediately for the call. Briefly and at top flight, the Number One of Boston related that he had just returned from lunch with Cardinal Gasparri, whom he at one time had rebuffed. He was told by Gasparri, he said, that the archbishops of New York and Chicago were nominated cardinals. He told me to rush with the story. I rushed.

It was the first dispatch to reach New York confirming the promotion. Now Hayes and Mundelein could tell everybody that they were going to Rome to be made cardinals. In fact, Mundelein had already started for New York and was on the train but could not tell anyone what he was going for. He told me when he got to Rome that he certainly wanted to release the secret but had to wait for my dispatch. When the Twentieth Century got to Toledo, the newspapers there streamed that there were yet "no red robes for Mundelein and Hayes." At Cleveland, my dispatch had registered. There the papers had confirmed the news. Then Hayes and Mundelein could open their mouths. Then there was rejoicing both in New York and Chicago.

Hayes went so far as to issue a statement on the signal from my printed dispatch.

"I was deeply touched by the statement from Rome to the Associated Press," he said, "that our Holy Father had conferred this dignity upon the great cities of New York and Chicago as a tribute to America."

They traveled all the way together. In Rome, Hayes was invited to stay in the North American College. He accepted. This was quite characteristic of him, because he did not know Rome as some of the bishops and archbishops who had received their training in Rome knew it. He apparently took the first place offered without thought of luxury. Mundelein, who had spent many years in Rome as a student in the Propaganda Fide College, knew the best places. He put up at the same hotel where O'Connell had given me the scoop just two weeks previously. O'Connell in the meantime had departed for America, for it is an unwritten law of cardinals that one must not steal the show of the other.

From the moment that Hayes arrived in Rome, the impending dignity of prince of the Church was upon him. But lofty as the honor was, he was still a New York boy. I remember how the rector of the North American Col-

lege seemed to coach him lest he fall short by some false
step of maintaining the rank and prestige of his coming
promotion. I remember how earnest and even zealous was
Monsignor Stephen J. Donahue, his secretary, now auxiliary bishop of New York, to protect him from the on-
slaughts of the newspapermen.

When Archbishop Hayes received the formal notification of his cardinalatial honor in Rome, he was required
in accordance with custom to make a short address of
thanks to the Pope and then express a word of gratifica-
tion to his own archdiocese. He thanked the Holy Father
in true gratitude. And when it came to talking about New
York, it was as if he had been suddenly overcome with an
ardent burst of nostalgia. In that modest reception room
of the North American College in the very heart of Rome,
everyone was carried back to all the attributes of the great
metropolis. Hayes repeated his favorite phrases of "our
beloved city," and "little old New York," and other folk-
loristic expressions of the giant ensemble which to him
was as close and familiar as if it had been a village.

But a few years later, he was to return to Rome to pay
the *ad limina* visit, a pilgrimage which all bishops pledge
on the day of their consecration to make to the pope every
five years. While no amount of rank and regal embellishment could change the humble character of Patrick J.
Hayes, this time he was to arrive with all the external ac-
couterments of a traditional Renaissance prince. This
was not of his own motivation; it was the expression and
symbol of the reverence in which he was held. George
MacDonald, devoted votary and trustee of St. Patrick's
Cathedral, chartered the second largest yacht in the world,
the *Innara,* to meet him at Gibraltar and take him to
Naples.

And it was no mere trip through the Mediterranean.

The *Innara* was transformed into a cardinalatial palace and was caparisoned much in the same way as the *Bucintoro* was as the ceremonial barge of the Doges of Venice. For this elaborate rigging, everything had been arranged beforehand. And though MacDonald had not thought of the *Bucintoro,* he did coincidentally create such a craft for his revered pastor. At the mainmast was hoisted with great ceremony in the presence of the New York prince of the Church, his own standard—a thirty-foot pennant where the Hayes coat of arms was emblazoned on a field of red. MacDonald did not know it, but the Venetian Doges flew exactly such a pennant, and its color was red, its length fully thirty feet.

They sailed into Naples. There the crews of the men-of-war anchored in the harbor were alerted if not startled by the unusual standard at the mainmast of the luxurious craft. Being Italians, they recognized it and hurried to get ready for a flag salute. A Soviet freighter also was tied up to the wharf. To the Cardinal, who had seen many ships in a lifetime, this was a novelty but hardly a surprise. It was doubtless a surprise to the Soviet crew as they tried to decipher the lavish heraldic bearings. They did not understand it. They did not salute. Italian officials came out to offer their greetings.

A special train was waiting alongside the wharf to take the son of the East Side of New York in his princely habiliments to Rome. This time, the shy and modest Hayes, who actually did not know where he would put up when he had come to receive his cardinal's hat, now entered the city of the pilgrims in royal style. He was welcomed in the royal waiting room at the station and given a royal escort to the luxurious Hotel Excelsior, where a whole floor had been reserved for him by his worshipful trustee, MacDon-

ald. Dining rooms and drawing rooms were all assigned
to him as if he were a sovereign.

He fulfilled his visit to Pius XI and made his report of
the archdiocese. This so impressed the Pontiff that he immediately gave orders that the work should be rewarded
by an unusual number of promotions for priests and laymen. He inquired of the trip on the seas. It was with
vibrant thrill that Hayes could tell the Pope of the *Innara*.
The Holy Father, usually more serious than expansive,
actually rejoiced with a refreshed stimulation when he
heard that his New York archbishop had traveled in a
modern *Bucintoro*. MacDonald in the meantime had
been doing his allotted turn as a papal chamberlain.
When it came to the notice of the Pontiff that, besides this
effort of official duty, he had unstintingly arranged all the
trip, he was struck by such filial devotion. The Cardinal
then related the qualities of his parishioner in works of
charity and in his unselfish co-operation in the affairs of
the Church. The Pope thereupon desired to make the occasion memorable. He bestowed on MacDonald the rank
of marquis.

As much in that atmosphere as anywhere else, it was
quite in the character of MacDonald, for, even without
rank he had always gracefully displayed a finesse and
savoir vivre which was outstandingly derived from a cultivated gentility and seignorial intuition. To begin with,
he was a handsome man—tall, slim, erect, and striking.
He knew the forms and conventions of the Old as well as
the New World. In this present voluntary responsibility
of patron of the Cardinal's travels, he had not left any
stone unturned to glorify the rank and high station of his
spiritual prince. Later, the *Innara* cruised the eastern
Mediterranean, stopped at Istanbul, and at Alexandria.

The Cardinal and his entourage toured Egypt and then returned for a sojourn on the Italian Riviera. The standard always flew from the mainmast.

In the work of the archdiocese Hayes put impressive emphasis on his priestly mission. Along the unwavering line of his attachment to simple principles, he had adopted the exhortation of St. Paul: "Now abide Faith, Hope and Charity; and the greatest of these is Charity." The penetrating influence of his boyhood hardships and adversity had chastened his soul to relieve the sufferings of the poor. This more than anything else whether the great ceremonies, the complex administration of the archdiocese, the extension of education, a building program, or whatever it was—this spiritual devotion in charity became the overwhelming motivation of his life. His paternal benevolence and toil had accomplished so much that he was universally known as "the Cardinal of Charity."

Charity, too, did not mean the simple offering of something for relief or as a palliative to conscience or even as a showy way of dispensing any overabundant possession of earthly goods. He did not mind these expressions of an individual's particular spiritual circumstance. But what he did with their offerings rested on his own conscience as a responsibility of trust. The needs of the poor and sufferings of the weak became a life work. He conceived it his mission so to meet their entreaties that the greatest good could be done for the greatest number.

It is accordingly one of his great achievements that he set up a charitable organization based on the most modern scientific knowledge, that has remained to this day a model in public relief. The depression years he faced with a grim bracing of his will. He distributed more than fourteen million dollars in less than twenty years. His own formula in carrying out this pattern was expressed when he said, "I hold it to be a shining truth, conceived in faith and proved in history, that Charity is the supreme test and goal of human relations." And then again, "A scientific charitable clearing house, such as the Catholic Charities, makes of Charity not only an earnest expression of the duty to God, but also a practical, sure way of helping where help is needed most. Here love and method go hand in hand."

Another evidence of the simplification of the abstruse nature of theological doctrine arose when his neighbor at his summer residence at Dunwoodie, John Moody, the great Wall Street statistician and publisher, approached him on the subject of conversion. Moody had been an Episcopalian all his life. He had studied profoundly in the history of Christian thought. Every word of the philosophy of St. Thomas Aquinas in many, many volumes had been thoroughly assimilated by Moody. He was in his sixties at the moment, so that his decision to seek conversion in the Catholic profession had been no snap conclusion. Moody expected to go through an exacting examination by a priest to test his true adherence to the faith. Instead, simplicity was the Cardinal's formula.

"John," he said as if summing up all his own knowledge in the theological and philosophical sciences and trying to crystallize it in some understandable form, "John, you will find everything in the penny catechism, and that is all there is to it."

Moody told me, after he had been received into the Church, that with all that he had learned in many decades of study of the great philosophers and theologians, the penny catechism did really epitomize the faith.

While the moment when Pius XI had held the red hat over his head as he knelt before him stood out as the apex of a career which had begun in dire penury and little hope, yet another moment quite as great studded the plain simplicity of his life. He was arriving in New York as he brought back the red hat on the liner *Leviathan*. He received a radio message from the Grand Street Boys Association, a group of New York men who had risen to civic and financial prominence in city affairs and who had played around the Brooklyn Bridge with Paddy Hayes.

"Regardless of race and religion," the message ran, "the East Side rejoices that in you it has given the world a Prince of the Church."

To thousands of messages he had received, he cabled a broadcast.

"My blessings to little old New York," it ran.

Scores of tugs came down New York bay to greet him. The state of New York was represented by Governor Alfred E. Smith, who was born in the very poverty and on the same streets as he was. They had attended the same parish church. Smith was accompanied by his entire official and military staff. The greetings of the city of New York were conveyed by Mayor John F. Hylan, another Catholic. Glee clubs sang "The Sidewalks of New York," which later on was to become the Smith campaign song when he ran for President of the United States.

When the new cardinal disembarked at the Battery, he received the traditional New York welcome when thousands of miles of ticker tape were flown from downtown skyscrapers as a triumphal welcome. The cardinalatial motorcade proceeded up Broadway and then turned up Fifth Avenue toward St. Patrick's Cathedral. Before it reached the edifice, this Prince of the Church descended. An ecclesiastical procession was formed. In his red robes he walked several hundred yards to the cathedral. Thousands lining the route burst into a welcome only accorded heroes.

Inside the cathedral he was escorted to a red canopied throne. Children sang. The frail boy of the East Side was enthroned in his red watered silk and his mantle of ermine. He had to say something to this outpouring of his own city.

"It is a New York welcome to a New Yorker," he said, speaking from the sanctuary, "a welcome to a New Yorker who loves his city, knows virtually its heart and soul."

He was New York.

6. Red Robes in the White House

IF O'CONNELL could endearingly be called Number One in Boston, we can without detraction from him or favoritism to anyone else designate *motu proprio* George Cardinal Mundelein, in his time, as Number One in Chicago. The two prelates had traits in common. Both were skillful administrators. Both knew how to hold a tight rein. O'Connell was a great builder and so was Mundelein. The Boston hierarch insisted on the recognition of his rank wherever he went, even to publicly putting priests in their places. The Chicago superior, while less pompous, imposed his princely privileges by his prelatial *savoir faire* of ecclesiastical precedence. We saw how O'Connell occasionally called the Massachusetts Legislature to Sunday school to get their lesson in public morality. Mundelein, in a less indirect way, extended his influence in the political field to embrace national and international issues.

O'Connell had particularly circumscribed his sphere of operations within the borders of New England. Now, while Mundelein exercised no ecclesiastical jurisdiction outside the province of Illinois and mostly was required to limit his administrative functions to the archdiocese of Chicago, he had so increased his prestige that every now and then he personally became an international controversy. What he said often exacted the attention of foreign

80

governments. Both our own political leaders and many of the foreign diplomats in Washington respected his pronouncements because of the arresting if not always realistic effect of them at home and abroad.

I first witnessed this talent of talking at or back to governments when he was made a cardinal with Archbishop Hayes in 1924. When the Chicago archbishop came to Rome to receive the red hat, he took the occasion very much in his stride. He was at home with people and prelates. With the newsmen he used to converse quite freely and openly, as if the occasion did not weigh too heavily on his nervous system. This was because he was quite accustomed to knowing what would be interesting for the papers to print. Since he had chosen the College of the Propaganda Fide as the residence where he would receive his *biglietto,* the occasion was far more cosmopolitan than the gathering around Hayes in the North American College. Men who had been students with him from Italy, France, Germany, Austria, and Hungary came to pay their homage. The ceremony was held in a large scholastic hall and therefore gave an appearance of being a highly intellectual convocation.

In his entourage was Father Quinn, an Irish priest who had come with him from Chicago. He watched the ceremony with eager anticipation. But in the end, he was not quite satisfied. He looked at it as just simply telling the Chicago archbishop that he had been made a cardinal, and why not let it go at that?

As Mundelein descended from the dais when the ceremony was concluded, Quinn approached his superior to kiss the ring and congratulate him.

"Too much fur-r-r and fithur-r-s," he said with undisguised Irish ruggedness. "Had it been me, I'd a jist taken the littur-r an' sed thank ye."

In a few days Mundelein's first international turn came to talk at governments. He was taking over his titular church and made the customary speech of acceptance of his Roman parish. This was before the Italian government had signed the Lateran Treaty which settled the quarrel between them and the Holy See. Mundelein told them that it was about time they gave back what they had stolen of papal territory. Of course, the Italians did not ever give back much, but in 1929 they did give enough back and made other concessions to satisfy the territorial demands and ecclesiastical exactions of Pope Pius XI. Not that Mundelein's words did it all. But they helped.

Though he was younger in years than Hayes, he was senior as a prelate because he had been an archbishop since 1915, whereas Hayes did not arrive at archiepiscopal dignity until 1919. For this reason, he took precedence over the New York cardinal and made all the speeches on those occasions where only one of them was indicated to respond. He was chosen to consecrate the new Knights of Columbus playgrounds, which were a gift from the order to the Pope, located right alongside the colonnade of St. Peter's and intended to serve the poor children of the neighborhood.

By a spontaneous decision, the Pontiff had promised to attend and bless the playgrounds. They were located just outside of Vatican territory. Up until that time, the popes had remained voluntary prisoners of the Vatican and had sworn, one after the other, never to set foot outside it as a protest against Italian depredations of the territory of the Holy See. Immense preparations had been made for the emergence of the Holy Father. Mundelein was to have the honor of formally receiving the Supreme Pontiff in his first step outside the Vatican since 1870.

But something happened. The *Giornale d'Italia,* a Rome newspaper, got the story and published it. The Holy Father had been scheduled to appear at five in the afternoon. The newspaper was on the streets with the news at four-thirty. It made it look as if the Pope were giving up the protest. It was translated as a clear-cut surrender to Italy. This was not the intention. Within the half hour the Pontiff changed his mind and decided, on the basis of this twisted interpretation, not to grace the ceremony by formally blessing the playgrounds. Mundelein was deprived of a historical privilege as host in welcoming a pontiff on soil outside Vatican limits. From that day, it took five years for the Pontiff to venture out again. In the new occasion, a treaty had bound Italy to accord him all the honors of a sovereign.

But perhaps the most repercussive international episode with which Mundelein is connected was when he addressed the Holy Name Societies of Chicago in 1938 and there called Hitler a paperhanger, and "a very poor paperhanger at that." This remark was cabled to Germany. The divine attributes of the Führer received a blasphemous shock. Something had to be done to wipe away this humiliating stain. Immediately, the press and radio machine of Nazi Germany was put in motion to excoriate and castigate the erring Archbishop of Chicago. Unforgivably defiant of Nazi scolding, he was sitting the next day complacently at his desk amused by the furor that his apparently innocuous remark had aroused. Retribution for the cardinalatial disrespect of the German divinity, however, must be inflicted.

In October of that same year, Mundelein presided at the Eucharistic Congress in New Orleans in the role of papal legate, which *de facto* and *de jure* means that he is the *alter ego* of the Holy Father himself. Important national figures attended the congress. When it concluded, it was part of his duty as legate to make a personal report to the Pontiff of what had taken place. But on his way to Rome he was invited by President Roosevelt to break the journey and be the guest of the White House. This was the first time in history that an American cardinal ever slept in the executive mansion. He was the first cardinal of the White House.

As he stayed on in the leisurely nothing-to-do of the evening, it was natural for the conversation between the Cardinal and the President to take on a leisurely tempo, too. Roosevelt knew how. Mundelein knew how. They laughed about the paperhanger incident. Then Mundelein opened the subject of diplomatic representation. He told the President that it would serve the government well to receive a papal nuncio in Washington. The Holy See was represented only by an apostolic delegate, who is without official recognition by our government. Mundelein desired diplomatic status for the papal representative. This would be a nuncio. He pointed out that there was substantial advantage in making use of the Vatican's world-wide diplomatic service.

The President replied that it was more important for the United States to have a representative in the Vatican rather than a nuncio in Washington. The pleasant evening ended when the President told Mundelein to be sure to convey his cordial greetings to the Pope and to discuss something of the diplomatic relations between the United States and the Holy See. He was to get the Pope's ideas.

Now Mundelein went off to Rome. Meanwhile, the President had telegraphed Ambassador Phillips, our emissary there, to leave for Naples. There he was to await the arrival of Cardinal Mundelein and accord him a welcome reserved by our diplomatic corps for very distinguished Americans. Phillips obeyed. Mundelein was welcomed officially by the American ambassador. It was the first time in history that any Roman Catholic ecclesiastic was so honored officially by the Department of State. Hitherto, American bishops, archbishops, and cardinals would enter Italy; visit the Pope, and leave Italy without the embassy knowing they were there and without the prelates bothering to find out whether the ambassador was even at home.

But the official fuss with which Mundelein was received was not to end there. He was the "so-called Christian" who had called Hitler a paperhanger. This would not and could not be forgotten. Actually, the Nazi press was following the movements of the Chicago archbishop with more thoroughness—albeit curdled with revenge—than was our own press. They had even scooped the American newspapers—either by irresponsible guessing, journalistic invention, or actual second-story intelligence on the conversation between the Cardinal and the President. Throughout Germany, it was headlined that Mundelein had been entrusted by the President with obtaining American representation in the Vatican and Vatican representation in the United States. This was not illicit. But Mundelein's mediation was all for a price, they said. Mundelein would deliver the Catholic vote to Roosevelt in exchange for the establishment of diplomatic relations between the Holy See and the United States. This was 1938. Roosevelt was serving his second term. At that time, no thought of a third term was born. The war had not yet begun.

From Naples, Mundelein was driven to Rome in the ambassadorial motors. With due formality and devotion, he was received in audience by Pius XI. It had been deep in the Pontiff's heart to establish diplomatic relations with the United States. But the hope would have to be postponed now. The Nazi charge that it was to be a trade had killed the prospects for the moment, no matter how disposed the United States was to discuss the subject. Mundelein told of the Eucharistic Congress. He related how he had stayed in the White House, a milestone in official recognition of a Catholic prelate. The Pope was pleased with all of it.

Mundelein arrived back in New York in November. Bishop Sheil, his vicar-general, had come on from Chicago to meet him. I saw them at the Hotel Vanderbilt. I knew privately about the conversation of Cardinal and President. I asked what would happen next in view of what the Nazis had published.

"The diplomatic matter is on ice for a long time to come," he said, smiling. "But Hitler is still a paper hanger and a very poor paper hanger at that."

Though Mundelein came of German stock, it was of that sturdy, pioneering line which established itself in the United States before the Civil War. He was the grandson of the first Federal soldier killed at Fort Sumter. Of all the Americans to reach the Sacred College, his ancestry on American soil dated a generation or two before any of the others. We can see in this heritage the deep roots of the hatred of dictatorial tyranny. It was quite in keeping for the descendant of a German who had fled the autocracy of the Hohenzollern rulers and their satellites to oppose the superman doctrines of Hitler.

Coincidentally, George William Mundelein was born in the same neighborhood on the East Side of New York as Cardinal Hayes, only it was five years after, and precisely on July 2, 1872. They have been called playmates, though this may be more of an affable stretch of memory than a real early companionship. The two boys did know each other. But they were so far apart in age in childhood that while their later careers ran quite parallel to each other, what suited one as a boy of twelve did not suit the other as a boy of seven. They both attended De La Salle Institute. Mundelein followed Hayes. Then again he came after him at Manhattan College.

Mundelein had thought of entering West Point and was actually tendered an appointment. He chose, however, to heed the call of the priesthood. Here is where he had his first touch with Rome. He was chosen as bright enough and scholar enough to attend the College of Propaganda Fide there. His native brilliance assisted him to do the course in three years. The degree of Doctor of Sacred Theology was awarded him in later years. He was assigned as secretary of Bishop Charles E. McConnell of Brooklyn. He became chancellor of the Brooklyn diocese in 1897 and was in 1909 appointed auxiliary bishop of Brooklyn.

The First World War, like the Second World War, furnished many nationality problems in the United States. It also extended these problems into the Catholic Church. With the strong Catholic populations of Germans, Poles, Irish, Italians, Lithuanians, Austrians, and Hungarians, it was often quite perplexing to a bishop to adjust his appointments of priests so that they would be wholly acceptable to the national sensibilities of his flock. Naturally, the greatest problems of keeping the parishes in spiritual harmony occurred in the big cities. Of these, Chicago presented the most labyrinthian enigma.

At that time the apostolic delegate in Washington was Archbishop John Bonzano. One of his heavy and exacting responsibilities issued from his duty of recommending the appointment of bishops and archbishops who were by their own national lineage and their innate tact able to cope with the problem of diverse nationalities. Archbishop James Edward Quigley, of Chicago, died on July 10, 1915. Bonzano was entrusted with gathering the data on a good as well as skillful high priest to fill the see.

The delegate himself towered as a personality. Whether it helped or not, he was gifted by possessing a most absorbing presence. He was impressively handsome. But his true gifts consisted in his power of persuasion and his rightness of judgment. He was made a cardinal eventually. I recall a reception which the American colony tendered him in Rome after his return. We were all from different places and there were two hundred of us. With a soul full of good intentions co-ordinated with a mind quickened with alertness, he was able to connect each one of us, whether he had seen us before or not, with some friend or relative of ours in the United States whom he had known. He knew people in Steubenville, Ohio. This power of his was regarded as almost within the realm of the prohibited profession of mind reading, which it certainly was not. It was just top-flight social charm. It was truly princely.

Archbishop Bonzano canvassed the entire American availability for a skillful archbishop of Chicago. Among others he had reported the capabilities of George William Mundelein, still auxiliary in Brooklyn. He was known as a great scholar and an efficient administrator. Evidence of his adroit tact had given guarantee of his ability to adjust delicate situations, for Brooklyn had even in those days enjoyed a certain priority in periodic eruptions. His German ancestry but lengthy American lineage helped to establish him as fitted to meet all national sensibilities. On December 9, 1915, he was promoted to the archiepiscopal see of Chicago.

The archdiocese was burdened with difficulties. The war was not destined to lessen them. Our entry in 1917 increased the tension. Besides, several mayoralty campaigns had suffered the irksome unpleasantness and anxiety of religious issues. Along came the stampeding and rampant "Big Bill" Thompson. He had been elected before the war and after the war made a comeback. In one of these campaigns he uttered the phrase for which he has been so ridiculed, "King George has got to keep his snout out of the affairs of Chicago." This was reported everywhere as meaning King George V of England. Everyone wondered in Europe as well as America why a mayor of Chicago would attack the King of England.

The late Melvin Traylor, Chicago banker, told me that it had not been Thompson's intention at all to attack George V. The religious issue had been injected into the campaign in a whispering underground. Thompson's opponent was a Catholic. The charge had been made that Catholics were all told to vote for the Catholic. Now Thompson decided to veil his attack on the archbishop. In citing "King George," he had meant George Mundelein, the archbishop.

The reference passed over everybody's head. But what happened? The various nationalities who were traditionally anti-British rallied to the Thompson standard for his attack on the British king. Thompson saw the effect of it. Craftily, he decided to let it go at that and continued to excoriate George V, even though he had never been an issue in the municipal affairs of Chicago.

Since that time, the Catholic population of Chicago has increased in greater ratio than the Protestant population. By the simple weight of superior numbers—should an election ever again be fought on a religious issue—the compactness of the adherents to the faith would render the result almost inevitably in their favor. Like O'Connell, Mundelein insisted that when professing Catholics

were put up for office, their characters should be above
reproach. When he found a man worthy of public en-
dorsement, he put no obstacles in his way. He had conferred on the present mayor of Chicago, Edward V. Kelly,
the honor of being a personal friend. Kelly consulted him
quite often on the forthrightness of Catholic men and
women for office.

His participation in political affairs was not always
given in a passive way. During the 1940 Presidential campaign, it was quite evident that he favored the re-election
of President Roosevelt. Even descending from Presidential prerogative, Roosevelt accepted an invitation to take
lunch with Cardinal Mundelein and was a guest at the
archiepiscopal mansion on North State Street. This was
not just exactly intended to give Mr. Roosevelt something to eat while he was in Chicago, though it undoubtedly did accomplish that purpose. More likely it was
that it suited Mr. Roosevelt to have a multitude of his
host's followers feel that if he was all right for Mundelein,
he was all right for them. As things turned out, Illinois
was returned in the Democratic column with or without
the influence of a nice luncheon.

The time and the particular situation in the archdiocese
happily dovetailed into his concepts of what ought to be
done. Little effort was lost in his getting his hands on
the controls. Just as Chicago is big, so he met that challenge of great magnitude in his projects for the care of
souls and the improvement of their cultural and intellectual aspirations. Chicago is now known as the most populous jurisdiction of any Roman Catholic authority in the
world excepting the domain of the Supreme Pontiff himself. It is credited with being the richest, too, and the
riches reside in the educational institutions, the churches,
athletic fields, and gymnasiums, a large majority of which

were undertaken and completed during the episcopate of Cardinal Mundelein.

With great enthusiasm, he told me of his project for the theological seminary of the archdiocese at St. Mary's of the Lake. It was to be a community of religion and scholarship. He called it Mundelein. What stood out more than anything else was his earnest intention to construct a group of buildings which would reflect the will and story of America while conserving the religious spirit in their use and even in their appearance. He told me that he had studied quite intensively and with innate pride the types of architecture which were natively American. What showed me his breadth of concept was his desire to include among his buildings an exemplification of the Quaker meetinghouse, because he thought of it as an American expression of history and of art. Most of the buildings were conceived in the colonial tradition, so that he succeeded in achieving a truly American feeling in the vast plan while still maintaining the theme of a truly intellectual and religious community. He was satisfied that he had combined a love of country and a zeal for the Church in the ambitious project now fully realized and standing as a permanent memorial to his patriotism as well as to his faith.

The site was located thirty miles from Chicago and included two arms of the lake. Over these he had erected strikingly monumental bridges. The whole tract was landscaped not in any nondescript fashion but in accord with the lay of the land, the contour of the lake, and the arrangement of the buildings. Over fifty thousand trees were planted so that while the view of Mundelein today is quite beautiful indeed, what it will be when the trees reach their spreading development in color and form can only be visualized as perennial and ravishing.

Willingly indeed did Mundelein assume the awesome responsibility of being host for the Twenty-eighth International Eucharistic Convention. This is the biggest gathering of lay and clerical members of the Roman faith in all the world. Here his talent for magnitude was profitably exploited. The Cardinal told me about his grandiose projects for the meeting. He had come to Rome to show them to the Pope, who was so overcome with their completeness and extent that he prophesied that the meeting would be the most encompassing the Church had ever experienced. This prophecy given at the time of its inception was abundantly fulfilled by a sterling manifestation of devotional solidarity. The vast plans were actually surpassed when translated into reality.

On the same site as the seminary Mundelein conceived the great gathering of the faithful which was to be the climax of the assemblage. Fourteen cardinals from all over the world attended. A million souls congregated in a specially erected stadium to kneel and prostrate themselves before the uplifted Host. The extent of the organization reached abstruse intricacies, and though a storm swept the lake region on the climactic day, the ceremony so carefully planned succeeded most eloquently in its meticulous enactment.

A happy circumstance which satisfied the desires of thousands of Americans emerged from the choice of the papal legate. The Pontiff sent Cardinal Bonzano. Of all the members of the Sacred College, this prelate was just as richly endowed to administer before great multitudes as he was to pour out a heart-to-heart satisfaction on a single individual. He personified pontifical authority as well as represented it. Mundelein had succeeded in having a special train built for him through the largess and generosity of rich Chicago parishioners. The outside was painted in cardinal red and bore the arms of the Pontiff and those of the Legate. The interior was also upholstered in cardinal red with the two coats of arms embroidered in profusion all about. Wherever the train stopped en route to Chicago, and on its return to New York, thousands gathered to welcome the Pope's own representative. Thousands genuflected before him as if he had been the Supreme Pontiff in person.

While Mundelein's influence set in motion many of the national and international currents which coursed through the nation and the world, his pastoral work in its magnitude was the equal of, if not paramount to that of any archbishop in the entire domain of the Roman Catholic Church.

In his twenty-four years of archiepiscopal administration, he increased the number of priests in the Chicago area from 790 to 1,779. The Catholic population grew from barely over a million to a million and three quarters. He died on October 2, 1939. He was a priest of wide horizons. His concept of religion was framed in a rigid devotion to country. He accomplished big things. He *was* big. He was as much at home in the White House as in the Vatican palaces. He never permitted his duty to the one in any way to minimize his obligation to the other.

7. What! Papal Legate from Philadelphia?

THE highest ranking prelate in the United States of today enjoys this dignified distinction because of his seniority. It just happens that he is the head of the usually quiescent archdiocese of Philadelphia. Primacy of position comes to Dennis Cardinal Dougherty because he has been a cardinal longer than any of his cardinalatial colleagues in America. After the death of Cardinal Gibbons in 1921, it was Cardinal O'Connell who graced the dignity of dean of the American hierarchy. This covered a span of twenty-three years. Dougherty assumed it in 1944 when O'Connell died.

A silent though not unnoticed reverence is paid to the senior cardinal. Wherever he is, he takes precedence over all other cardinals, archbishops, and bishops in America. His word carries weighty significance in the councils of the bishops when they meet for their periodic convocations in Washington. He is ex-officio chairman of many of the boards and committees among them. The position of honor is always reserved for him no matter what ecclesiastical function he attends. All of these privileges and prerogatives he will enjoy as long as he lives. Among the American cardinals he is *primus inter pares*.

But the rank he holds, while venerated, carries very little, if any, real authority in the Church assemblies. It would certainly raise him to a position akin to "Pontiff of the West" should real power be vested in the rank. As it is, his administrative authority is very definitely limited to his own archdiocese and in a lesser degree to the Metropolitan Province of Pennsylvania. Should he wish to propose a move which might benefit the whole Church—unless all the factors for its accomplishment existed in his own jurisdiction—he would have to seek approval of the bishop or archbishop who did have jurisdiction. This never occurs in the endeavors of Cardinal Dougherty. He is a high priest who stays strictly within his own prescribed domain.

His eighty-one years have been most benevolent in withholding the usual adversities of age. He was born on August 16, 1865, in Girardville, Schuykill County, Pennsylvania, which is now in the Philadelphia area. Today he takes active command of the pastorship of nearly a million communicants. He is built quite stockily. The four score summers do not seem to reduce his functional vitality. For the one score of years I have known him, he has always emitted a buoyant tone of assertive life. Perhaps most men do not change very much in the mature period of their span. Certainly Cardinal Dougherty is one of those who can maintain an even tenor in countenance, as well as spirit—as if his strength were to be perennial.

Though he is not tall, he gives an impression of massiveness. Certainly what he lacks in height he more than balances with a robust frame which confirms the tradition about him that few men could outdo him in his earlier days in a test of strength. Usually his face is expressive of tense decision. His square jaw bears witness of a tenacity which has kept him fighting through many encounters where the rights of religion had to be defended. His step is steady, though hardly spirited. His gestures bear testimony that life goes on in an even tempo, though he can show displeasure. None of his movements are quick but each is regular, as if to indicate that time must be measured but not wasted. Tenacity, scholarship, studied judgment are the attributes which have evolved from this highly experienced and deeply grounded prince of the Church.

His life was to take him around the world several times. He could be called a wanderer from Philadelphia, though he returned to it as the head of the archiepiscopal see. Even his education started with leaving Philadelphia, when he attended the Jesuit College of St. Mary's in Montreal, Canada. Among other accomplishments, one thing St. Mary's did was to furnish him with an excellent command of languages and especially French. He also speaks Spanish and Italian with quite as much fluency.

For his preliminary theological training he returned to Philadelphia, where he attended St. Charles Seminary. He studied there two years and was chosen for his further theological and philosophical work to go to the North American College in Rome. From this institution he was graduated in 1885 but was four years too young to be ordained. He pursued his further studies in the College of Propaganda Fide, which is the highest ecclesiastical institution in Rome. There he obtained the degree of Doctor of Sacred Theology. He was forced to wait for ordination until he was twenty-five. It is not without its significance that his historical turn of mind induced him to choose the Basilica of St. John Lateran as the scene of his ordination. This is the primatial church of all Christendom and known traditionally as "Head and Mother of Churches."

All of this learning was destined to make him a likely choice for a professorship in a theological seminary. He returned to Philadelphia and was immediately assigned by Archbishop Ryan as professor of theology at St. Charles. Twelve years were spent in the teaching profession. He had registered the imprint of both his personality and his knowledge on the thousands of students who had passed through the institution during his teaching years.

But the knowledge of his learning could not be kept within the limits of the archdiocese. Besides, he had left a great reputation in Rome itself. His leadership with students, his profound erudition, and his authority as a theological analyst, together with his talent for languages, brought him to the attention of the supreme pontiff, who was then Leo XIII. And it was well for the Pontiff, too, because in 1903 he had decided to take the administration of the Philippines out of the hands of Spanish bishops, who had ruled the Church there for three hundred years.

Acute trouble had developed in the islands following the cession to the United States in 1899. It was inevitable that readjustments would have to be made between the new civil authorities and the bishops. The rule, both political and ecclesiastical, had been autocratically Spanish. Spanish institutions in education and in administration had dominated the islands with no other motive than the personal aggrandizement of the rulers by the exploitation of the Philippine people.

Complicating the purely administrative functions necessitated by the change was an independent religious movement which started in northern Luzon. Right Reverend Gregorio Aglipay, who had the official position of ecclesiastical governor of the diocese of Nueva Segovia, organized a schismatic movement from the Roman Church, which then had been the faith of 90 per cent of the population. The movement gained in adherents. The purely schismatic nature of the offshoot posed a serious problem for the Holy See.

First, it was necessary to attempt to prevent the spread of the schism, which had become known as the Aglipayan Movement. It had actually gone beyond the realm of a schismatic church and could easily be classified as heretic, though the Roman authorities preferred to attempt a return to the Roman fold rather than pronounce an out-and-out excommunication. The new church proclaimed its adherence to modern science and even announced that its belief attributed greater authority to science than to Biblical tradition. Aglipay denied the performing of miracles and also repudiated the scriptures which related those of Christ. With such a radical departure from Catholic doctrine, it did seem strange that the cult held to the Roman ritual, though Spanish formulas were substituted for the Latin ones.

This was certainly a problem to be met by the best tact and perspicacity in Vatican missionary extension. Surveying the field for some ecclesiastic to measure up to this peremptory exaction, the Pope decided to call Father Dennis Joseph Dougherty, professor of dogmatic theology, from his chair in St. Charles Seminary. He was to go to the Philippines to arrest the Aglipayan schism. Recalling the former Spanish bishop at Nueva Segovia, the Pontiff designated Dougherty as the new bishop. He was the first American to be appointed under the new policy the Pope had established in substituting American for Spanish administrators.

The new bishop started out for his thorny assignment with more apprehension than joy. He was not a bishop at thirty-seven just to wear a miter. His innate restlessness for solving the knotty complexities spurred him into the field. His square jaw was not a mere facial embellishment but redounded more to his inherent and bracing aggressiveness than anything else. His thorough groundwork and profound erudition in doctrinal theology made him impregnable for the faith against any schism or heresy. His gift for languages was turned to good account, since he could speak to the native clergy and their communicants in a tongue they could understand.

When he arrived at his see city, it was not long before the effect of his vital energy was noticeable. He reopened the theological seminary of the diocese at Vigan. He had recruited five Philadelphia priests to go with him into the chaotic labyrinth of crosscurrents. To these he assigned the task of organizing the new seminary and of enrolling a sufficient number of students from among the Filipinos themselves. These he intended to use as the nucleus of a new and militant native priesthood. He later invited missionaries from Belgium to assist him. Then he decided to induce the Fathers of the Divine Word of Steyl, Holland, to come out and battle for the faith. A large group of them accepted.

Now, there was much church property, too, which the schismatics took over. Bishop Dougherty protested that the churches, schools, and charitable institutions which they seized were by right the property of Catholic communicants. They were built as Catholic institutions by adherents to the Catholic faith. Appeal was made to the American civil government. The civil authorities avoided any responsibility in deciding such a delicate issue. The entire matter was referred to the Philippine courts. Each case was decided on its own merits. Most suits were won by the Roman diocesan jurists. In this way the Bishop, who was now weighed down by a net of entangling problems, was able to salvage a number of Catholic churches and institutions. This enabled him to establish the administration of the diocese on a firmer basis. In five years the seminary he had opened was graduating enough priests to shepherd the spiritual welfare of the flock with abundant grace.

Five years of tireless travail and anxiety resulted in a successful accomplishment of the mission. Accordingly, Leo XIII recognized his dovetailing fitness and facile tact in delicate situations. Bishop Dougherty was promoted from the see of Nueva Segovia to that of Jaro. Here the problem of the schismatics was greater. Other jurisdictional and administrative obstacles made Jaro a much heavier task than Nueva Segovia. But he had found the key for solving these abstruse irregularities in the religious irresponsibility of the agitators of the new cult. He worked closely and tactfully with the American authorities. His efforts were finally crowned with a success which had the attributes of the triumphal.

Conflicts between the Philippine insurrectionists and the regulars had destroyed a great many of the churches and other institutions in the Jaro diocese. Bishop Dougherty had to rebuild his own episcopal residence from the ground up, as it had been a complete wreck. Intermittently, he returned to the United States to collect funds for the restoration of the institutions. His policy concentrated on administering to the physical sufferings as well as the spiritual shortcomings of the natives. He built a new seminary because he had early conceived the key problem of the Church as based on the training of a sufficient number of native clergy. A new hospital was constructed at Iliolo, the largest in the East.

But while these efforts were proceeding in the ordinary though toilsome course of his episcopal administration, the innumerable law suits which were fought to retain possession of the institutions built under the Spanish regime took considerable toll in energy and anxiety. Since the American civil government had washed its hands of any interference in the conflicting claims of the Catholic faith and the Aglipayan sect, recourse to the law courts entailed an interminable amount of legal preparations. The Philippine courts had established the principle that the churches belonged to the people, so that it became the task of Bishop Dougherty to prove that the Catholic Church was actually representing its own communicants, who had built the edifices. The legal entanglements were endless. Nevertheless, it was gratifying to the Bishop and to his superiors in Rome to learn that over the period of years that he was resident bishop in the islands, he had won nearly all of the cases.

Finally and by the order of President Theodore Roosevelt, steps were taken to reach a settlement on Church property between the United States government and the Catholic Church. William Howard Taft, later President of the United States and still later chief justice, but at this time the secretary of war, visited the islands. The situation relating to Catholic religious orders was explained to him. He returned home by way of Japan, China, and India. Passing through the Mediterranean, he stopped off in Italy and there was received in audience by the Pope. A final agreement was reached in which the various religious orders were given possession of the lands and institutions they had formerly held.

All of these happy developments out of the somewhat chaotic state in which Philippine religious affairs had fallen were quite inevitably entered on the credit side for Bishop Dougherty. The succeeding popes and especially Benedict XV had watched his labors. He recalled him and appointed him bishop of Buffalo. This may have been a short respite, though it was no respite for the amount of parish extension and building operations which were inaugurated in his new diocese. His ability had been already measured. The Pontiff knew Dougherty as an ardent, persistent, and ceaseless toiler. When the see of Philadelphia was vacant in the spring of 1918, it was Dougherty who, from all the names in the vast American hierarchy, received the call. He was chosen archbishop on July 10, 1918.

Emotionally as well as ecclesiastically, the promotion produced an abundance of joy in his soul and a volume of satisfaction in the hearts of his Philadelphia communicants. This was his native city. He had come back to assume the throne of its cathedral. This had been a goal of which hitherto he had not permitted himself to dream. He knew the problems of the archdiocese well. He had lived there as an infant, gone to school there as a boy, studied there as a youth, and taught there as a man. He was now in the very prime of his life. He had reaped a wealth of spiritual and administrative experience in both hemispheres. Now all that he had learned would be bestowed with unstinting effort on the archdiocese he had long wished to serve.

The summit of a career was now being reached. In terms of the length of time that members of the Catholic hierarchy wait their promotions, Dougherty's successive elevations were rapid. Finally, he was chosen a cardinal. This lofty dignity was the first ever bestowed in the archdiocese of Philadelphia. He had been archbishop only two years and nine months when the elevation came. He went to Rome to receive the red hat. In the elaborate Hall of Benedictions on March 10, 1921, Benedict XV held the red hat over his head. He was a lone American taking his cardinalatial honors that day. The lordliness of the red robes had still to await their imposition on Hayes and Mundelein, though the latter had been an archbishop then for six years. Dougherty's variety of administrative and even diplomatic talents had brought him the honor.

When it was decided to hold the Thirty-third International Eucharistic Congress in Manila, Philippine Islands, the designation of a papal legate to bear the papal blessing from Rome on the Pontiff's own authority seemed to center on one personality. The post of *legatus a latere* is one of the most highly prized by all prelates. The legate speaks with the authority of the Holy Father himself. He is entitled to the same honors as if the Pontiff were present in person. Often at such huge gatherings communicants genuflect before him as they would in the presence of the Holy Father. It was to Dougherty that the honor went. He was the most endowed by experience and knowledge to grace the great gathering with credit to himself and honor to the Supreme Pastor whom he was to represent.

When the call came, Dougherty prepared to go to Rome to kneel before the Pontiff to receive the pontifical blessing. He was accompanied by a number of the priests who had served in the Philippines and some intimate relatives. His entrance into Rome was simple enough, but after the Pontiff's authority was delegated to him the Italian government began paying him the honors due a sovereign. Leaving the Hotel Ambassadeurs with his entourage in his full cardinalatial robes with *cappa magna,* he was escorted to the station by a platoon of full-dressed motorcycle police. As he descended from the papal automobile, masters of protocol from the Italian foreign office escorted him into the royal waiting room, where full-dressed carabineers in quaint Napoleonic uniforms stood at attention and formed a guard of honor. A special saloon car was assigned him for his trip to Naples, where he boarded the liner direct for Manila. During the long journey the steamer flew the papal flag. Masses were said every day. The luxurious craft gave every appearance of being a floating cathedral.

On his arrival at Manila he found that exceptional preparations had been made by the civil authorities. He was welcomed at the Admirals' Landing by the mayor of Manila, Juan Posadas. Philippine troops, boy scouts, school cadets, and student nurses lined Dewey Boulevard all the way to the ancient cathedral. There Mass was sung and the congress began its four days of devotions and spiritual manifestations. The first day was designated as men's day. The second day was set apart for the women. The third day was concentrated on children's activities.

The fourth day brought the climax of the immense concourse of the population. It was estimated that a million pilgrims had gathered for the celebration of the final Mass and the bestowal of the papal benediction. At dawn aerial bombs were exploded to give the people the signal as if for a great spiritual awakening. The bells of the churches rang. The site of the multitudinous convocation stood along the sea front at the great oval outdoor meeting place, the Lineta, transformed for this day into an immense amphitheater. The altar, covered with a golden *baldacchino,* shone brilliantly in the morning sun as an immense procession of clerics and laity began pouring into the great meeting place designed for the climactic ceremony of the apostolic blessing.

This procession had passed through lines of cheering multitudes who had stood along the route to render homage to the representative of the living Vicar of Christ in Rome. Two columns of the militant faithful marched in reverent step along the wide boulevard leading to the Lineta. On the left was the women's column, twelve deep. On the right were the men in phalanxes of twelve also. Children numbering forty thousand, the girls dressed in white and the boys in their colorful native costumes, marched in serried companies. Banners were held aloft registering the common faith of all the congregated hundreds of thousands.

The improvised amphitheater became a sweeping mass of song and chant. Voices were raised to the glory of the Universal Father. Prelates high in the hierarchy of the Roman Church ranged about the specially constructed altar. All eyes were focused on what was to transpire there. The Mass was sung with a religious fervor which encompassed the moving souls of one million children of man. The tension reached uncontrollable emotional heights. Presently it was the moment for the benediction —the benediction right from the throne of the Holy Father.

Here the man who had toiled to restore the Church in the Philippines to its militant strength and now was the embodiment of the authority of the Prince of the Apostles lifted high the monstrance. Cardinal Dougherty with solemn strain moved the sacred vessel first on the one side and then on the other as if to give each one of the great million there assembled the personal joy and privilege of bowing to its spiritual essence. This was the culminating moment of the gigantic assemblage emblematic of the reverence paid by four hundred other millions spread over the world's extent.

Then the multitude waited to listen to the voice of the successor to St. Peter himself transmitted from far-off Rome right into the very heart of the Far East through the ether. Men, women, and children listened with quickened emotion and soulful consecration. The voice from Rome welcomed the sons and daughters into the spiritual feast as the common father of them all. Heights of Christian devotion were reached. The broad expanse of the Pope's domains had been united in the blessing.

What Dougherty experienced coursing through his veins and through his soul has been experienced by no other American. It has not fallen to the lot of any other hierarch in the Catholic Church in America to represent the Supreme Pontiff on such a world-wide mission. Legates have been appointed from among the American cardinals but none has had the supreme spiritual experience of carrying the authority of the Pope to the far ends of the earth, and of bestowing his apostolic blessing as if it had been transmitted by the living hands of the supreme shepherd. It is quite true that Cardinal O'Connell was appointed on a mission to Japan but that was more diplomatic than authoritative. Mundelein was the legate in New Orleans but was limited to the jurisdiction of the United States.

Dougherty's work in Philadelphia reflects the active, dynamic force which characterized his restoration of the faith in the Philippines. Diligence in furthering the causes of education and of charity is witnessed in the great institutions which dot the area from one end to the other. To be pastor of a million souls requires experiences which bring reciprocal spiritual reactions to the needs of such a multitude. Dougherty has learned them. He knows how to meet them.

8. Medieval and Modern, and Vice Versa

W ORLD WAR II, with many other disruptions, also hindered the creation of cardinals. When the pope holds a consistory to make his worthy choices princes of the Church, the function is supposed to be none other than joyous. With war on, no function could have been joyous. Death reduced the Sacred College from fifty-seven to twenty-eight, though the maximum number is seventy. In August 1945, the war over, the Pope studied the new situation all over the world. Drastic dislocations had taken place. The Holy Father took inventory of men and movements all over the world. On the basis of what he had found, he made up almost a new college of cardinals.

Reapportionment, so common in our Congressional system due to changes in population, was adopted in the Pontiff's formula, based instead on modern Catholic strength rather than historic precedence. Traditional primacy had awarded more than fifty seats to Italians as late as the middle of the last century, with only twenty left for the rest of the world. By the turn of the century Catholic strength had grown so much in the New World that it was compelling to allot a number of seats to North and South America. Before World War I the number of

107

non-Italian cardinals had increased to be about equal to those of the Italians—thirty to thirty-five each. After World War II, North and South America should have still more, and with them recognition should be accorded Africa, the Middle East, China, and Australia, where the growth of the Church had flourished in contrast with saturated Europe.

By Christmas the Pope was ready. He had canvassed the field. He had gathered together a tremendous directory of the talents, scholarship, achievements, and spiritual riches inherent in the prelatial resources of his extensive and universal domain. The task had a magnitude for one mind which rarely if ever is found in the administrative courses of world-wide empires and continents. This all-encompassing responsibility, gigantic as it was, passed un-noticed by the multitudes who followed the proceedings throughout the world. The Pontiff sought the top men everywhere. This was his world-wide task. On December 24 the historic announcement was made that to fill the Sacred College to its full complement, he had nominated thirty-two new cardinals, and only four of them were Italians. The rest came from sees in Europe, but more, many more, from the Americas, and all the new countries where the faith was prospering.

Four cardinals had been allotted to the United States. Francis J. Spellman, Samuel Alphonsus Stritch, Edward Mooney, and John J. Glennon, archbishops of New York, Chicago, Detroit, and St. Louis respectively, received the call. One was given to Canada when James Charles Mc-Guigan, archbishop of Toronto, was nominated. This was the first time that Canada had received a cardinal outside Quebec, the stronghold of French-Canadian Catholicism. Other nominations went to Peru, Cuba, Chile, Brazil, and Argentina. Besides, the Pope extended cardinalatial patronage in otherwise unrepresented countries by appointing princes of the Church in Mozambique, Portuguese Africa; in Sydney, Australia, and in China. Automatically this kept the number of Italian cardinals at eighteen and increased the number of non-Italians to fifty-two, reversing the ratio of a little over a century ago.

Thirty of the new cardinals were present in Rome to attend the consistory, which the Pope had fixed for the week of February 18, 1946. The appointment of thirty-two cardinals simultaneously made the highest number ever honored at one time. Even though two were unable to come to Rome, and a third contracted illness while in Rome, it was still the greatest number which had received the red hat at any consistory.

New and extensive arrangements had to be made to take care of the traditionally formal proceedings with their staid medieval etiquette and rich pageantry. Hitherto, when only three or four cardinals were raised at one time, Vatican prelates took the ceremonies in a normal stride as if they had been waiting for something to do. But with thirty cardinals, they had to call for help from other colleagues not in the ceremonial career. For instance, in the simple act of notifying each cardinal-designate, it had been customary for a papal messenger to leave the Vatican from the Pope's secret consistory in a papal coach drawn by four black horses. The messenger, who was always a prelate, was driven to the temporary Roman residence of the nominee and carried the official notification of his elevation. This time there were too many places to go to. The procedure, however, had already been intermittently disrupted. In this consistory it was not used at all, because automobiles, albeit bearing the papal arms, were substituted for the papal blacks.

Several lavish halls were chosen where the new cardinals

would receive their notification. The Americans were appointed to the Chancellery Palace, the British Empire nominees to the English College, the Spanish to the Spanish Embassy, the French to the French Embassy, the Chinese cardinal to the Oriental College, the South Americans to the Latin-American College, and so on around the representative strongholds for which Rome is so plentiful and cosmopolitan. I broadcast the American ceremony for Radio Station WOV, New York.

On the Wednesday afternoon when the Pope placed a red biretta on each of the new cardinals, a spectacle of the world-wide expanse of the Catholic Church was presented. I had seen the ceremony a score or more times. On this day, it was as if the Catholic domain had come to do homage to the Supreme Pontiff in one single convocation. The new princes of the Church, in purple robes, with a short cape of ermine superimposed—the former because it was a penitential season and the latter because it was prescribed for winter—had taken on the seriousness of this first postwar outpouring of world-wide Catholic representation. The Pontiff, high upon his throne, the golden miter on his head and the short red velvet cape bordered with ermine over his shoulders, personified the centripetal point of all the converging currents and forces which bind the chief shepherd to his far-flung flock.

But the great and lavish event was the public consistory on the Thursday. This took place in St. Peter's. Papal masters of ceremony had been hard put to accommodate the crowd and prepare the setting for such an assembly of the nations. They had brought out all the special stalls from the basement of St. Peter's, covered them with brocades and damasks in richly embroidered tones. Multitudes, of both the high and the lowly, crowded wherever anything could be seen.

Pius XII entered, borne aloft by red-liveried ushers on his ceremonial throne, escorted by an elaborate procession of prelates and soldiery in resplendent uniforms. Two huge ostrich-feather fans swayed alongside as a symbol of regality. When he reached the papal altar, he descended the *sedia gestatoria* to take a throne before the altar seven steps above the dais. From this he performed the ceremony of formally placing a ceremonial red hat over the head of each new cardinal in turn.

Each, in turn, genuflected on the first step. Now he arose. Then he ascended the steps and knelt before the Pope. His six-yard train was stretched out down the steps by the ceremoniers. He kissed the slippered foot of the Pontiff. He arose and genuflected again. Then he kissed the Fisherman's ring on the Pope's third finger. Genuflecting a third time, he embraced the Pope. Once more he knelt. At that moment, the Pontiff placed the ceremonial red hat over his head repeating the formula *"Accipe galerum rossum"* (Receive ye the red hat). When the Holy Father concluded, the new cardinal was assisted to his feet. He descended the steps to embrace all the old cardinals as brethren. Seated on the brocaded stalls at right angles to the throne, threescore cardinals, old and new, the highest number I had ever seen congregated, except for a conclave to elect a new pope, represented the modern power of the Church. Concluding the rite, the twenty-nine new cardinals prostrated themselves before the Altar of the Cathedra full-length upon the floor as a symbol of humility before the Almighty.

When all the historic precedents had been recalled and had served to identify the consistory of February 1946 as the greatest in the long course of the Church, added human and spiritual values were awaited from the epochal event. It was true that at no previous consistory had thirty-two cardinals ever been created. It was true that it was the first time that all of the five continents were represented. It was true that the Western Hemisphere had been accorded greater importance than ever before. It was true that its geographical and racial representation had subscribed to the doctrine of universality of the Catholic Church.

But there were also qualities that without detracting from the bold relief which all these precedent-breaking factors gave to it, enhanced its importance in greater measure than the fact that some of the things were the first time in history. Ally and enemy had been brought together to mold a new world in the spirit of Catholic brotherhood. In the teaching and the precepts of the Church, they all believed that the common denominator in fraternal love could be found among them. Pope Pius XII as supreme pastor emphasized this principle in his first address before the new cardinals. He underscored the supranational character of the mission of the Church. This was truly the first meeting after the catastrophe of World War II where leaders of men met to urge the nations to lay down the sword forever and to fashion the world for a new reign of peace through the regeneration of the spirits of mankind.

This feeling of brotherhood was evident from that very first meeting. In purple and ermine, cardinals from Germany sat next to those from Britain, France, and the United States. Cardinals from Hungary and Italy marched side by side with those of Portugal, China, Canada, and the countries of South America. It was emblematic of the occasion that boundaries and racial hatreds did not exist at all, even though there were men among them of all colors and varying origins. China's cardinal was given the same station as the cardinals of Spain, Italy, or

France. Cardinal de Gouveia of Portuguese West Africa brought out, in penetrating impressiveness, the universality of Catholic teaching when he was accompanied in all the ceremonies by his black African secretary in prelatial robes.

Even before the consistory had taken place, French cardinals had extended their hospitality to the German cardinals, all of whom passed through Paris on their way to Rome. En route and in democratic humility they had shared their food baskets with them. Cardinal von Preysing of Berlin, Cardinal Frings of Cologne, and Cardinal von Galen of Münster all received a brotherly hand. The French government, too, had helped in providing safe and direct passage for them through to Milan.

And in the ceremonies, from the moment that the first new cardinal approached the throne, the living expression of this world's currents—whether it were joy or sorrow, the pride of victory or the dejection of defeat, the clash of an old civilization with the new, or of one society with another—or whatever it was—this living expression seemed united in the physical symbols of their spiritual obedience to their common Father.

Inevitable diversity of personality and presence was bound to emerge from a score and a half of men providentially chosen as the most outstanding of the pastors from nearly a score of nations and races. Differences of countenance and of outlook, of speech and of manner brought out the strangeness of the one to the other. From these exterior differences they were to pass as if from lack of understanding to full understanding, all within the orbit of their common faith.

Cardinal Agagianian, patriarch of Armenia, bearded, olive-skinned, and slightly rotund, wearing the traditional Oriental garb of flowing robes and turban, impressed his almost Arabesque and dignified bearing on pontiff and peasant alike midst the prelates of the West. In decisive contrast, the four American cardinals with the wiry alertness of the New World seemed to raise spirits of hope with their buoyant and confident dash among the members of the Old World beset with confusion and dejection. The new princes of the Church from France and Spain and Italy brought their secular touch to the traditional ceremonies as if they had always been used to cardinals.

The sight of a German bishop in the same procession as his former mortal enemies pricked attention. And yet here was a German bishop who had defied the Nazis throughout their long repression of twelve years. Here was Bishop Clement Augustus von Galen, son of a German count.

In this world convocation, von Galen, erect and confident, drew a spirited applause in the very depth of the ceremony, just as he was about to kneel before the Pope. Unpretentiously, he was on the verge of running away with the show. He had been remembered for his defiant and dauntless courage. And as a fortunate distinction, which allowed everyone to recognize him even though they had never seen him before, he stood towering above all the others. He was six feet eight inches in height. His face was set and determined. One could without tax on imagination conceive this unbreakable shaft of strength standing before an arrogant Nazi *gauleiter* and making him feel abject.

But the applause was not for his physical noteworthiness. From the beginning of the Nazi suppression of religion he launched out in vehement attack against their pagan dogma. As early as 1934, when the doctrines of a German racial god were promulgated, he declared in pastoral letters and exhortations to the flock that Nazism was contrary to Christianity and that it denied the teaching of the Nazarene. In 1935, when even more repressive measures operated against the Church, when priests were arrested and thrown into concentration camps, he cried out that Nazism had embraced idolatry, and charged that the Nazi leaders had made an assault on the Christian Church which in its pernicious effect was the worst in history.

It was not strange that Nazi vindictiveness rose to maddening irresponsibility against von Galen during the war. The Gestapo hounded him wherever he went. Its stooges were assigned to listen to every word he spoke, whether from the pulpit or in private. This did not lessen his condemnation. It strengthened it. He deplored the acts of violence perpetrated by the secret police on the clergy and peaceful citizens alike. Finally, in 1941, he was confined to house arrest and remained under this Hitler surveillance until 1945, when the Allies entered Germany.

His unbreakable courage and firmness in the faith brought him the applause, first in the Hall of Benediction and secondly in huge St. Peter's. Pius XII, who had to welcome all these varying personalities, embraced him with solemn joy. The Pope knew the terrors and torment he had suffered. He had fought the good fight. He had shepherded his flock even when the prison and the concentration camp seemed to gape open for his determined will and strong body. Kneeling before the Pontiff, he fulfilled the aspirations of his people to share in the common inheritance of that freedom of the faith which he had so valiantly defended.

Fatefully, his cardinalatial elevation was not long to endure. He returned home to Münster and contracted a blood infection. He died on March 22, just a month after he had received the red hat.

Propitiously fifth in the procession marched, with liturgic pace, the archbishop of Cracow, Monsignor Adam Stephen Sapieha. He was the lone representative of Poland, but the significance of his presence outshone his singularity. The last time Cracow was honored by a cardinal was almost half a century ago. Then that part of Poland was under Austria by the famous third partition. Cracow's cardinal then was Puzyna. It was he who had opposed the election of Cardinal Rampolla as pope in 1903 even after the latter had received the necessary two-thirds vote. He told the Sacred College that his sovereign, Emperor Franz Joseph of Austria, imposed a veto on Rampolla. This was both climactic and valid, because the aging sovereign did possess the power to turn down a successful candidate. The Sacred College was forced to reject Rampolla and then proceeded to elect Pius X, whose first act as pope was to abolish the veto of the Austrian emperor.

And after the long years Cracow had a cardinal again, and this time he was a true Pole owing no allegiance to a foreign intruder. And the contrast between the new and the old told the story of the rise of democratic Poland. Puzyna had always visited through the archdiocese in a coach of state, drawn by six white horses with outriders and trains of carriages. His residence in the archiepiscopal palace was one of the last strongholds of medieval splendor in Poland. Puzyna lived in the medieval age with an elaborateness which resembled the courts of the Hapsburgs themselves.

But the lithe and ascetic Sapieha did not revel in the lavishness of the past, though he came of noble birth. His father, a count, was known for allotting lands to the peasants and instituting other reforms. For his paternal benevolences he was cynically called "the red count" by his less altruistic fellow landowners. The new cardinal, therefore, knew the hardships and toil through which Polish peasantry strained to live. Sapieha had suffered the miseries of the Polish people under the domination of the Germans. He had fired the national spirit. What he had done in condemning Nazi suppression of worship stands out as one of the war's most courageous acts of Polish defiance.

Despite German surveillance, Sapieha continued unseen in all his daily devotions, which had been savagely prohibited by the Gestapo. He said Mass, baptized infants, joined men and women in marriage, administered communion in secretly hidden vessels and listened to confessions. It was all underground, but he held fast to the faith. It had to be underground because any assembly of Poles was forbidden. The occupying army was always afraid of outbreak of the national spirit if they allowed a gathering of any kind. When Sapieha knelt before the throne, the Pontiff's face deepened. It told in undisguised lines how the sufferings and hardships of Poland had found consolation in the hearts of all men of good will. Here in the person of Sapieha was dramatically embodied the Polish fight for the faith.

Then, too, for the first time in any consistory the British Empire was represented by a cluster, and *as* a cluster, of three cardinals—Griffin of Westminster, McGuigan of Toronto, and Gilroy of Sydney. While national assertion arises in many of the dominions, here British solidarity was crystallized. The three cardinals were adroitly assigned by the Vatican ceremoniers to receive their notification of elevation all together in the English College. One speech of thanks to the Pope was made, and it was delivered by the senior archbishop, McGuigan of Canada.

Today, with Villeneuve of Quebec, the British Empire is assigned four cardinals. This is not unusual if we include Ireland, as in the quite recent past often the British had two cardinals in England. The memory of Newman and Manning remains deep. Later there were Bourne and Gasquet. Today Ireland is without a member of the Sacred College because of the recent death of Cardinal MacRory. It would have been interesting to speculate what the suave master of ceremonies would have done had there been an Irish nominee. Skillful and responsive as they are to national sensibilities, they would likely have assigned the Irish cardinal-designate to the Irish College, where all ceremonies relating to the Church in Eire have taken place, rather than include him in the British cluster.

And quite as striking as anything else was this admission of Australia and, as we said, of British Canada. Significant were they of new fields won. Their presence denoted the fruition of pioneering Catholic expansion in lands opening for cultural as well as religious strengthening. Since the Pope deemed it wise to appoint a cardinal for China, it would not be too anticipatory to expect a cardinal for India, which is also rising in its susceptibility to Catholic expansion. Should the bounty of the Pontiff in assigning the red robes extend to the round-the-world sweep of the Church in British dominion, the Commonwealth of Nations would be represented by seven cardinals.

Speculatively in my previous volume *The Listening Post* I had presaged a greater recognition for the countries of the Western Hemisphere. The assignment of generous cardinalatial honors to the United States and Latin America, therefore, did not surprise me. The sees to be graced were foretold with almost mathematical accuracy, though this, perhaps, was more good fortune than perspicacity. Certainly the United States was destined to be held in high esteem. With the allocation of four cardinals, the honors have not ceased, as there will certainly be more in the offing. For South America, too, the same largess will prevail. Presently, Peru, Chile, and Cuba are represented for the first time in the senate of the Church. More favor is extended to Argentina and to Brazil. In the Western Hemisphere, the equilibrium of Catholic strength is gradually being realized. This consistory registered its greatest New World readjustment since the United States was recognized by three cardinals in 1903. From three then, the number in the Western Hemisphere reached fourteen with these new appointments, a redistribution which coincides with the relocation of Catholic strength.

But at this compelling consistory, too, one other function took its place among so many, though quite apart from sacred rituals. This was the royal reception. Medieval royal pomp and pageantry constituted much of its impressive thrill. It was accompanied with all the glory of a past age; and what we wondered was—whether or not the elaborate trappings we were witnessing were the last bold effort of a passing formalism to represent a way of life which was losing its identity in the modern assault. Such was the reception tendered by Crown Prince Humbert of Italy in the Quirinal Palace to the members of the Sacred College of Cardinals. Thirty-six cardinals came.

Humbert later was sworn in as king of Italy on the abdication of his father, Victor Emmanuel III. As king he reigned for just one month and was deprived of his throne in the plebiscite of the Italian electorate on June 2, 1946. The royal function we attended, therefore, was very likely to be the last in the ecclesiastical and imperial atmosphere which Rome alone possesses.

The royal residence provided a superb setting for the elaborate scene. This palace, the most spacious and lavish in Rome, was begun by Gregory XIII in 1574 and had remained the town residence of the pontiffs until 1870, when the Italian armies occupied the capital under King Victor Emmanuel II, great-grandfather of Humbert, who seized it and made it his royal mansion. Then it was that Pope Pius IX took refuge in the Vatican. The frescoes, friezes, tapestries, damasks, and sculptures were all conceived under the patronage of the popes. The spectacle of an Italian chief of state entertaining the Sacred College in a house which had originally been constructed as the private residence of the popes cast a strange paradox over the enchanting and highly colorful scene. Here it was heroically true that the old had actually mingled with the new. It was the first time in history that the Italian royal house had welcomed the Sacred College in what was for centuries the home of their own spiritual sovereign.

The Quirinal Palace occupies several blocks. From its windows can be seen the whole of Rome to the west, with St. Peter's in the distance. At the time of the setting sun, a scene of rare picturesqueness provided a respite for the popes, who almost every evening would look toward the Vatican and see the horizon dotted with pines silhouetted so vividly against the Italian skies. Set in the center of the panorama were the great basilica and the Vatican palaces.

At this reception, the cardinals arrived at short intervals through the main entrance into the wide courtyard to the foot of the grand stairway. As each in turn descended his car, a royal fanfare was sounded by the trumpeters of the royal guards, or cuirassiers of the king. A platoon of other cuirassiers stood at attention with drawn swords. Each guard was over six feet two inches. He wore a black tunic with red piping, white breeches, and high boots with spurs. Silver epaulets adorned his shoulders while strands of white military braid extended over his chest. The whole was crested by a brass and silver helmet of ancient Roman design. A heavy strand of black horse-hair stretched from the top of the helmet down the guard's back to his waist. Physique, smartness, precision, and the drawn sword made them look invincible.

At the foot of the stairs Count Suardi, the royal master of ceremonies, and several chamberlains welcomed each cardinal. With a sovereign's guard of six cuirassiers the cardinal was led up the wide stairs. On either side, a line of cuirassiers, each with a drawn sword in one hand and a lighted candle in the other, formed a guard of honor.

At the head of the stairs the prince of the Church was conducted into the frescoed Hall of the Corrazzieri, where another platoon of these massive men stood rigidly at attention. At a command, all raised their swords to salute him. Most of the cardinals stood for a moment to admire "The Ascension," a fresco by Melozzo da Forli.

With his royal escort, each purpled prince now passed through to the Hall of the Ambassadors and thence to the Throne Room, rich in brocades of gold and damasks of red. Here Crown Prince Humbert as regent of Italy and Crown Princess Maria Jose greeted him, assisted by the Duke of Aosta, the Duke of Genoa, and the Duke of Ancona, with several princesses of the blood royal. Despite the soldierly bearing of the cuirassiers, but in keeping with the subdued military prowess of the Italian royal house, every one of these royal princes discarded his accustomed uniform and wore conventional black morning coat with striped trousers. The princesses wore long-sleeved and high-necked dresses of varying color and material.

In the Throne Room, dozens of cardinals, bishops, and archbishops in violet *ferraiuoli*, ambassadors, ambassadresses, ministers, royal ladies-in-waiting, prelates of the papal court, and members of the royal household gathered. Conversation was brisk and brilliant. Cardinals turned to ambassadors and ladies-in-waiting to ambassadresses to comment on the epochal events in the epoch-making consistory. Both the Crown Prince and the Crown Princess engaged each cardinal in turn.

At six-thirty the vast crowd, which had reached about three hundred by that time, was led through the great halls into the state dining room. This was hung with priceless tapestries and red damasks. The ceiling was embellished in red and gold stucco. Three huge crystal chandeliers spread their delicate kaleidoscopic tints over the scene. In the center of the vast hall was a huge round table fully twenty-five feet in diameter covered with a cloth of golden lace and adorned with five silver candelabra on which scores of candles were burning. Red and yellow roses were interspersed in clusters between the candelabra.

The cardinals sat around the table in threes and fours, and between each three or four was either a royal prince or a royal princess. On the right of Humbert sat Cardinal Enrico Gasparri, nephew of the late Secretary of State; on his left, Cardinal Tisserant, the prefect of the Vatican library. On the right of the Crown Princess was Cardinal Agagianian, and on the left, Cardinal Massimi of the Roman Curia, spoken of as a probable secretary of state. Cardinal Spellman sat three places away from Humbert alongside his most intimate friend of many years, Archbishop Borgongini-Duca, nuncio to Italy.

The scene combined a medley of color. More dominant than the damasks, frescoes, brocades, and lace were the flowing purple *ferraiuoli* of the cardinals. Adorned by golden cords holding the pectoral cross, the richness of the princely tint set the aura for the entire scene. Never had so much cardinalatial grandeur honored a royal table during the whole history of the long dynasty of the House of Savoy. As each ecclesiastical prince conversed with another or with a royal prince or princess, the spectacle was lifted from its static splendor to heights of dynamic vitality portraying in color and tone the lofty stations of the assembled. The past was united with the present, the spiritual with the temporal.

Two other commodious tables were set alongside the great table. At the table on the right sat other Vatican prelates and lesser princes of the Italian realm. At the left table were ambassadors, ministers of the Italian government, and men high in the academic and literary life of the nation. United States Ambassador Kirk occupied a place not far from former Prime Minister Orlando. Beyond the state dining room, in another spacious hall, also adorned with damasks, frescoes, and tapestries, a sumptuous buffet awaited the chamberlains, the ladies-in-waiting of the royal family, and the newspapermen.

Coming from a world which had strained its resources to enact a democratic way of life, we were all overawed and even perplexed with a spectacle which restored to our minds, in vivid enactment by living *dramatis personae,* the florid civilization of the Renaissance. It gave us a close-up of royal grandeur, albeit in subdued form. This reception to thirty-six cardinals by a reigning monarch in 1946, nevertheless, represented the wavering strength of a royal institution which right then struggled in the travail of its last gasps.

The royal reception was undoubtedly the last.

Consistories will go on.

9. Unlike Any Other—Past or Present

STREAMLINED protocol and perhaps a new manual for modern princes of the Church could conceivably emerge from the spirited and man-to-man conduct of Cardinal Spellman. His daily routine would absorb the vitality of two or three ordinary men. His contact with the public is unentangled and close-up. He knows how to meet personages big and little. His eagerness to engage in good works crowds a personality already abundant in achievement. His own dynamic spring to life, as buoyant as it is unpredictable, avoids the pattern set by the usually staid and dignified members of the Sacred College. Not that he lacks dignity when dignity is prescribed, indeed not. Nevertheless, he meets the modern world head on, accepting its challenge with but a savory modicum of the ceremonial vestiges of the medieval and even more recent past. In him, a new and modern manual has its makings.

This acceptance of the world today emerged from Spellman when he was a simple priest. He met and talked with people on common ground—learning their difficulties and hearing their complaints. When he became a monsignor, he spoke to the same people. The promotion developed no change in how he was going to take the

124

world into account. He was made a bishop, which, while it broadened his field, tightened his older contacts. When he was elevated to the dizzy height of archbishop, an identical routine of service ruled the day. He performed the same offers of kindness as he did when unimportant and lowly. When he became a cardinal, the same free and welcoming marks stood out in bold relief more than ever.

I have been present at every ceremony in the career of Francis Cardinal Spellman. I knew him as a simple priest. We ate lunch or dinner, irregularly but often, in the rather modest restaurant in Rome known as La Rosetta. He was as jovial with the manager as he was congenial with the waiters. He became a figure and landmark of the place to such an extent that the enterprising proprietor hung his picture up in the garb of a simple priest, which was quite a distinction in Rome where simple priests are almost as plentiful as parishioners.

Work constituted life for him. He had been a reporter, an editor, a teacher, and a diocesan administrator. Work was the force driving him forward. From the time when he woke up in the morning until he went to bed in the late hours of the night, his day was a constant succession of tasks. Though his position made him chaplain to the Knights of Columbus playgrounds in Rome, the children were only there in the afternoons, and so Spellman found himself more work for the mornings and the evenings as well.

He lived in one room in a very modest hotel, the Minerva. He never changed his residence either in good times or bad. He would usually say Mass in the Church of St. Mary near by. Then he would hike over to the Vatican across the Tiber and work there all morning, doing even the most humble of secretarial jobs—copying orders, typing instructions and speeches, and translating encyclicals and other documents. While he seemed to work for work's sake, yet he was always accomplishing something which became at least a minor, and not infrequently a major milestone in Vatican procedure. Press releases were unknown in the chancellery before he originated them. Translations into all the languages of important documents to avoid garbling the official word was instituted by Spellman. A relative mechanization of the offices with typewriters, teletypes, and telegraph instruments took place while he was there. His chaplaincy, though a job in itself, began to take second place to important tasks he was assigned in the secretariat of state.

I have told in *The Listening Post** how he was chosen to smuggle an encyclical to Paris to avoid the Mussolini guards. I described how he startled Monsignor Borgongini-Duca, the papal undersecretary of state, with his athletic prowess. The story of how he was gum-shoed by stooges of Il Duce and turned, offering to take them on collectively or individually, has also been related. Other such events in his career were also chronicled in the earlier volume. *Life* magazine reprinted most of them in two issues at the time when he was to become cardinal.

Working in the Vatican and evolving better methods of doing the business of the chancellery inevitably focused papal attention on him. Inevitably, promotion was destiny. Pius XI made him a bishop, auxiliary to Cardinal O'Connell, as we saw. As a bishop, he still lived in the Minerva until he would leave for his post. It was there that he received all his presents on reaching this first strategical promotion. I recall the boxes of fine vestments—the rings, the pectoral cross, and the rich miters which were presented to him. He had them all carefully placed in the modest room, somehow. He had stayed in this hotel

* *The Listening Post*, New York, G. P. Putnam's Sons, 1944.

receiving his friends and proceeding on his charted ways as if the elevation to episcopal rank had not even taken place.

Viewing so many precious things among these expressions of friendship he was receiving, I searched Rome for a large jewel box for him, as my own humble token. I discovered how difficult it was to pick a present for a bishop. When I found it, I sent it to him with a note affirming my feeling that in serving mankind so well, he had served God supremely, too. He was far more impressed by the note than the jewel box and asked me to autograph a photograph instead, using the same words as in the note. This photograph was always displayed when I visited him. What became of the jewel box has passed into the annals of history as one of my lost relics of a reflected glory.

Even as a bishop, too, simplicity of manner was the more emphasized. He continued the same modest chores for a while. All the preparatory work for his consecration he did himself, without even benefit of valet or help of secretary. St. Peter's having been chosen as the scene of these rites, a lot of things had to be done. There are no pews anywhere in the vast edifice. Chairs were hauled in and tribunes erected for the distinguished guests. This work he supervised personally, aided by his friend Enrico —Enrico Galeazzi, supervising architect of the huge basilica.

Besides, there were invitations to be sent out to thousands of Vatican prelates and functionaries and to members of the American colony in Rome. This he did himself, and with happy result, for when the ceremony took place the entire apse of St. Peter's was filled. This was no mean accomplishment, since it takes about three thousand persons to make a showing even in the apse of St. Peter's. And what is more—since most of the American colony

understood little about the elaborate ceremony of consecrating a bishop—he provided each guest with a booklet
giving the entire procedure and the meaning of the forms
and symbols used.

He erected a special tribune for the members of the
American Embassy. Headed by Alexander Kirk, who was
then the counselor of embassy but who later became ambassador, the entire personnel and their wives occupied
the tribune. Incidentally, it was the first time that any
American official had ever attended any kind of function
in St. Peter's since the United States was represented by
a minister to the Holy See in 1868. Counselor Kirk was
not a Catholic, but he accepted his role as highest-ranking
civilian present with affable geniality and reverent deference, and performed the required obeisances with such
perfection that Captain Francis Brady, our air attaché who
later became a general, and his wife, who were Catholics,
watched him to get the cue of what they were to do.

Many episodes made the ceremony prophetic. It was
not without significance that he had chosen as his consecrator the mild, ascetic, and meditative Cardinal Pacelli,
who was then papal secretary of state. Pius XI was then
in vibrant health and had given his especial approval to
having the consecration take place in St. Peter's. The
presence of the Secretary of State certainly added grandeur to the occasion and placed it in that category where
it could truly be said that the Holy See had definitely
taken the new bishop into the inner circle. Providentially, Pacelli became the next pope.

And it was not alone the presence of the Pope's chief
adviser, but Cardinal Lauri was there as well. Lauri had
been chosen as the Pope's own legate to represent him at
the World Eucharistic Congress in Dublin in 1930. Spell-

man had gone to Dublin as secretary to Cardinal Lauri. In that capacity he had occupied a position right up on the high rungs of the hierarchical ladder, even though then many others were clustered at the same point. It was a spot, nevertheless, where he certainly could be seen if anyone looked to the top of the ladder at all.

Then, too, as co-consecrators, he had chosen two intimate friends, and even these were in positions that controlled the nerve centers of Vatican co-ordination. First, Archbishop Borgongini-Duca, papal nuncio to Italy, supported him on the right, while Monsignor Giuseppe Pizzardo, papal undersecretary of state, accompanied him on the left. Then, as an added elaboration to this personified authority, Monsignor Carlo Respighi, papal master of ceremonies, directed the sacred function. Others from around the papal throne occupied places in the sanctuary, bestowing a truly pontifical milieu for the rich and engrossing ceremony. The scene impressed itself insistently that the very participants in the consecrating act would have been the identical persons were the Pontiff himself to have graced the occasion with his presence.

And when the Bishop-elect made his profession of faith and gave his responses to the consecrator in almost catechismic form, the contrast in the rhythm and tone of the Italian with the American signified the worlds and centuries. Pacelli's flowing tones as he recited the Latin formulas moved with a smooth and liquid cadence of one born and fashioned in the Roman rite. One conceived voice and tempo as if at the dawn of the ritual. His Latin tones echoed and re-echoed through St. Peter's as if they were bringing to life all of the long centuries of the faith. One can live the centuries to listen to the ritual—there.

When Spellman pronounced his responses, we were

conscious of a new world. A world joined to the old in this very ceremony. We were conscious of America, for though the words were all in Latin, a native tang lifted the language of the Church from its epochs of beauty and harmony to a new life imposed by the virility and dash of the West. Even when Spellman recited the simple one-word responses of "Credo" and "Voglio," vowels as well as consonants danced to revitalize the scene. We felt as if Latin had taken on a Western vigor which raised it from mere recital to a living symbol in the rite. And just as the flowing tones of the Italian hierarchs had brought to life the centuries, so the virile and conquering notes of the New Englander personified the spirit which had battled with the wilderness and subdued a continent. It was St. Peter's, but America was truly there that morning.

And it was also somewhat peculiarly ominous that when the consecration ended, in his full canonicals and escorted by his co-consecrators, he led the procession of these papal dignitaries through the aisles to bless the people. The miter so emblematic of the bishop's rank was upon his head. From the thousands of men and women he had won to him, the sighs passed like gentle zephyrs, for the thousands were all his friends. As they bowed their heads to receive his blessing, they silently applauded his rise to episcopal rank.

In a few weeks, the new bishop and myself were traveling companions on the maiden voyage of the *Rex*, the first 50,000-ton Italian steamer, which was setting out to capture the record for the Atlantic crossing. He was returning to Boston to take up the duties of auxiliary bishop. James J. (Jimmy) Walker, former mayor of New York, was aboard. Then the gay-living public servant was enjoying one of the lowest popularity ratings in his colorful career. Not many months back, he had been forced to resign as mayor and had sought solace in travel. On the *Rex* he was planning a comeback.

He was to land in New York when the New York city Democratic convention was meeting to choose a candidate for mayor. He planned to be that candidate. It was held that a deadlock would occur and James J. Walker would arrive at the psychological moment just off the record-breaking *Rex* and stampede the convention. But such a well-laid plan demanded perfect timing and could tolerate no hitches. The hitch was early born, however. At Gibraltar, on the second day out, the *Rex* broke down.

While we were waiting, the days passed aimlessly except in the anxiety to know just when the *Rex* would sail. Walker and Spellman had met before when the gay and dazzling politician had visited St. Peter's. On the very threshold of the edifice, Walker had brought forth one of his brilliant pleasantries when, fully in tune with the reverence due to the huge basilica, he had remarked:

"They must have passed the hat around a good many times to build this."

But now, on the luxury liner *Rex,* no one knew much what to do. Spellman decided to take a trip into Spain and asked me whether he could take my young son Dino, then aged eight, on the jaunt. They started out but in the afternoon returned to the *Rex* because the car, too, had broken down and before they had even reached Malaga. Gaining the promenade deck, Spellman met Walker. They sat down in the lounge with no other purpose than to pass the time on the lingering and disabled steamer.

Jimmy began by telling the new auxiliary bishop that he had tried all his life to live an honest life but that, like all human beings, he had had his weaknesses. Spellman as a priest had understood the existence of human frailties and

> Had tried each art, reproved each dull delay,
> Allured to brighter worlds and led the way.

Jimmy at the time was regarded as an erring son of the Catholic Church by Cardinal Hayes, who was then archbishop of New York. What he was telling us may have had some relation to this strain with his chief pastor. He wanted to get back in his good graces, and though he was not seeking any intercession from Spellman, he *was* seeking solace. It was therefore quite in conformity with sacerdotal generosity for the new auxiliary bishop of Boston to admit the humanity of sin, big and little, and the divinity of forgiveness.

Six or seven newspapermen in resigned mood and aimless effort joined the light and congenial circle. Joe Phillips of the *Herald Tribune,* John McClain of the *Sun,* Skipper Williams of the *Times,* and others listened, much more intent on being amused than edified, because Walker had a devouring charm and a sparkling humor in all his narration. Seldom did he speak without emitting a wisecrack. It was quite obvious that all the newsmen admired him with a zeal enriched by true affection.

Then Jimmy went into his problems with the newspapers. These he treated as if all the newsmen understood his heart and sympathized. They did. But his discourse was directed to Spellman; the newsmen were in reality a silent, though pleasingly intriguing claque. He lamented that not a single newspaper had ever supported him. He cherished the friendship of all the newspapermen. We smiled assent. Then, he observed, an obvious streak of hypocrisy ran through their natures. While they were warm and admiring friends, yet when they wrote, they wrote as if they were enemies. As men they were friends; as reporters they were enemies. We all understood as well as he did that the newsmen had to comply with the editorial policy of the paper; we smiled again.

"I know," said Jimmy in cynical jocosity, "that the publishers never tell these friends of mine what they should write. That's what they call freedom of the press. But it is really only freedom of the publishers. The newspaperman may not take orders from the publishers, but he certainly knows which way the boss is looking and writes on the beam where his eyes are fixed."

Then, drawing himself up in his chair, but without showing the slightest change in his humorous manner, he quietly delivered his gnawing though understandable analysis.

"If you want my opinion of a newspaperman," he said, "he is nothing but an intellectual gigolo."

All of us laughed and so did Spellman, who counseled that an honest confession is always good for the soul.

Now, Jimmy wanted the *Rex* to hurry because his entree into the convention was timed for a voyage of seven days from Naples. On the third day, it was too much. He would not wait any longer and decided to leave the *Rex* and rush off to Cherbourg, where he took the German liner *Europa*. Spellman stayed on the *Rex* and so did the rest of us, except Joe Phillips, who, with orders from his paper, went off with the wishful candidate. A day or so after, the *Rex* was ready and we started again—and beat the *Europa* by two days. Jimmy had lost his chance of the stampede. The convention was over when he landed.

It was one day before we arrived in port that the new bishop came up to me and showed me a telegram. It was the now famous telegram which he had received from his ecclesiastical superior, Cardinal O'Connell.

"Welcome to Boston," it read with more than a touch of subtlety. "Confirmations begin on Monday. Report to chancery for instructions."

Spellman was returning to his native Massachusetts with no little concern and a fair amount of anxious foreboding. He knew that he was to be assigned a room in the diocesan seminary. It might mean that though he was a bishop and outranked its rector, he would courteously have to abide by the discipline of the seminary. That fear was removed, however, when he was assigned O'Connell's private suite there and was allowed to come and go as he pleased. It is also the custom for an auxiliary bishop to be assigned a parish which he should administer and which in turn should make him worthy of his hire. Now, while the confirmations had been assigned, the parish had not been assigned. It later developed that Spellman was to bestow nearly all confirmations that year while the Cardinal limited himself to a few swanky churches and institutions.

Eventually O'Connell softened and sent him to take over the parish of Sacred Heart in Newton Center, near Boston. But the cardinalatial gesture was more generous in the form than in the substance. The church was burdened with a debt of $69,000. Now, while Spellman appeared to have a roof over his head by becoming pastor of the church, he could have little use for the roof since he would be out on confirmation duties most of the time and collecting the debt in the rest. O'Connell surely knew of his boundless energy. Certain it is that whatever the strain, the auxiliary braced for the shock and met all requirements. The debt was cleared. The parish flourished.

When Cardinal Hayes died and left the archiepiscopal see of New York vacant, speculation buzzed everywhere on the next appointee. Pius XI was still living, and looking over the promising prospects of men of stature for the post is reported to have actually decided upon Monsignor John T. McNicholas, archbishop of Cincinnati, known in Rome as a profound scholar and firm administrator. Before the formalities of the appointment went through, Pius XI died, and Pius XII succeeded to the papal throne on March 2, 1939. Seven weeks had transpired in the new pontificate when the striking news reached America that the new pope had chosen Francis J. Spellman to be archbishop of New York.

The new archbishop was welcomed in his see cathedral of St. Patrick on May 23. Work began immediately after his installation. The drive that was in him soon permeated all the nerve centers of the archdiocese as if he had turned on a switch. An increased tempo derived from the new voltage. Pastors, assistant pastors, and the religious orders caught the dynamic power transmitted from the archiepiscopal residence. Priests set out to be closer to their flocks. A quickening in all aspects of religious life in the parishes was evident. Reports were required more regularly. Work, pastoral work, charitable work, and religious devotions became the watchword throughout the New York territory. Pastors had to keep regular hours so that their parishioners knew where and when to find them. Assistant pastors were not allowed to own cars, much less spend the time in pleasure jaunts in them.

New churches must be built where old ones were in ruin or where none existed. Those already built must be kept in a smooth-running state meeting modern exigencies. Repairs must be made the moment they were necessary. So thorough were the Archbishop's inspection tours that he detected a leaking roof, a worn-out floor, a displaced waterspout, or a door or window needing paint with the sensitiveness of a setter. The great religious and educational organism of the archdiocese must function for service. The men to minister to the welfare of the flock, spiritually, as well as socially, must always be on their toes. The sleepless and perpetual watchfulness of the Archbishop imposed it.

And while the immense religious complexus functioned in charitable works and spiritual fruitfulness, Spellman extended his efforts outside the purely pastoral fields into the realm of public affairs. It was on his initiative that Myron C. Taylor, former chairman of the board of the United States Steel Corporation, was appointed personal representative of President Roosevelt to the Pope. It was Spellman who had worked out the whole proceeding. The appointment did not create an embassy to the Holy See. It simply placed a spokesman for the President near the Pope. Taylor was accepting no salary. It was a personal function for the executive; no appropriation or Congressional action was therefore necessary, nor was the Senate asked to approve the appointment.

Meeting Spellman on one of his afternoon walks along Park Avenue (though he usually chooses Fifth Avenue), I congratulated him on the success attained in securing a diplomatic representative to the Pope.

"As an achievement," he quietly replied to me, "I regard my part in the appointment of Myron Taylor as a progressive step for America in world affairs."

When the added burden of appointment as bishop to the Catholics of the armed forces came to him, he did not look at it as a mere trinket or a piece of costume jewelry to adorn his cassock. He set out to make his contribution to the religious exigencies of the soldiers in every part of the globe. He organized a central office for the appointment and dispersion of chaplains in New York City. Then he began that series of visitations to the various theaters which were to raise the spirits of the men in the field, give encouragement to the chaplains, and bestow a not uncertain measure of calm on the parents and loved ones back home.

If it can be said of him that he spurred his own priests to greater exertion, in a far more intensive way did he goad and drive himself to almost inhuman efforts. The hours of the day did not divide themselves into work, recreation, and rest for him. He did not know a moment when his tireless energy was not in use. It was true that he had set out to make a visitation, but many acts of pastoral benevolence occurred to him all along the vast routes he took. He had work to do, but he also went out to search for more things that might bring solace in the field or consolation at home.

He possessed the stamina of the hardiest fighting soldier. He could toil for long hours in the Arctic cold or the tropical heat. The Army had given him a schedule, and never once did he fail to fulfill that schedule. Whether it meant lack of sleep, irregular meals, scanty rations, or inclement weather, he was always equal to the ordeal and overcame every hazard which the exactions of military life imposed upon him.

In his trip to the Aleutians in August of 1943 he encountered enigmatic extremes of heat by day and cold by night, of fog, mist, and dampness, of snow and sleet on the high levels, and of rough travel in that barren and bleak stretch of islands. The austere fare provided on land and sea, designed to give the soldier and sailor the greatest stamina and energy, was hardly adapted to one arriving right from the cozy hearth of home where edibles were always adjusted to the man. Yet he thrived on the rugged rations, carried on his daily program of multiple visits, officiating at masses and meeting the chaplains with their problems and complaints. I saw him on his return to New

York. He was just as vital and robust as when he left. Immediately he resumed his work just where he had left off.

Demands for the spiritual needs of the soldiers took him on a second odyssey which covered 45,000 miles and required seven months of constant day-by-day and hour-by-hour work and travel. He flew to Spain and from Spain flew to Rome. The remarkable feature of that jump—which has been overlooked—was that Rome was an enemy capital. Spellman had a right to go there. By the Lateran Treaty with the Holy See, Mussolini had agreed to the safe passage in peace or war of bishops and archbishops of the Roman Catholic Church whenever they wished to visit Vatican City to pay their homage to the Pope.

Spellman was the first man to test the validity of that treaty. He was met at the civil airport and driven to Vatican City under a guard of Italian police. He conferred with the Pope. Then he was off to Algiers, Egypt, London, back to Africa, thence to Jerusalem where he celebrated an Easter Mass, thence to Malta, Syria, Turkey, Iran, Iraq, and finally a tour around the whole of Africa. The entire voyage was done by air. He had called upon and conferred with Eisenhower, Winston Churchill, Field Marshal Smuts, King Farouk of Egypt, President Inonu of Turkey, and Emperor Haile Selassie of Ethiopia.

And while he was on these missions of good will to the various countries, he had found time to administer to the desires of individual soldiers of all faiths. Precisely here are found his most appealing attributes. Administratively, his job required him to make the necessary contacts with army officers in the higher commands, with chaplains who directed the religious work of divisions, army corps, and whole armies. This task he inevitably fulfilled. But he went much further than that. He stepped outside the formal role of archbishop to become a simple priest in companies, in battalions, in small detachments on outpost duty, in supply depots, in hospitals. He was a man to men.

And it was not that he embraced them in condescension. Indeed he spoke their language with all its short cuts and phonetic economy. He knew how to make parables out of their chores, their daily life, their struggle with nature, their quarrels with man, and their zeal for sports. He had been an athlete himself. The nomenclatures of baseball, football, and the gym often enriched his word pictures and brought his thoughts closer to them. Family talk was second nature to him. Instead of highly involved language, they always listened to speech which was home to them. He shined his own shoes.

He sat down with them in their tents on a cot or on the ground. He ate with the privates as well as with kings and emperors. A rough table in the field was often his only desk, and when no table at all was available he made a table out of his own brief case. He plowed through mud without any thought of his archiepiscopal appearance. When seats were scarce in cars, he was never slow in offering others the better places. In hospitals, he stayed to administer spiritual comfort to the sick and the dying into the long hours of the night. This was a rite that no amount of fatigue could undo.

He went among the fighting men to perform humble tasks. He undertook a most formidable enterprise. He offered out of his own volition to write a letter for each one of them to their parents or sweethearts. He had them write their addresses on slips of paper. He himself collected the slips as if he were a mere messenger. He walked or rode from unit to unit covering hundreds of miles a day. Every bit of this required physical effort, a faculty he had never stinted in dispersing even after long hours in the field. Endowed with this rugged and almost indestructible constitution, he eagerly put it to work without flurry of rank or fuss of person. The buck private was accorded a benevolence not inferior to that of a general, and quite often superior. For Spellman had an innate impulse to do something for somebody all the time, and without their asking.

When he returned home in September, he brought 14,-000 slips with the addresses of the parents and sweethearts of men he had seen. True to the spirit and letter of his promise, he sent a personal note to each of the addressees. He had traveled 45,000 miles and had been on an unending whirl, day and night, for over seven months. After getting off the letters, he resumed the administration of the archdiocese and engaged in strengthening morale on the home front. He went out to campaign for the Third War Loan.

A third trip was made in July of 1944. The grueling he had received on the previous trips did not dampen his ardor nor yet suggest to him that he had done his bit. This third trip covered some of the ground of the second trip; but this time, with the Allied advance, he was able to officiate at Mass on German soil. He visited Pope Pius XII again. He had luncheon with King George VI, Field Marshal Alexander, and General Mark Clark. This was when a bomb exploded just two hundred yards away from their table in the field. His journeyings covered 19,000 miles this time, but he had to keep up schedule and collect messages and fulfill all those innumerable little favors he had wished on himself by his own inherent eagerness. The uncomfortable and exacting result was that when he arrived in New York on October 16, he had not slept for three nights. But, his spirit mingled with steel, he attended the Mass celebrating the diamond jubilee of the revered Father Martin J. Smith in his church of St. Francis Xavier.

When the war turned to the Pacific, his duties summoned him on that wide expanse. He had done enough to prove that distance was no great obstacle to him. The sudden end to hostilities while he was en route did not terminate his mission. He performed the same routine as on his European tours. He took the administrative side of his task in his usual stride, meeting with Admiral Nimitz in Guam and with the top-ranking chaplains of his faith in their turn. But the big job was again to minister to the men. He officiated at Mass in Tokyo Bay, at Kwajalein, Saipan, Tinian, and Iwo Jima. And still he collected the addresses, and every address meant an additional letter to write. But work was incentive to action. From Tokyo he traveled all the way around the world, by way of India, Egypt, Rome, and Lisbon. He returned to write another ten thousand letters to friends and parents. On the day of his arrival, he appeared before the New York Committee of the Laity to launch a three-million-dollar campaign for the Alfred E. Smith memorial of St. Vincent's Hospital.

And then came that great moment when he was to be made a cardinal. This had been rumored ever since he had been promoted to archbishop in 1939. Whenever I visited the archiepiscopal residence or saw him on his walks along upper Fifth Avenue or Park Avenue, I invariably asked him what he had heard, if anything, about a new red hat. I knew that if there had been anything in the wind, he was in duty bound to keep silent, because a new bishop, a new archbishop, and much more a new cardinal must wait for a news dispatch from Rome before he can even tell his friends or accept their congratulations.

This is the rule. He would have to parry with me, changing the reply to suit the varying occasion.

"You know as much about it as I do," was a frequent eschewal of his.

"I've got enough trouble keeping a black hat before wearing a red," was another characteristic evasion.

"Who wants a red hat anyway when you have to wear a khaki one?" he snapped jauntily when he had donned his uniform for overseas. "Red's too good a target."

On one occasion he said that it was quite possible he never would get a red hat.

"Archbishop Hughes was never created a cardinal," he added. "And he was New York's greatest archbishop."

But the most significant remark he made in dodging talk of the red robes was back in 1940. I suggested that it was time for a consistory and that certainly he could not be left out.

"I don't know why not," he returned in reverent jocosity. "You know, Tom, that on an average a man has to be seven years an archbishop in New York before he gets to be a cardinal."

Back in 1940 no one thought it was going to take more than a few months. New York had been recognized from away back in the last century as a cardinalatial see. Certainly of all the archbishops in America the archbishop of New York would be the first to get the call. He would get the call, but the Pope was not holding consistories for the creation of cardinals. There was a war on, too, for making cardinals. It had not taken seven years before Francis J. Spellman was made a cardinal, but it did take nearly six.

Inordinate and intricate preparations face a cardinal-designate. Rather than have his red hat sent from Rome, he naturally wants to go there to have the Pope place it on his head. This pleases both the new cardinal and the Pontiff. To get things ready and to make the trip takes a lot out of a man. A natural though sometimes unwarrantable anxiety bestirs him betimes. For him, it is not the easy, happy jaunt to Europe it seems on the outside. There is really nothing to worry about, however, since it is the highest honor any ecclesiastic could achieve within the favor of the Pope. Everything will certainly take its natural course. But he worries nevertheless.

Transportation in postwar times was disorganized for civilians. This was vexing. And then air travel had come in. This made it nerve-quickening even if it was time-saving. Travel agents had to be consulted, routes studied, available aircraft canvassed, and pilots mustered—for it had to be a special trip. Could it or could it not be done? It could.

Then clothes must be provided. It had been customary for previous American cardinals to order their clothes in Rome by wire from a favored ecclesiastical tailor. The Rome tailors had run through their stocks. Mussolini had decreed red watered silk a nonessential. But Spellman was heir to the vestments of Cardinal Hayes. He was able to collect his entire wardrobe before he set out. This included the *cappa magna* of red watered silk with its six-yard train, ermine capes, black cassocks piped in red, red cassocks, lace rochets, violet cassocks and capes for the penitential season, stockings, shoes, and slippers. In all, while a cardinalatial vestiary consists of $10,000 worth of clothes, the New York archbishop was spared that toll, emerging fully invested with bare alteration charges.

To get to Rome with all this indispensable paraphernalia just when both air and sea transportation was still harassed by wartime restrictions imposed a lot of arranging and adjusting. Everyone knew Spellman liked to fly, but with this weight in finery, I had thought that he would have to go by steamer. Instead, and not a little to my surprise, he decided to go by air as did the other three American neo-cardinals.

As an affable gesture toward him, but a slight problem in transportation just the same, notables of the archdiocese decided to accompany him. Naturally enough, he invited several members of his immediate family. Besides, a score of newspapermen had harassed him with a benevolent threat that they intended to go along, too, whatever way he traveled. Pressing on him was the time he could spend for the trip. With all these snags and hurdles, fly he would. Family, friends, notables, officials, and newspapermen made up a party of seventy people. It took two planes carrying thirty-five persons each to carry the load. Cardinal Glennon and his entourage traveled in the Spellman fleet. As correspondent for the International News Service I was assigned a place in the first plane.

The newspapermen and several prelates, including Bishop McCarty of New York, traveled in the first plane. Archbishop Spellman and Archbishop Glennon with Bishops O'Hara of Buffalo, Kelleher of Boston, Bergan of Des Moines, and several priests and a score of laymen, including the Spellman family, flew in the second plane. Among the latter's passengers, James A. Farley and Frank C. Walker, both former postmasters-general, bestowed an air of ex-officialdom even if not officialdom. George Mac-Donald, utility magnate who holds the post of highest-ranking layman because he is a papal marquis; Joseph V. McKee, former mayor of New York; Attorney George J. Gillespie, and John C. Kelly brought a civic tone to the plane's ecclesiastical and journalistic manifest.

But the little turn which started considerable hubbub amongst the passengers—the majority of whom were mak-

ing their first flight, and, still more tart, their first trans-
atlantic flight—was contained in sealed envelopes, one of
which was given to each passenger. In it, we found a
bronze medal of St. Christopher. Everyone knew that this
was intended providentially to invoke a safe journey. We
also found a one-dollar bill. At first, and without due
Christian deliberation, I could think of nothing but that
it might have been some kind of Gaelic fetish, since most
of the party were of Irish origin. I thought that it could
be one of those ancient rites which provided travelers into
the unknown with a token of provision. This was the
token.

But, fondling the strip of money with perhaps more
miserly intent than spiritual devotion, I came across the
signature, "Francis J. Spellman." It came to me at once.
This, then, was the short-snorter which all travelers almost blatantly boast about when they have crossed the
Atlantic by air—a dollar bill signed by the other passengers. The archbishop had saved me and doubtless had
saved many others in our aerial caravan from the humilia-
tion of being caught without a short-snorter after having
crossed the Atlantic. This willing gesture penetrated the
most crusty natures of our profession, and though we may
not have said much in public, we certainly thought in private that it was very companionable of Spellman to have
thought it up.

From the time we left New York, he seemed to be always puttering about to do something for us. They were
not things that one would write about in the papers, so
that suspicion that he was doing it for headlines never
existed. We landed in Ireland and were received by
Prime Minister de Valera almost as diplomats. We rode
on the Irish presidential train from Limerick to Killarney.
As satellites of Spellman, we attended all the civic func-

tions as visiting dignitaries. In Paris we were guests at the American Embassy. And then that we might see the glories of the Alps from the air, he asked the officials of the air line to change the route to Rome and pass through Switzerland. And this was the most overpowering sight of the whole excursion—to see Mont Blanc, the Matterhorn, the Dent du Midi, and Monte Rosa, with glaciers and craggy mountains all mixed in, in the very firmament of heaven. We owed Spellman a great deal for this.

What captured the usually cynical hearts of the newsmen, too, were his efforts to get them all the news. With all the responsibility of the ceremonies on his hands, he took on the added task of acting as his own public relations official. Here was a puzzling undertaking even for a skilled professional. He met the newsmen every evening, gave them the news of the day, and told them what was going to be done the next day. He went much farther than that. He accepted the arduous chore—for that is what it was—of securing for between sixty and seventy newsmen of all countries the required tickets for the important functions. Their places were so distributed that they could observe the ceremonies as if they had been members of the papal household.

The lay and clerical constituents of the Cardinal's party will never realize the debt of gratitude they owe him through his labors to gain for them what was, perhaps, the greatest spiritual experience of their lives. He specifically chose the great churches of Christendom in which to say Mass, which not alone added to their devotional riches but also filled them with those great emotions which come from the witness of monuments which record the master course of the faith. They saw and worshiped at St. Peter's, St. John Lateran, St. Paul's Outside the Walls, St. Clement, Santa Susanna, and many others. Their truly untiring pastor even took them on tours through these great landmarks in which he personally explained the importance of the shrines, their relics, the frescoes, sculptures, friezes, paintings, and mosaics.

His abundant energy was generously distributed on this trip, too. Even with the pressing tasks of taking part in the sacred functions, he found time to visit his old friends in Rome—humble as well as mighty. He even went to the hospital to take the get-well-quickly word to Willard de Lue, correspondent of the *Boston Globe* who was struck with an acute ailment in the rush. He personally asked the Pope to present the medal commemorative of the consistory to each member of the party—newspapermen as well, non-Catholic as well as Catholic. What he did came as a spontaneous expression of human fellow feeling. These voluntary deeds were outside any requirement of what a new cardinal should or should not do.

The dignity with which his presence was latently endowed carried him along in the arduous ceremonial and was by no means inferior in its human appeal to the willingness of his heart to help and to co-operate. In his great cape of purple and gold, he awaited his personal notification in the Hall of a Hundred Days, where frescoes of flowing line and harmonious color told of stirring events in the battle for the faith. Here he seemed to lay to one side the pleasantries with which his personality spreads joy for others. Now it took on that halo of marked and stern responsibility in the great honor that was then bestowed. To him it was not the glory of being raised to princely rank. To him it was the command so to order his labors that they would render him worthy of the glory.

On the day on which the Supreme Pontiff placed the biretta on his head, he approached the throne with benign submission. The Holy Father received him as if his whole store of joy was suddenly released. There was the bond of faithful affection between the elder brother, the Pope, and the younger brother, the Cardinal, for that is the relation between the Pontiff and the members of the Sacred College. Spellman's robes of purple seemed to drape about him as if to them he was born. The superimposed mantle of ermine gave approving finality that he had reached the highest state of a prelate. As he knelt before the successor to St. Peter, the red biretta was placed upon his head, the assuring gesture that he was a prince of the Church. In humble reverence and still kneeling before the Vicar of Christ, he removed the red emblem, kissed the Fisherman's ring of the Pontiff, and descended the throne, bowed in humble obedience in soul and heart.

In overpowering St. Peter's on the Thursday of the public consistory, he seemed transformed as he took the oath in the Chapel of the Most Holy Sacrament. Attired in the same purple vestments, with his train borne by attendants, he trod the long march up the aisle with his brother cardinals immersed in the profound depths of spiritual submission. Again he performed the service of obedience to the Supreme Pastor. Again the devoted affection between the bestower and the bestowed revealed itself in the joy and the signs of emotion which each felt as the crowning act of placing the ceremonial red hat over his head was performed. Again he embraced the Holy Father. His long purple train was now folded and placed over his arm. Step by step, he descended the throne, thence to embrace each member of the Sacred College in turn, a symbol that he was received into the brotherhood of the chief advisers of the pontiff, the Sacred College of Cardinals of the Holy Roman Church.

More telling than all the outward expressions of the devotion of the elder for the younger stood out the lavish bestowal of the Pope's own cardinalatial hat upon the youngest American cardinal, Cardinal Spellman. This was an overwhelming mark of affection. It was born of a penetrating and decisive feeling, enabling the Holy Father to choose decidedly from among thirty-two brethren the brother who was the most beloved. This act of pontifical grace told in bolder and more impressive terms where the New York archbishop stood in the affections of the Sovereign Pontiff. Everyone watched with bated breath as the elaborate ceremonial headpiece was placed in his hands by the master of ceremonies, Monsignor Toraldo. Cardinal Spellman trembled with emotion. The Pope had chosen him for the highest honor in the consistory.

The homage of the lowly as well as those of high estate was accorded him. He was the most revered at the reception tendered the Sacred College by Crown Prince Humbert of Italy. At the reception of Franklin Gowen, U.S. chargé d'affaires during the absence of Myron C. Taylor, it was Cardinal Spellman who was chosen by the Crown Princess Maria Jose to accompany her in to tea. He received the greetings and tokens of devotion from princes, dukes, ambassadors, and ministers. The present prime minister of Italy, Alcide de Gasperi, sought him out for special obeisance. Former Prime Minister Orlando held long conversations with him.

But this was not all. When he proceeded in his great *cappa magna* of watered red silk to take possession of his titular church of St. John and Paul, and while the affable Archbishop Borgongini-Duca, nuncio to Italy, had come to do him honor with other Vatican prelates, the plain people crowded the church. There was not a jot of vacant space in the imposing edifice. Just as when he was consecrated a bishop, they were the faithful and devoted little folk who had served him in his younger days in

Rome. Their friends had come, too. The vast throng had heard the name of Father Spellman in the years when he was toiling as a humble shepherd of souls among the poor boys and girls who came to the social centers over which he had been placed in spiritual charge. This he held as a sterling token of their devotion.

That physical ruggedness which had served him well in his travels to all the theaters of war with the armed forces stood him in good stead on this trip, too. We had unpleasant weather all along the route. The hotels were without heat. When he got to Rome his schedule called for speeches and the officiating at Masses in cold and wind-swept churches. Three days after we arrived, four out of every five of the cardinalatial company were down with colds, including Cardinal Glennon. But Spellman continued in the midst of all these defections as if he were impervious to cold churches and unheated hotels.

We returned through Spain and Portugal, and there he had appointments. We arrived in Gander, Newfoundland, on the return trip at four A.M. New York time. This time, his plane had arrived ahead of us. At the airport hotel, our first sight was to see the cardinal seated at a desk attending to his correspondence and answering telegrams about when he would arrive in New York and what preparations could be made for his welcome. We all had breakfast there. He sat at a table without any rank or fuss. Our plane was scheduled to leave an hour ahead of his plane.

We were all getting ready to board a bus for the field, which was several miles from the hotel, when who should appear to go with us to see us off but Spellman. A blizzard was blowing now. He wore a simple black cassock and a small skullcap. Everyone else had on either a great ulster or a heavy trench coat. The wind pierced the bones. It was no day to go out at all unless one had to, and especially not at five in the morning. I asked him if he did not think it prudent to let the blizzard blow by itself and stay indoors, until it was time for him to take off. I suggested that at least he put on a cape.

"I don't need one, Tom," he quipped.

I was surprised that he did not need one when even the youngest among us were packed in camel hair, sheep fleece, and chinchilla.

"Well," I countered, "you surely are wearing some very heavy underwear? In a blizzard like this, *you'll* be down with a cold, too."

"Oh, no," he whipped back. Most rhetorically but without saying another word, he took my hand and placed it between his shoulders. I was astounded. His clothing was very light. I could feel the warmth of his healthy fiber. I knew then that he could stand things.

We all boarded the bus. Unceremoniously he took a seat on the aisle over the wheel. In a few minutes we were at the airport. We all got out near the plane. He stood around in the uncomfortable blasts and shook hands with each one of us. Then our plane was off. We saw him boarding the bus to return to the hotel alone. Hard-boiled reporters saw it. They breathed a sigh. Personages never treat us that way.

And more than anything else, when we saw Francis Cardinal Spellman of the title of St. John and St. Paul in his humble black cassock in the blizzard, shaking hands, we saw him in one of his loftiest roles.

10. No Runs, No Hits in Cassock

THE Roman Church has had, on one side, its crusaders and men of action; on the other, its mystics and philosophers. While there was a fighting Paul, there was a martyred Peter. Pope Gregory VII ordered kings and emperors, forced the proud Henry IV of Germany to prostrate himself before him at Canossa. Correspondingly, St. Thomas Aquinas, cloistered and in solitude, expounded Christian philosophy in writings which are greater than victorious wars and skillful diplomacy. Pope Alexander III humbled the haughty Emperor Frederick Barbarossa to kiss his slippered foot. St. Francis of Assisi by the power of his own humility has handed down to mankind the lesson in practice of "Blessed are the meek."

In modern times, Pius IX and Leo XIII both faced a turbulent world and fought with strained virility. The former defied King Victor Emmanuel II of Italy; the latter spurned Bismarck. They were followed by Pius X. So humble was he that not only once, but often, he pawned his gold watch, unselfishly, to give to a needy family, rarely to get or do something for himself. He eschewed the worldly to attain the unworldly. So spiritually rich was his life that Pius XII is now elevating him to the honor of a saint. Then came Benedict XV and Pius XI. The first raised the Vatican's cry against Russia; the second defied Hitler and Mussolini.

And while these contrasts in action course through the life of the popes and even of the saints, they also run through the structure of the Church—a fighting priest here, a devoted scholar there. We learned how Cardinal O'Connell almost with no holds barred reproved a papal secretary of state, condemned a state lottery, and in acrid vein repudiated men unfit for public office. Cardinal Mundelein with more wit than malice made Hitler fighting mad by calling him a paperhanger. He influenced Chicago politics and entertained a President of the United States.

And yet besides these prelatial warriors there are the mystics, the philosophers and scholars, too. There are the hosts of professors in universities and the companies of monks in monasteries, whose daily lives are lived in communion with the Infinite. They are unsung but not always forgotten. In our day out of this vast number who laboriously yet unostentatiously perform their devotions and indulge their meditations comes one who with silent tread, and unheralded, becomes a cardinal. He is Samuel Cardinal Stritch, archbishop of Chicago—a mystic, a scholar, a philosopher and writer, who exemplifies in his daily turns the same beatitude as St. Francis.

In my last talk with Cardinal Stritch, which was after he had been raised to the purple, I found him exploring the stratosphere of thought with a humility bowed to timidity lest he offend. Garbed as a simple priest, he was working in the chancery. His serious and shy countenance denoted a submissive heart. Of medium stature, his locks of white enhancing his paternal mien, his eyes laboring behind heavy lenses, he avoided all effort of show. His voice was soft and persuasive, seeming to admit that others have a right to talk, too. He conversed slowly as if meditating on the correctness of his thought. His material is pondered, and because his knowledge is great he is able to sight all the angles from which a subject can be viewed. And when he has surveyed the field, he knows how to eliminate the nonessentials. He knows the relation of each angle to the other and then to the whole.

I recalled to him the great name he had himself created by his love of scholarship, a yearning for learning. When he was elected bishop of Toledo by Benedict XV, the word was thoroughly spread through the Vatican that the promotion had been earned by his profound intellectual penetration. There has been no slackening of his zeal for knowledge ever since he was a boy. His meditations in the realms of theology and of philosophy have been equaled by few scholars of our day. Since he was singularly a churchman, he concentrated in the moral sciences and doctrine.

Always within fixed bounds, his studious efforts did not wander into fields of science other than those which had a bearing upon him as a priest and shepherd of souls. He loved the arts, especially those arts which could redound to the benefit of religion. Music, painting, and sculpture received a cherished place in his searching endeavors. Architecture received the rank of a major course in his personal curriculum. He sought to dwell on the lines and form of the great cathedrals in Europe. And this knowledge which he had acquired served him to good purpose because it was not long after he had assumed the episcopal throne of the see of Toledo that he was called upon to build a new cathedral.

His knowledge of architecture was so thorough that he could call upon it for the detailed design of shrines and chapels as well as the general design. The cathedral stands as his most cherished work. He told me that it was the realization of all his knowledge and artistic inclinations. Its Spanish lines show how he was influenced by what he had seen in Toledo in old Spain, in Granada and other places. It took the knowledge of great cathedrals to have constructed an edifice such as the cathedral of Toledo is.

Samuel Alphonsus Stritch was born in Nashville, Tennessee, on August 17, 1887, of Irish parents. The name Stritch may seem more like German than Irish, but it is of ancestral Gaelic lineage. His father, a schoolmaster, was born in Ireland. His mother was a Malley. Deep family attachment to the Catholic faith steered the son's education in the beginnings of spiritual experience. The altar rather than the playground held the greater attraction. Early he assisted the priest at Mass.

While he was deep in his high school studies, he announced to his mother that he intended to be a priest. She discouraged his boldness in such a youthful decision.

"Mother," he replied, "you should not interpose yourself in the call of God."

At fourteen he was ready to begin his college studies, whereas the average age is eighteen. He entered St. Gregory's College in Cincinnati. Phenomenon that he was proving to be, he was ready to take up theology at sixteen. The bishop of Nashville, Thomas Byrne, thought of him as a prize for the priesthood and sent him to Rome. Misgivings filled the hearts of his parents in speeding their son across the world alone. But he consoled them in the thought that he would get there and get there all right. This turned out to be an understatement in prophecy.

Wanting in years and sparingly given a physique as if he had partaken of all for the mind and little for the body, he presented himself as a not too hopeful prospect for the rough handling of the North American College. He arrived when the college was still in summer session, so that he was received in their suburban retreat at Castel Gandolfo, where the pope also has his summer residence. When the rest of the students saw the undersized and apparently undeveloped youth entering the grounds, they thought that a tourist had strayed away from his traveling troupe. To make the judgment all the more conclusive, he was wearing knickers. Adding injury to misfortune, it was the fate of young Stritch to be nearsighted. He wore a pair of heavy lenses protectively rimmed.

When it was learned that he actually was seeking to be a student in theology, the rest of the college quite naturally, for such an unprepossessing appearance, put him under a subconscious but rigid probation. It was soon learned that he had a great deal of knowledge. It was learned also that he had a command of Latin which could put the older students to slight embarrassment if not to shame. Of course, the knickers were replaced by the cassock, and it was inevitable that Stritch looked more of a theologian than they did; for while he was but a boy, his lean frame and ascetic countenance combined to make him look theological even though they were of juvenile issue.

This summer retreat was set in a vast grove of umbrella pines in the Alban hills. The neighborhood abounded in Christian shrines. This was an accepted home for the young but avid student. He explored the cathedrals and the churches round about. With a guide and carrying a torch, he ferreted into the labyrinthian passages of the caves of Grottaferrata, in which is enshrined the miraculous Madonna under the protection of the Basilian monks. The Appian Way ran right alongside the grounds of the college. Every monument, relic, and ruin made a chore for Stritch, for he was never satisfied until he had deciphered all the Latin inscriptions on them.

Most students of the North American College engage in the same sports they knew at home. Baseball was, of course, the sport which had the major call, because it was easy to pick up sides and collect a playable aggregation to oppose one another. A few played golf. Those who played tennis had no way of gratifying their athletic inclination because there were few, if any, tennis courts in Rome in 1904 or 1905. And his classmates tried to work young Stritch in on the game of baseball, first, because they wished to have enough players, and secondly, very secondly, because they were touched with an altruistic spirit of giving the frail theologian a little outdoor exercise for his health.

Bishop James A. Griffin, of Springfield, Illinois, was a classmate of Stritch. Griffin was a good player, and as is the custom, a good player was generally charged with picking a side. Stritch would always be the last man left. Griffin is sympathetically responsible for the story that while he admired the top ratings of Stritch in class, he could not hide his disappointment over his lack of athletic bent. When Stritch was the lone survivor of the pickings, and it fell to Griffin's lot to pick him, Christian compassion surpassed baseball intuition as he included him on his side.

With Ralph Hayes, now bishop of Davenport, Iowa, he set about to teach Stritch something of the technique of practical baseball, as much for the acquisition of a new player as for a love of bringing him into the social orbit of the class. Griffin had taken a great fancy to Stritch, which at least reached elder-brother patronage if not paternal protection. He did not want him to be an outsider just because he could not pitch or catch. Griffin and Hayes made patience a virtue, but try as they would, they could not teach the unsporting Stritch a sport. They showed and showed how everything could be done and done easily. And though their patience seemed inexhaustible, the effort was foreordained to come to an end. One day Griffin drove a cannon-ball drive in the direction of third base where Hayes was fielding. It rocketed directly toward Hayes and missed his head by only the fraction of one of its seams. Stritch saw the quasi calamity. It had fortunately been indecisive for Hayes, but it was decisive for Stritch. He was through with it. It was as if he had excommunicated baseball for its willful disregard for the sixth, eighth, and tenth commandments.

In those days, too, the students could take the train from Castel Gandolfo and run down to the seashore to the beach at Anzio. This was the identical beach over which thousands of American soldiers passed in mortal combat in 1943. Today many thousands of white crosses are mute evidence of the sacrifice they made on the Anzio beachhead. But in 1904 and 1905, Anzio was a peaceful fishing village and the beach was the finest near Rome. Stritch could swim. This one lone athletic faculty gave him the right to accompany the other students on their occasional summer jaunts to the sea for a respite from the heat of the Roman campagna.

In the autumn the students returned to Rome for the rest of the year. The college building lies in the very heart of the city. Somehow baseball had to go on even without Stritch. With studies and devotions cramming their schedule, these men destined for the priesthood found their only outlet in baseball. They still picked sides and played in the Borghese gardens, Rome's public park. It was a strange sight to watch these sacerdotal as-

pirants in their cassocks—for they were not allowed to go
out except in cassock—trying to pitch, catch, field, and
run bases. They tucked the skirt of the cassock into their
belts. While this may or may not have improved their
running speed, it certainly dislodged their dignity.

It was a strange sight for Americans, but—Italians
looked on too. Sports in Italy were then almost unknown.
They looked on and wondered. Then they passed by,
thinking that Providence should be thanked that no Italian ever engaged in such a spectacle where a cassock was
being worn and taken off at one and the same time. For
that reason, the students of the North American College
were colloquially regarded as "not a little odd" by the mis-
understanding Italian populace. Stritch used to go along,
but never did he have to join the spectacle because he
could quite skillfully undertake the unathletic though
necessary role of scorekeeper—and in a cassock properly
worn.

The nature that was in him was absorbed with the
command of giving the spirit the fullest exercise of its
power. He seemed to argue with himself whether this or
that would improve his spiritual substance. Bishop Griffin recalled that the students of the college quite often
visited the villa of Merry del Val, when he was secretary
of state, which also was located near the papal summer
residence. The Cardinal had a predilection for the Americans and, as we said before, often invited them to tea.
His presence impressed them with its commanding dyna-
mism, brought out in its pleasing emissions and intellectual depth, as it did me, from the first time I saw him.
But Sam Stritch in those teen years was not sure whether
a cardinal should engage in the diversions of ordinary
men.

Merry del Val would talk tennis, hunting, horsemanship, and would listen to the Americans tell him about baseball. Customarily he offered them an exhibition of his marksmanship. On one occasion when Sam was present, he set up a row of Italian pennies, which were the size of a silver dollar, and placed them on edge on the garden wall. He then went to the other end of the garden, took up the rifle, and shot each of the ten pennies one after the other as if he had been an expert at a military fete.

This display by a prince of the Church did not coincide with the lofty concept which Sam Stritch entertained for them. He told Griffin he thought it a surrender of cardinalatial dignity. His bent was at this point circumscribed by dogma and doctrine. On these, his being breathed and lived. I have wondered what effect it would have had on him then had he visitéd the papal villa in Castel Gandolfo and there seen the portrait of Pope Clement XIV mounted on a white mule and escorted by mounted monsignors. It was a papal custom. Nevertheless, this enclosure of his personality within the spiritual orbit had set his course. He feared becoming worldly; avoids worldliness today.

What demonstrated his meditative nature more than anything else was his custom of staying in the chapel of the college and virtually fondling its sacred objects with worshipful affection. This attribute, together with his record in scholarship, induced Archbishop Kennedy, the rector, to choose him for house sacristan. Here he had charge of all the precious symbols on which his heart truly dwelt. For most of the students, it was not a position to be sought because while the very exalting touch of the vessels and linens lifted the spirit, the rather irksome task of paring the candles and fitting them into the candelabra discomfited the flesh. In fact, the office was performed in a dark, cell-like room which constituted the college sacristy and was colloquially (though unfittingly for young Stritch) called "the grease room." Besides, gratuitously enough, an added pleasure was bestowed upon the sacristan in that it was his duty to polish the silver candelabra.

But whatever chore was to be done about the chapel found its ready acceptance in the heart of little Stritch. He lavished hours of time and a soul full of care there. He saw that the marbles were kept immaculate. The decoration of the altar with flowers was a favorite job on which he put a quantum of thought and deliberation. His artistic nature came to light in the arrangement of colors and of forms. He had become so engrossed in his office that the chapel became in a very special way one of his most contemplative exertions.

Bishop Griffin was a traveling companion with Stritch, then a bishop, too, on a visit to Rome in 1925. They naturally visited the college and went to pray in the chapel. They talked about old times in the manner of "old grads" coming back to college for a class reunion. When they had finished their collegiate pilgrimage, they returned to their hotel in a horse-drawn hack. Its leisurely pace was propitious for meditative reminiscences. Both were silent while pondering over their re-enacted educational and religious experience. Finally it was Stritch who broke the silence.

"I still think," he said with a feeling of nostalgic pride, "that I kept those candlesticks shined up better in my day, don't you?"

Pius X was pope when Stritch was a student in Rome. Though they were two generations apart, yet their natures ran parallel with each other. Pius X, as we saw, was a meditative, communing personality. His spirit dwelt more on the ways of heaven than those of the earth below.

The world and the quarrels of men and nations were abhorrent to his soul. The power of love was mightier to him than the mightiest army. He conceived the currents of human affection as coursing through the hearts of mankind and winning them in love for one another. With love, unostentatious and sublime, he knew that humanity could be saved.

Young Stritch often cherished the pattern of this contemplative spirit. It found ready sympathy in his own soul. Stritch was not one to devise means by which man became the enemy of man. Pondering on how to make man just became a passion. He sought out the great books on philosophy and ethics so that he might delve as deeply as he could to discover the key that would turn man from evil to good. The contrite heart and humble spirit of the Pope, who pawned and pawned his watch, revealed to Stritch a nature which, in its silent and reserved way, was winning the souls of mankind to a religious surge creating more good than the glittering blandishments of rough-heeled conquerors. Meditation on the good fitted into the personality of Stritch. It was for others to engage in worldly spectacles and to seek to reform humanity by going along with humanity. For Stritch, the mode of life was to regenerate mankind with the substance of the spirit which could penetrate the soul and restore that soul to a rich, healthy, and eternal existence.

When he was finally ordained, he embraced the occasion with inherently grave presentiment. As a priest he would return to his diocese. His name as a scholar had already been known there, but what he had done in Rome in receiving first the degree of doctor of philosophy and secondly the degree of doctor of sacred theology only enhanced his fame.

Far from being without honor in his own town, he was

covered with it. Bishop Byrne, who had chosen him for his talents beforehand, was all the more convinced of them and gratified by them now. It was not without a certain measure of pleasure and self-satisfaction that he appointed him a curate in the Cathedral of St. Patrick in Memphis.

The happy combination of an encyclopedic knowledge and a meditative mind served to enhance his priestly potentialities. This was the more noticeable because he so outshone his own colleagues by what he knew. His analysis and logic in spiritual abstractions was easily discernible in his preaching. He now possessed those faculties which would recommend themselves to a bishop who was seeking in his diocese a likely man for episcopal honors. The bishops are always looking for men who would make good bishops so that the continuity of administering the faith is the better maintained. In the case of Stritch, he was made a pastor, then he became chancellor of the diocese. As an added extolment of his ability, he was made superintendent of the parochial schools. This was to give him the touch of the levers of administration.

When he left Rome, this reputation for knowledge and for priestly talent had been registered in the minds of the prelates of the Consistorial Congregation, which is charged with the responsibility of recommending to the pope the names of candidates for the episcopate. What with this reputation and the skill he had shown in the diocesan chancellery, he was definitely enrolled in Rome, too, as a coming bishop. The turns in his own development were coinciding with the requisites of the pontifical advisers. It was on November 30, 1921, that he was chosen to assume his episcopal throne. I remember that day and how at the North American College his name had been glorified as one of the greatest scholars ever to have entered its halls. Now he was but thirty-four. At that moment he was the youngest bishop in the world, though later Kearney of Brooklyn was made a bishop when he was thirty-two.

Some fourteen years had passed since Sam Stritch had lamented the worldly spectacle of a cardinal shooting a rifle. Now, however, succumbing to the persuasive power of his athletic classmate, Bishop Griffin, he admitted to a necessity for physical exercise. He was induced to take up golf to meet this necessity. He learned, but he never embraced the game with the enthusiasm of an addict. While he and Griffin were on a vacation in Florida with other prelates, the group decided on a game of golf. Stritch begged off and was found at the end of the game under a tree reading the less relaxing pages of an encyclopedia.

The diocese of Toledo was just ready to embark on a period of expansion; and this opportunity was thrust upon Stritch. Like so many of those who have been able to lift up the goal of mankind and to project its future on a course of common well-being, so the new bishop took hold and led his flock into a promised land of religious plenitude. His endeavors, whether in the interest of the personal lives of his people or whether it was through the instrumentality of new institutions, always kept to the bond with his own nature, namely, that by enriching the spiritual, all other things, whether material, social, or educational, would fall into their proper place in the progress of the diocese.

And so he ordered the formation of various organizations to encompass the spiritual welfare of the people. There were organizations in which the women of the diocese were shepherded and still others where the men could share in the bounty of the spiritual stores which he himself could bestow. But he did more than that. He was naturally engrossed in the education of children and young men and women according to the teachings of Catholicism. With a concentrated diocesan effort, he was able to muster the resources to build a million-dollar high school. He established a teacher's college and built seven new churches. Then, to crown a short episcopate of but eight years, he constructed, as we said before, his own cathedral. This was a life's work in a short span. Now he was called to another promotion. On April 26, 1930, Pope Pius XI chose him to be archbishop of Milwaukee.

Milwaukee was rich in educational institutions, churches, and a famous cathedral. It was such a completed material structure that it gave to Stritch the great opportunity for the intensification of the spiritual values in the faith. He made good use of these riches in buildings and grounds. As if to bring the men of the archdiocese into a compact phalanx of spiritual power, he launched a campaign for the expansion of the Holy Name societies, which are the living expression of militant Catholic action. The membership was increased from 15,000 to 50,-000. Similarly, he desired to enlist the youth into a spiritual crusade. Units of the Catholic Youth Organization had been established in but 125 parishes when he took charge of the archdiocese. In nine years he increased these to 547—272 for boys and 275 for girls.

And it was in Milwaukee that his preaching began to find response in the times. He saw the danger which was to be exerted by a rampant overlord who was poisoning religion in Germany. Thousands of his flock were of German extraction, but his condemnation of Nazi doctrine found willing acceptance among his communicants, whether they were of German antecedents or not. He made great efforts in the realm of charity, consolidating the various Catholic societies under one organization. By this method the efficiency of the organization increased so that it was able to dispense two million dollars in charitable works in nine years. While his work in the Milwaukee diocese did not record the construction which featured his Toledo endeavors, what was accomplished in the spiritual realm was quite appealing to Rome. His work had pleased three previous popes, and now it was to please a fourth, Pius XII. On the death of Cardinal Mundelein, the call was given to Stritch. On March 7, 1940, he was enthroned to rule over 1,652,587 Roman Catholics in the archdiocese of Chicago and more than 2,000,000 in the province of Illinois, over which he assumed the title of metropolitan.

The design of his life and endeavors in the rich though turbulent jurisdiction of Chicago was slid into, rather than was fitted into, the complex mélange of interests there. Chicago has all the problems of the great urban centers, with the slight difference that it has them bigger. The Apostolic Delegation in Washington always was cognizant of the many-sided and many-angled nature of a keeper of Chicago's morals. To begin with, a multiple national-origin feud sways back and forth. Catholic Poles are jealous of Catholic Italians and Catholic Italians are jealous of Catholic Irish and Catholic Irish are jealous of Catholic Germans and so on with Lithuanians, Czechoslovaks, and Hungarians, too. The strictures between these groups are carried to the point that there will be four or five Catholic churches in a very small area, where one church would do but where four or five have to be built because of national distinctions.

Unlike Mundelein, Stritch keeps a wide distance between himself and the politicians of Chicago. His loftiness of thought conceives it as his function to promulgate the principles on which a righteous political life could be built. He prescribes his course as completely outside of the political conflicts which devil the region. Mayor Kelly, as we saw, was a frequent visitor with Mundelein, but he hardly ever sees Stritch, much less visits the archiepiscopal residence. Mundelein used to recommend either directly or indirectly whom he regarded as worthy for public office. It is outside archiepiscopal dignity today to interfere in the political quarrels which sweep the city.

Stritch, too, had given a great deal of study to economic and sociological problems. According to Bishop Griffin, this began when he was a student in Rome. He commenced his humanitarian projections with a profound absorption of *Rerum Novarum,* the encyclical on labor by Pope Leo XIII. He followed this up with a weighted deliberation on all the pronouncements of the Catholic Church. Especially was he imbued with the principles enunciated in the labor encyclical of Pius XI, which sought to establish the principle that labor was now not a chattel, as had so often been claimed, but was life, and that the dignity of the worker should always be defended. He based his own pronouncements on labor mainly on these two papal letters.

But with all these multifarious interests, I asked Cardinal Stritch whether or not there was any great problem in Chicago which stood out beyond the others. In his soft and measured speech, he said that it was his belief that all problems were dealt with in the course of their existence and efforts made as circumstances demanded to meet these problems. I enumerated various telling chores like the problem of nationalities, the labor problem, the race problem, and the problem of child delinquency. But the Cardinal was quite calm. He appeared to be satisfied that what had been done and what was then projected to meet all of the social and spiritual disturbances which plague Chicago was at least equal to the call. It was really an exemplification of his nature that put his inherent confidence in the showing of the way. Then it was the responsibility of the individual to follow. To this end he kept in close contact with all the various lay organizations of his charge, invited their leaders to conferences with him, and while he checked their activities, he also indicated for them the definite lines on which their progress should be made and their activity undertaken.

I talked about the features of the Chicago archdiocese with one of my fellow newsmen there. He brushed all the usual archdiocesan activities to one side.

"The most outstanding fact about the Chicago archdiocese," he said quite sincerely for a member of the profession noted for its cynicism, "is the happy balance of the hierarchy. While Peter had his Paul, so Cardinal Stritch has his own crusader, too, and right in his own time. He is Bishop Bernard J. Sheil."

Talking with this one and that, I found the crusader a complement for the mystic. Sheil cannot be denied as a power in Chicago. He is the senior auxiliary bishop, was made auxiliary under Mundelein. Sheil and Stritch are poles apart in personality. They do not do things the same way. We have seen how Stritch hovered and pondered over his books, spurned a baseball bat, polished the candelabra at the altar, and read an encyclopedia under a tree while others played golf. Sheil is the antithesis of this.

Sheil was born in Chicago in 1888. He roughed it with the boys of St. Columbville parish. He learned early to use his fists, catch and throw a ball, sprint from the cops, and to stick by the gang. He went to St. Viator College and then to St. Viator Seminary, both in Bourbonnais, Illinois. He was a good quarterback on St. Viator's football team. But he was more than that. He achieved one of the records of all time in baseball and merited a classification in Bob Ripley's "Believe It or Not." And this was it—he pitched a no-hit nine-inning game against the University of Illinois and lost. It was in the last inning that he gave a walk. Then the shortstop missed a grounder and the ball went careening into the outfield, where the players, who evidently were tense and nervous, did not know what to do with it. The man on first base scored. Sheil is still an athlete and can shoot a game of golf in the lower eighties. When it takes too much of his time to go out to a course, he takes out his athletic nostalgia in a handball court.

I first met Bernard Sheil in Rome in 1924. He had accompanied Archbishop Mundelein to the consistory which created him a cardinal. Mundelein had drafted him as his secretary, though he actually held the post of chancellor of the archdiocese. He was thirty-six then and had already passed through a variety of curdling and even macabre experiences which stamped him as a man who had met the challenge of life. One day Mundelein brought him back from his private audience in which he had presented Sheil to the Pope. He was full of joy. He had already told the Pope about Sheil. Pius XI was a great athlete himself and had won records in mountain climbing which have never been broken or even equaled.* He was thrilled with the account of Sheil's athletic prowess, though he knew little of either baseball or football but favored them just the same.

But where the Pope was truly moved was in Mundelein's description of the work of Bernard Sheil in the Cook County jail in Chicago, where he was a chaplain. He had administered the last rites to a score of condemned men for as much as the faith allowed. In war, men slay in

* *A Reporter at the Papal Court,* New York, Longmans, Green.

battle heat. No one unless he has experienced death in cold blood can feel the awe and remorseful struggle to witness a life snuffed out without premeditation and certainly without malice. How much worse for a chaplain! He must call in all his strength to give what consolation there is in the blackness of the impending tragedy. Not once but a score of times had Sheil suffered the anguish for the mistakes of humanity in the very cry for vengeance of an outraged society. Here was the steel for character.

Mundelein could not hold Sheil down to a desk job. He promoted him from chancellor to vicar-general, but in 1930 Sheil founded the Catholic Youth Organization. The inspiration had come from the oft-recurring specter of the agonized faces of young men on the gallows and in the cells. Sheil wanted to save men for life here and then for eternity. This youth organization was to channel youth in healthy endeavor—both physical and spiritual. A hundred thousand youth of Chicago now belong to Sheil's outlet. Not all would have gone wrong. It is for those who would have gone wrong that it was all worth it.

But where a spreading contrast keeps the personality of Stritch and Sheil on widely spaced parallel lines which never meet but are certainly going in the same direction is precisely in their public approach. Sheil goes to boxing matches. More than that, he sponsors boxing. He has been called the Catholic Mike Jacobs. To the cardinal-archbishop who shrank from the thought of seeing a prince of the Church shooting a rifle *in private* we may balance the acts of his senior auxiliary who would promote a prize fight *in public*. Stritch believes that it is his duty to map out for his flock by spiritual communion the way to Paradise; Sheil gets out on the way and does some spade work.

While Sheil's youth organization has many activities—

such as open-air camps, pilot training, social service, and various study clubs, the achievement by which it is kept before the public is precisely its boxing teams. Sheil came on this by what can be called amateur and accidental psychological and social research. He was trying to get the devil out of unruly boys. He always found them wanting to fight somebody, perhaps as an outlet of their early-acquired grudges against society in general. Well, why not regulate this urge and harness it? He called in the late Packy McFarland, former boxing champion, to help him out. The boys liked this novelty. To them Sheil is known only as "the Boss." Under "the Boss," organized boxing replaced indiscriminate fighting as the escape valve for these combative and perhaps vindictive energies.

The idea of the youth organization found favor among several Catholic philanthropists. It was put on its feet financially. Fulminantly, its beneficent effects spread to other dioceses. Now, it is a recognized Catholic adjunct in youth training. This has brought Sheil into greater boxing limelight. In priestly garb, unprepossessing in stature but pleasing in nature, he gets around. His five-feet-eight presence at amateur boxing functions such as that known as the Golden Gloves contest has developed to the point that it is almost protocol that he should be there. He is regarded as a patron of the manly though barely prelatial art. His pictures at the ringside in company with boxing celebrities and sports writers are published all over the country. And the devil seems to be on his good behavior whenever he is around.

The youth organization, first an infant and now grown to rompers if not to long pants, has begun to shift a little for itself. This self-propelling propensity has allowed Sheil to crusade on another battle front. He has mixed it up with the adult crowd and has rubbed against the sweat and dirt in overalls as the champion of labor—and organized labor at that. He lined up with John L. Lewis when the permanently scowling leader founded the C.I.O. He kept friends with John L. though the shaggy-browed organizer walked out on his offspring and made it a foundling. Sheil helped nurse it and became a favorite with it. He is buddy-thick with Philip Murray, its present president.

Chicago's auxiliary also gave his good will to the American Federation of Labor. William Green, its president, is one-two-three on Sheil's list of intimates. While the labor leaders cannot call him "the Boss," because they have bosses in their own hierarchy, they do call him "Bishop," which is no slight anachronism where fights are virile and talk strong. He calls them John, Phil, and Bill.

The reason that the tie-up with labor remains compact lies in the out-and-out comradeship Sheil has shown. As between capital and labor, the bishop is no two-sides arbiter. His impartiality is partial. He has uncompromisingly taken up labor's battle. And these labor forces, too, either by design or accident, fit into his own racial concepts. They decry race discrimination and this is one of Sheil's pet preachings. And he touches the warm heart of labor by championing no mere abstract theories of justice. He steps out boldly and calls out the figures. The abolition of the Little Steel formula found its principle public support in Bernard Sheil. Some of his speeches before labor organizations sound like the labor leaders themselves.

"It is interesting to note," he said in an address before the Building Service International Union convention, "that according to the statistics of the War Labor Board, there were fourteen million American workers averaging only seventy cents an hour in March 1945. With time and a half, and double time, on the basis of a 56-hour week, these purportedly highly paid workers would receive about $45 weekly. From this amount came the withholding tax and war-bond reductions, leaving them with the magnificent sum of about $34 as take-home pay."

At the annual convention of the C.I.O. in Chicago in 1944, Sheil was presented as the chief speaker. Certainly nothing could be more significant as a testimonial to his labor leanings. His address was spiced throughout with those labor aspirations which a receptive and grateful audience could only welcome by spontaneous shouting and clapping and whistling traditional with labor's boisterous expansiveness and more than incidentally emblematic of a companionable unanimity with the Bishop.

"Labor knows that the common man's desires are not excessive," he said. "They consist of a home, a piece of land, a stable job, and an opportunity to educate his children. Labor knows that organization is the most efficient and most enduring way of achieving these things. Labor knows, then, that for the future peace and for the extension of democracy, labor unions are an absolute necessity."

And in that same convention he fulfilled the hopes of the leaders and of the delegates by putting his own stamp of approval on the guaranteed annual wage, a labor hope that looms disconsolately on the industrial horizon.

"The wage scale must be regulated with a view to the economic welfare of the whole people," he decreed as if it were *ex cathedra*. "I believe that the guaranteed annual wage for the working man is just; it is socially necessary; it is economically feasible; it is a democratic imperative."

Sheil got into such depths in the labor whirlpool that he tried to bring John L. Lewis and President Roosevelt together after the fall-out, when Mr. Roosevelt chided the C.I.O. and the A.F. of L. with "a plague on both their houses," before the 1940 presidential campaign. Lewis was president of C.I.O. then. In Chicago, Sheil is consulted by a number of leaders and often invited in to rally the membership to serried efforts when a campaign is in the offing.

At the C.I.O. convention, too, he chose to carry his attack against the National Association of Manufacturers. Nothing could have sent his hearers into greater rhapsodies of satisfaction than an ecclesiastical chastisement of the bosses, a thing so rare in the labor orbit that it had the effect of being a great event.

"It is time we realized," said the prelatial patron of labor, "that the National Association of Manufacturers is not the only repository of wisdom in America. What many of our industrial leaders fail to see is that economic democracy is part and parcel of the entire democratic climate. They cannot see that social legislation is only a means to a wider participation in democracy. That is why full employment is necessary, that is why an adequate unemployment compensation plan is necessary; that is why the 65-cent minimum wage law is necessary; that is why a permanent F.E.P.C. is necessary. That is why labor's just demand for increased wages should be met at once."

And as if to utter an economic heresy while still keeping to ecclesiastical orthodoxy, he told them that they should have a part in management.

"Normally, there should be a partnership of labor and capital," he proclaimed with pontifical authority. "This partnership has been prevented by modern economic conditions. Labor has been excluded from its rightful voice in management."

Sheil comes out four-square for racial equality. A large share of the social service efforts of his youth organization is devoted to helping the Negro. He was one of the prime movers for President Roosevelt's Fair Employment Practices Act. In all his public action his stand has been firm, definite, and determined. I once attended a luncheon of the Chicago Council against Racial and Religious Discrimination. Dr. Preston Bradley, the famous radio preacher, presided. Sheil was one of the chief speakers. Bradley in introducing Sheil paid him about as lavish a tribute as could be paid when we consider that oftentimes Catholic and Protestant divines, in contradiction to Christian exhortation, delight in calling each other by un-Christian names.

"Without detracting anything from the great prince of the Church, the Cardinal," proclaimed Bradley, "I do not think that there has been a churchman throughout the whole Chicago area, either Protestant or Catholic, who has been a greater influence for economic and social justice than Bishop Bernard J. Sheil. He has been courageous and adventuresome in tolerance for every people and faith."

The Bishop has pronounced views on most public questions. He was one of the first to propose sharing the atomic bomb.

"Yielding of the bomb secrets to international control," he said, "is now the most practical way of arriving at international harmony. We can choose to build one world or we can choose to have no world at all."

He has stood out against anti-Semitism.

"The only Jew the gentile needs fear," he declared, "is the imaginary one he has created in his own mind."

For the failure of churches to arouse the people to a sense of religious responsibility, the Bishop blames a blind spot tinged with respectability and hypocrisy.

"Too much respect for the local banker, industrialist,

or politician," he said, "has caused them to be silent when
the teachings of Christ should have been literally shouted
from the housetops."

The working day of Bishop Sheil squirms through a
maze of the most difficult exactions. As pastor of St. Andrew's parish, he makes his parochial rounds first thing.
Back to his home, he packs up to be whisked out to a
confirmation ceremony somewhere in the Chicago area.
For with Cardinal Stritch and Bishop William D. O'Brien,
he helps administer the thousands of confirmations for the
archdiocese. Next, he must return to the city and take his
place as the executive head of the C.Y.O. This would be
a full-time job for any man. The recreational and cultural activities of one hundred thousand Chicago boys and
girls exacts its toll of toil. Some days, he addresses a luncheon. Then back to the C.Y.O. and perhaps another confirmation. Meetings, conferences, and civic gatherings
extort with benevolent acquiescence more of his self-
generated energy. Thrown in may be a rally with a labor
union. The rounds are continuous, week in, week out.

No wonder we can attribute to him the Paul of Chicago's Peter, Cardinal Stritch. While the wiry senior
auxiliary curls his way with bountiful vigor through the
streets and boulevards, whether they be swank or slum,
the chief pastor of the archdiocese plans the course of his
populous flock, the most numerous and variegated in all
the world. Deep spiritual communion runs through the
daily labors of the Cardinal, filled with its multitudinous
mélange of problems either to solve or circumvent. In
chancery and chapel, in the colleges and the cathedral, he
gives out his acquired store of inspirational bounty and
leavens the religious life of students, priests, and laymen.
His is the humility of being the least. Though master, he
is the servant. He knows how blessed are the meek.

11. No Mannequin He

THE cannonade of public clamor has struck no ecclesiastic with as much impact as it has Edward Cardinal Mooney, archbishop of Detroit. Other divines have had battles to fight—rackets, political rings, gambling, divorce, and controversies on education—but none has been forced combatively into the blinking glare of the national searchlight as has Mooney. He has had to fight race wars. He has had to defend the Church in labor wars. There was nothing more controversial to incite his own flock than the labor battle line—where he had big Catholics on the employer side and a vast population on the labor side. Henry Ford II, John Raskob, and the Fisher brothers of Fisher bodies are all Catholics, and plenty of other big tycoons as well. The Catholic labor population runs over a half million. Mooney was not by nature a spectator. He joined battle, rocketed his bombs, and emerged, his hands gnarled but head unbowed.

Ordinarily this would be enough to tax the strategic resources of any prelate, whether he had been used to preaching his way to episcopal success or whether he had favored the sterner method of giving orders and exacting obedience.

But as if trial and tribulation were to be set upon him, the problem, the *problem* of Father Coughlin had to be saddled on Mooney's overburdened back. Coughlin became a national issue. It was one of those dilemmas involved in a dilemma. The cry went out from everywhere, "Why doesn't Mooney shut him up?" If Mooney did shut him up, then another cry would come from another direction tagging him as an American Hitler or Mussolini who would not allow his priests to preach what they thought. If he silenced him, it was wrong. If he let him talk, it was wrong.

It was worse if he paid no attention to Coughlin, because the one side charged him with cowardice and the other with lack of courage. If he censured the radio priest, the radio priest made capital out of it. On one occasion Coughlin with crocodile mimicry even lamented lacrimoniously his own crucifixion, where cruel forces had nailed him to the cross, put a crown of thorns on his head, and cast lots for his raiment.

When Coughlin was riding high and when millions of dollars were pouring into his Shrine of the Little Flower at Royal Oak, Michigan, I talked exhaustively with Mooney on this uncommon ecclesiastical embroilment. This was in 1939. A special post office staff had to be recruited to handle the Coughlin mail. The basement of his nine-million-dollar church was devoted to business administration—opening the mail, sorting it out, endorsing the checks and putting them in the bank. The Coughlin organization ran gift shops, sold religious objects, ran a restaurant, and operated a gas station.

Now, these things did not worry the Archbishop much. What worried him most was what Coughlin used to say over the air. In fact I asked him, if it should come to a showdown and he would be forced to remove Coughlin from his pastorate, whether it would embarrass him in keeping up the nine-million-dollar edifice and the enterprises annexed thereto.

"No," said the Archbishop, "that would not worry me at all. As a parish, we could easily get someone else to fill it."

Coughlin's tactics, his unreliability, and his veiled threats over the radio put the chancery on the gridiron. Usually, when a parish priest gets a call from a superior to correct his ways, he hastens to put himself right. Whether he gets a mild scolding or painful scalding for something he has said, the result is the same, for he usually admits he is sorry and penitently promises that he will not do it again. But with Coughlin that was not the case. He wanted to know by what authority the Archbishop dared touch him on the shoulder. If he was told it was the Archbishop's ecclesiastical right, he then would ask that he be shown the passages in the canon law on which that authority was exercised. Coughlin always wanted a crisis in public, because he craved a show and longed to depict himself as a victim. Naturally, Mooney was not playing into his hands.

The Archbishop had hoped that Coughlin would wear himself out with the public. But the more the Archbishop wished, the more the newspapers paid attention to Coughlin. It had been part of Mooney's strategy to leave him alone and to trust that the public would tire of him. Coughlin would not let anybody forget him, much less the public—as long as he could use the air.

"If people would not make so much fuss about Father Coughlin," the Archbishop told me, evidently thinking somewhat wishfully, "then this phenomenon would vanish in its allotted course. But it's the papers and the magazines which really make Father Coughlin. There would be no problem at all were it not for the controversy stirred up about him."

But the hope that the pastor of the Shrine of the Little Flower would have his day and then decline was bound to fade as long as Coughlin could arouse even though he did not amuse. His statements were generally so inaccurate that Mooney feared some involvement of the Catholic Church. When Coughlin went on the air, here was a job to be done—he had to be checked up. And the more the radio priest found himself becoming a nuisance to the chancery office of the Archbishop, the more he liked it. He was an adroit strategist in working his advantages and imposing them on his superiors.

Mooney sent out his consultors to persuade Coughlin to make use of the "friendly" advice of other prelates before he delivered his blasts. This was to insure accuracy of statement as well as doctrine. Coughlin feared "friendly" advice. He was constitutionally elusive. His own personality was bifocal, for while on the one hand he regarded himself as a big power politically and a towering giant intellectually, on the other he always pitied himself ignominiously as victimized. And then, either for personal consolation or public justification, he skillfully contrived to imply by innuendo that it was the Archbishop who was the Pontius Pilate.

It turned out to be a source of prankishly puerile pleasure to Coughlin to learn that Mooney could not leave Detroit without having him on his mind. Sometimes it seemed he was more than a trifle mischievous when he would plan a sensational exposé when the head of the archdiocese was on some episcopal mission. On one occasion Mooney attended a gathering of Catholic bishops in Buffalo. Just as he got there, he received a telephone call. This was from the Detroit chancery to advise him that

Coughlin was going on the air the following Sunday to say that there was a bill before Congress which provided for the abolition of all parochial schools throughout the United States.

It would be hard to conceive a bit of news which would so drastically upset any Catholic, and especially an archbishop. Mooney asked his chancery to inquire where Coughlin got his facts. This meant waiting around in Buffalo for another telephone call. In due time, it came —Coughlin got his facts straight from Washington. Now Mooney had to check the story himself. He got the officials of the National Catholic Welfare Conference in Washington on the phone. He told them to investigate the claim of Coughlin. They turned things upside down to track down the disturbing bill. They called senators and representatives as well as the clerks of the House and Senate. They did track it down. There was no such bill.

All this time Mooney was waiting in Buffalo; finally he was called from Washington by the N.C.W.C. They told him what they had found. They were sure of it. No trace of such a bill existed. It would have been human to be annoyed if not downright enraged at all the extra dislocation of his trip. Not phlegmatic by nature, he was nevertheless composed though he waited minutes to be sure of this composure himself. Now he had to telephone the Detroit chancery to tell Coughlin that he was shooting off on a tangent. On the wire he was cold and adamant. Coughlin was told to lay aside his clandestine discovery. This was the order, criticism notwithstanding.

Now, though he was legislating on Coughlin Sunday after Sunday, he had no intention of accepting him as an unfortunate though irremovable annoyance. This is what Coughlin would have liked and it would have run everybody ragged. Taking no advantage of rank, Mooney wanted to make it fair, for fairness had become, if not an instinct with him, at least an irrevocable habit, cultivated since he was a boy. Avoidance, too, of autocratic dictation was a *sine qua non* in him, for he is neither autocrat nor dictator. His priests have told me that he gives each his justifiable say. They enjoy maximum license. Coughlin had translated license into archdiocesan weakness. Conclusively, Mooney's problem was to square his principles of fairness and freedom with any disciplinary action directed at Coughlin.

He was laboriously searching for a formula. *"Geduld bringt Rosen"* is a German proverb, meaning "Patience brings roses." Patience to the impatient is characterized as slothfulness in action, but in Mooney it is the concomitant of action. He cultivates events and currents just as the gardener nurses his plants. He devises for time to wait for action or action for time until the one is co-ordinated with the other. As the patient gardener combines with the elements to bring his roses to a pleasing full bloom, so he painstakingly collects all the ingredients of the problem, places them in their proper relation, and then works it all out to a logical result. The method could almost be called the Mooney formula.

With Coughlin, the accompanying currents were so diverse and opposite that he had to await the converging of many inconsistencies, religious and otherwise, so that the radio priest and his supporters would themselves be convinced of the rightness of a final judgment. He did not want to put him off the air on some simple excuse. Certainly plenty of those existed. He desired something that would pointedly reflect against Coughlin's right to speak as a priest and to use the cloth as a means of furthering his own personal ends. Coughlin was saying more than enough to annoy the Archbishop. His attacks on the

Jews, his tirade against public men, his charges against various banking institutions, and his condemnation of United States foreign policy were not alone disturbing, but in many cases they overstepped the bounds of the Catholic line of action and stated Catholic principles.

When President Roosevelt appointed Senator Hugo Black to be an associate justice of the United States, the *Pittsburgh Post* had published the charge that he was a member of the Ku Klux Klan. This aroused more than a ripple of complaint. Coughlin went on the air about it. He proclaimed it an "act of personal stupidity" on the part of President Roosevelt. Mooney told him this was no way for a priest to talk about the President. Here was the beginning of Coughlin's turn toward the exit, even though he did not know it.

Henry Ford happened to be meandering aimlessly about Washington Boulevard in the neighborhood of the Detroit chancery in 1939, too. It was as if he had a day off from the plant, because he decided casually to drop in and have a visit with Mooney. No appointment had been made. Henry Ford asked to see the Archbishop. The Archbishop, never having met him, decided there was no time like the present.

Mooney is a much easier man to talk to than Henry Ford. Quite understandably, he is also a better talker than Henry Ford. He has to meet more people. The Archbishop has made a fine art out of conversation and knows plenty of things to talk about. The pioneer auto manufacturer knows motors and knows them from top to bottom. He is as laconic as he is inventive. Everything was quite cozy about the meeting. Henry Ford threw his hat down and took a chair alongside the prelate's desk. Mooney sat in his usual working togs of black clerical garb. That morning he could be taken for a simple priest.

And though the auto sage had just wandered in casually, this time he did have something to say.

"Well," said Ford after they had talked about Detroit, the weather, and where they had come from, "I dropped in more than anything else to tell you that I like your man out there at Royal Oak."

"Well," said Mooney in return. "Some like him and some don't. Varying opinions are one of the reasons why press and people talk so much about him."

Ford then went on to explain with evident singleness of purpose how Coughlin had been a great influence by his radio addresses in keeping down Communism. At that time there was something about a company union which Ford was planning to organize, and it was alleged that Coughlin was trying to work himself into the gearing there. Besides, his anti-Semitic attacks played the same melody as that of Henry Ford. All these coincident views got the one to like the other, albeit *in absentia* and by proxy. The Archbishop, however, could not quarrel with Ford. He was not in his jurisdiction even as a layman, much less as a priest.

But World War II was coming on. The Coughlin radio talks against American foreign policy finally convinced the Archbishop that time was getting abreast of action and that with the country in full swing toward a strong policy of defense and eventual intervention, a defeatist force like Coughlin could not be on the air, especially since he caused a certain reflection on the Catholic Church. Currents and events were converging. This was the moment. Time and action were co-ordinated.

And the Archbishop, while his position required that the initiative should be his, did not make it a personal matter at all. Incidents and forces had now made it all too plain that Coughlin had written his own indictment. In fact he was virtually self-condemned by preaching obstruction when the country was mustered for defense against a mortal enemy. Consequently, no one now could impute the Archbishop's action to personal animus. The formula had reached its mathematical inevitability. Fairness was safeguarded—fairness to the country and the Church as well as Coughlin. Accordingly the archdiocesan synod, which corresponds roughly to the cabinet of the archbishop, inserted in its regulations for sacerdotal guidance a new instruction.

The instruction forbade the clergy of the Detroit archdiocese to belong to political parties. They were not allowed to make political speeches without the archbishop's consent, nor could they endorse or repudiate candidates for public office. A further instruction prohibited priests from writing in newspapers, magazines, and other periodicals on political subjects unless they had previously obtained the consent of their superior.

Now, while this procedure is considered usual practice in most jurisdictions, yet in Detroit it had to be put in a formal regulation.

And thus was the case of Father Coughlin disposed of. This put him off the air. A few months afterward the periodical *Social Justice,* issued under the Coughlin aegis, ceased publication.

The long, tortuous procedure in handling the Coughlin case justified the results. It had called for the skill of a surgeon in public affairs who could remove painlessly and without much disturbance to the entire body some disruptive anachronism. It could not be the hacking abandon of a woodman chopping down a tree. This faculty of knowing how to unravel an enigmatic entanglement deftly had grown on the character of Mooney from boyhood on. He was now a man of stature. His polygonal experiences in life had given him a technique on how to meet tough times.

Mooney was as humbly born as his parents were religiously devout. As most things in his life have borne their true returns, so his birth in poverty in Maryland in 1886 gave him forbearance he might not otherwise have had. When he was four, the family moved to Youngstown, Ohio. His father worked in the tube mill, making steel pipe both big and little. Anybody making anything in steel is bound to get strength from strength. It is the size and power of things in steel mills that gives those sturdy men a sense of handling big things. To take a long steel plate, two feet wide and twenty feet long, heated to almost white heat, wrestle it with the tongs and pass it through a bender which curls it into a round steel tube and welds the seam makes mastery. There is enough in that to make a man feel a conqueror.

Young Mooney, growing up past his infancy, saw his father do these mastodonic acts. The power of what his father could do impressed him. He knew that he could do things, too, albeit in the long and distant future. His father died while he was still young, so that to the already hard lot he had encountered in being the son of a mere tube mill worker, he now must join the team of his mother, his six brothers and sisters in keeping the family going. Mrs. Mooney worked hard. She made bread and Edward delivered it.

He was known as Eddie and had a full day. He went to St. Francis School, morning and afternoon, played with the other kids a little, and then went home to deliver the bread. There are those still living in the old neighborhood in Youngstown who were kids with him. He was the one who always settled the fights—generally after the fight had been duly fought, which certainly showed far more shrewdness than had he done it before the fight began. Some, nevertheless, he did settle outside the ring. He had the usual rub with the other boys, too. His humble home was set in a poor neighborhood, inhabited entirely by Irish workers in the steel mills. Literally, its location lay on the other side of the tracks. So Irish was it and so definitely was its frontier fixed that it was known as Kilkenny.

Here was a setting to place a child in and see what he would turn out to be—his mother a widow, the other children still infants, the neighborhood poor, and the times hard. This would defy all the recent precepts for bringing out the best in a child. According to what we are told, here was practically everything to give a boy a subdued personality, to break his will and prevent him from ever expressing his inclinations. What was the result? Reinforced by straining eagerness to meet the hardships, his will increased and likewise his strength. A natural bent to be right and a definite surge of spiritual power within him set him on the road to the priesthood. He consulted his parish priest, Monsignor Edward Mears, pastor of St. Columba parish, where the Mooneys went to church.

Mears treated him as if he were another boy just looking for an easy life without knowing anything about it. Mears was always glad to find a boy who wanted to be a priest. He would be inwardly overjoyed. But he would paint such a picture of clerical adversity that it would appear as if he were actually dissuading the young aspirant from taking holy orders. In Mooney, who had suffered hardships all his life, he found one who would take anything—just because he believed.

Sarah Heneghan Mooney, his mother, nourished an uncontrolled pride within that Eddie had decided to become a priest. The loyal ties of family continued to bind the little group. They all helped. They were all glad that Eddie had chosen a life of self-abnegation. It now appears the more sincere in all of them because, taking the probability of fame, they dared not even dream that he would become much more than a solitary pastor of a church. And at that, to them this loomed as a worthy ambition.

To start this theological education, Eddie returned to Maryland. He took his higher studies at St. Charles College in Ellicott City. In due time he was admitted to St. Mary's Seminary in Baltimore. Watching his work all the time and acting much as a parental as well as a spiritual father, Mears looked upon him as a good prospect to stake. Accordingly, he worked up enough enthusiasm in St. Columba parish to send Mooney to Rome to finish his theology and philosophy at the North American College, which turns out in due course most of the bishops in America. Definitely, this was a turn in which the currents were carrying Eddie Mooney along. He was eventually ordained in Rome and said his first Mass at the basilica of St. Paul's Outside the Walls along the way that Peter and Paul had taken when they first came to Rome to establish the faith.

It is only looking backward that we can see how another incident gave him a second unseen and even undreamed turn along the way. Monsignor John P. Farrelly was rector of the North American College. This meant nothing at first except that he should do as Farrelly told him. This was not difficult for Mooney, since he was of a docile and eager nature. But before he was graduated, Farrelly was chosen bishop of Cleveland. At that time Youngstown was in the Cleveland diocese. When Farrelly took over his see, he wanted a headmaster for the new Cleveland Latin

School which he decided to establish. As rector he had learned that Mooney was good in scholarship. He sent for Mooney from Rome and made him headmaster of the new school.

Mooney made a great success of Cathedral Latin School. And again it was still a formative period in his development. He had a great faculty for handling boys. They say he was strict, but it was severity highly tempered with justice.

"Any boy with more than thirty demerits in a year," announced the priestly headmaster, "will receive a fond farewell from Cathedral Latin."

Another prescription for making stand-out graduates— which is still a prescription at Cathedral Latin—was coined by Mooney.

"We are going to make true Catholic gentlemen in this school," it decreed. "They will not be men who are merely 75 per cent gentlemen."

But the road was not always to be without snags. In 1922, Farrelly died and was succeeded by Bishop Schrembs, learned but somewhat pompous, earnest but ambitious, firm but perhaps too firm. He changed the system at Cathedral Latin by turning the teaching over to the Brothers of St. Mary. This sent Mooney back to Youngstown to become assistant pastor at St. Patrick's parish. Here he seemed to be shelved.

But the threads he had carried from Rome were now drawn taut again as he found himself cloistered in St. Patrick's parish. Fatefully, he was called to become spiritual director of the North American College. St. Patrick's thus turned out to be just a suspense. He picked up the threads again. Now, in Rome, he virtually resumed where he had left off in Cleveland. He was back again with boys, even though they were older. He was back solving their

problems—family ties, money strains, their heavy responsibilities in the priesthood, their studies, and their personal
conflicts. Those who were under him there attribute to
him a sense of balance in directing them which became an
oracle as the years increased in arithmetical progression.

Monsignor Allen J. Babcock, rector of Mooney's Cathedral of the Sacred Heart, attended the North American
College when Mooney was its spiritual director. In my
many conversations with Mooney at that time, he was then
showing a human sympathy which was drawing men to
him. He had a faculty of getting close to your heart. Back
in Detroit in later days, I asked Babcock whether the men
in college did not feel that same mutuality of spirit which
I felt. The cathedral rector, who possesses a drawing personality in his own right, too, said that while Mooney
penetrated all men's souls outside the college, what he did
inside the college was deeper because the problems were
closer, more direct, and oftentimes more dramatic.

"The spiritual problems we faced," said Babcock in his
suave, velvety voice, "were the more easily overcome when
we talked to him. We all had gained such confidence in
him that we reposed our difficulties, whether spiritual or
otherwise, in his judgment. Willingly did he undertake
to advise us on studies, on the trend of our missions, and
on what to do about the folks at home. His priestly affection stayed with us all because it was deep, sympathetic,
and real."

The North American College is really the center of
American Catholic activity in Rome unless we have an
ambassador to the Holy See. The rector makes it a practice to invite high-ranking cardinals and other Vatican officials, sometimes for lunch, other times for dinner. This
serves the many-sided purpose of getting Vatican gossip,

of making new contacts, and not infrequently of creating considerable diversion from the staid academic atmosphere. The secretary of the congregation for the Propagation of the Faith, Monsignor Marchetti-Selvaggiani, was guest on several occasions. But on one visit in particular he was looking for good talent and diagnosed Mooney as being a suave and skillful diplomat—a talent which Mooney did not know he had, for diplomacy as a profession had never made the slightest dent in his cerebral plasm.

The monsignor reported his find to Cardinal Van Rossum, who was his superior, the prefect of the congregation. I have told in another volume* how Van Rossum saw Mooney and found the diagnosis correct. He wanted a man like Mooney to go to India as apostolic delegate. He wanted an American. This was because he had a difficult job to do in adjusting some Portuguese dioceses which were all entangled with some Indian dioceses. Certainly so far as professional diplomacy was concerned, a diplomat could not have been outside preconceived partiality in the problem. Mooney had no preconceptions. That fact, coupled with his ability to work out simple symmetrical plans disinterestedly in the many-angled controversy, settled the issue. They had probably calculated that the less their new man knew about formal diplomacy, the better it was. Mooney was their man.

Van Rossum reported it to Pius XI, who was then pope. The Pontiff also saw Mooney and talked with him. Again the judgment of the preliminary estimate was confirmed. In due time Van Rossum called for Mooney and told him that the Pope had decided to appoint him apostolic delegate to India.

* *The Listening Post*, New York, G. P. Putnam's Sons, 1944.

"I must obey the Pope's wishes," replied Mooney, his thoughts more or less out of hand through the impact of such a call.

Then he braced a little.

"I am surprised," he said, "but I am afraid I shall not live up to expectations."

"Don't be afraid," returned Van Rossum. "You will."

Mooney was made an archbishop to accord with the new office. He went out to India. This new experience and a broadening horizon was to deepen his soundings and equip him more than ever for greater tasks. His concept of even-handed justice made his mission successful. This was 1926; Mooney was forty. In 1931 he was sent to Japan. Again it was a life which was showing him the many-faced prism of humanity. The student whom Mears, Farrelly, Marchetti-Selvaggiani, Van Rossum, and finally the Pope had chosen for humanitarian and Christian reinforcing was now silently though unknowingly preparing for a greater destiny. Truly, a divinity shaped his ends!

When his work was done in Japan, he was recalled and promoted to be resident bishop of Rochester, New York. He held the rank of archbishop but ruled a bishop's see. When Detroit was made an archdiocese in 1930, Mooney, who had become very much of a favorite with Pius XI, was chosen as its first archbishop.

The new archdiocese needed an administrator who though spiritually fortified could work a few miracles in the mundane plane as well. Certainly, here miracles were needed in the mundane plane. Mooney had told me once that it was all very well to depend on divine guidance in matters of the Church, but divine guidance did not mean that one should just forget everything and let Providence do it all. He feared that if Providence found that He was carrying all the load, then He might be justified in letting one down. Then the devil could draw his dividends.

This was when he had returned from his diplomatic explorations in India and Japan. He admitted that he had had a delicate time in the East, which was his way of saying that it was nip and tuck all the time, first with the Portuguese and then with the Japanese.

"We are endowed with reason," he said as I met him in Rome. "We have got to make use of that reason and work out our own problems. Certainly, we can put our confidence in spiritual inspiration; but God does not look kindly on us when we take advantage of Him. The job, the work, the toil has to be done, and Providence exacts all of it from us if we are to share in His bounty."

And by the time he assumed the administration of the restless area of southern Michigan, he was ready, reinforced with the crystallized synthesis of all his composite personality, girded to meet all kinds and conditions of men and all kinds of problems.

"I carry the Gospel of Christ," he said when he was installed as the new archbishop. "This is the Gospel of brotherly love and peace—not peace at any price but peace at the price of doing justice, of practicing charity, of exercising the discipline of conciliation and restraint, of pursuing the way of mutual understanding, of using methods of calm discussion and responsible agreement, of standing faithful to the given word."

This constituted the blueprint of his studied action, confirmed later by his decisions as a shepherd and administrator. So deep was the impression made by this pronouncement on his present chancellor of the archdiocese, Monsignor Edward J. Hickey, that this affable and magnanimous official has memorized it as a constellation for charting his own actions.

Mooney had resolved to administer Detroit this way and this way only. He was new there. He asked the various chancery officials about the state of things. Collecting the various opinions, he found himself in a big job and on a tough spot. He had come through adversity as a child, struggled to get an education, mixed it up with fresh kids in the Cathedral Latin School, was shoved about and then worked his way back to Rome, was assigned a chore he knew very little about but came out on top, and finally was given a diocese to administer. And though there was sweat and midnight oil in all of these, none of them compared to the mountainous pile of rock that faced him in Detroit.

To begin with—and it was enough to give any man a lump in his swallow—the archdiocese was bankrupt. It was insolvent to the staggering total of $25,000,000. Mooney knew that he needed more than a purple cassock to wipe out such a long streak of figures in red. And then he was told that he would have to declare himself on the labor situation in the Detroit area. For a third boulder, he was told about the radio station at Royal Oak. We have seen what he did about that, and incidentally according to the blueprint. And fourthly, there were plenty of wild horses in the archdiocese and it was quite necessary for him, if he wanted to keep control, to tighten the reins.

The old problem of paying off the debt was the first that Mooney tackled. The old bugaboo of keeping out of debt which had been rubbed hard in his own toughened flesh by his own hard-working mother and brothers and sisters came right back as the first thing to do. Detroit had got quite riotously into debt, and it was his knotted task to get it out. Bishop Gallagher, who had preceded him, was happily strong on glorifying the Church but unhappily had overstretched himself on a building program.

It is said that he tried to finance the enterprises through insurance companies. They had settled on a scale of annual payments with low interest, but told Gallagher that he had to put Coughlin off the air. This he regarded quite understandably as an unjustifiable interference in his own ecclesiastical province. He refused. He did not live to see it through. The bills were now coming in for Mooney.

It would not be beyond the realm of possibility that had Mooney issued a call for funds, he could have gathered checks of one-million-dollar denominations from the great Catholic tycoons of Detroit. It was not because it was too easy or that he deliberately wanted to make it hard, but he steered quite clear of any big donations. Not a single big donation has been accepted since he took charge. He deliberately discouraged big donations. His plan was to get the whole archdiocese right into the problem. He wanted the modest shopgirl and the humblest street cleaner to be in with him on getting the Catholic Church out of the red in Detroit.

The Archbishop invited me out to dinner one evening in the palatial mansion which had been built for Bishop Gallagher by an admiring communicant. It was not Mooney's style, because he had never brought himself to the high or low level, whichever it may be, of languishing in excessive luxury. He said that since it was built, Gallagher could have done none other than accept it just as *he* then had accepted it and was living in it. That night, he talked somewhat generally about seeing bankers and financial overlords. To me, it was a rather strange twist in his career, and I sympathized with him for being out in a wilderness which he had never charted. He had never had anything to do with finance before.

But what did he do? Mooney had been used to spending no more than a hundred dollars a month and earning it before he disbursed it. Now he had to raise millions without the joy of spending it. He took the archdiocese as a whole. He mapped out a financial campaign which would attempt to bring an annual return to liquidate the debt in five years. He persuaded eighteen Detroit banks to go in with him. He could show them plenty of collateral if—and there is where the snag comes in so many financial deals—*if* they were convinced that he himself was a man capable of putting through a donation campaign that would meet the payments. They accepted the risk. He kept after it—month after month, year after year. The debt was paid. The archdiocese of Detroit is today solvent and paying as it goes. Out of it all has come the realization of another attribute. Mooney, they say in Detroit, is a financial wizard; but, for all the wizardry, none of the money is ever his own.

Restless and turbulent is what Detroit is in its labor strife. When one dispute is settled, another has already started. Time was when Ford, Chrysler, General Motors, and Packard got along with labor because they were able to hold its smoldering temper in check. But along came the Wagner Act confirming for the men of labor their right to band together to bargain for better conditions of work. Hitherto that right had been disputed. The Wagner Act put it in the lawbooks. Unionism made a leap forward. To consolidate the labor forces of the great industrial enterprises, the C.I.O. was born. Now it was a greater problem to hold that smoldering temper in check. The automobile industry of Detroit furnished the world's biggest union—the United Automobile Workers Union. They talked back to Ford, Chrysler, General Motors, and Packard. The companies were astonished at the effrontery. They resented the assault. The strife was on.

And here is where Mooney came in.

What stirred the thought of Mooney and his chief assistants were the purely social, ethical, and moral aspects of unions. They knew that large bodies of Catholics had already joined or wanted to join the automobile union and other unions, too. Plenty of doctrinal authority existed to allow workers to join unions and remain squarely with the faith. The oft-quoted encyclical of Leo XIII, *Rerum Novarum,* and that of Pius XI, *Quadragesimo Anno,* urged workmen to form unions. That made it final.

But the U.A.W. was a subsidiary of the C.I.O. This was something else, because men there were with not-unselfish intent who threw acid on its face and made it look Communist. It would not have been a difficult task to handle the issue on its merits. Mooney had plenty of avenues open to him to find out just how Communist C.I.O. was. That was easy; but it had to be made difficult because Coughlin launched right into the labor battle and wanted to take charge of some of the fighting. He wanted his own shock troops. It was at this time, too, that the Ford Company was thought to be in league with Coughlin.

At his radio microphone in Royal Oak, Coughlin denounced the C.I.O. He charged it with Communist infiltration and doctrine. Catholics should beware of the infidel doctrines, he warned. To make it clear, he declared that they could no more join the C.I.O. and stay in the faith than they could embrace the Mohammedan faith and remain a Catholic.

This broadcast aroused Mooney more to righteous indignation than displeasure. He realized that Coughlin had quoted the famed encyclicals of the popes in such a way as to suit his own immediate aims, which, according to some, were to penetrate the union field with his own *agents provocateurs.* In the interest of encyclical rectitude and square Catholic principle—Mooney moved, and moved with virile pen if not mailed fist.

"Catholicity and Mohammedanism are incompatible on the basis of the clearly stated fundamental principles of both," thundered the Mooney statement throughout the archdiocese. "Catholicity and Communism are incompatible on the same basis. But no Catholic Church authority has ever asserted that the C.I.O. is incompatible on the basis of its publicly stated principles."

For directness and decisiveness, this statement left no misgiving or doubt about where Mooney stood. It was true that it had been occasioned as a reproof to Coughlin, but it was a straight-out declaration on what Mooney thought of the unionization of labor.

And we can see how this could be expected of a son who had seen his father gnarled and bowed with toil. For in his father's day, in the hot, stifling air of the tube mills, men worked twelve hours a day drawn up in a sweating phalanx alongside the white-hot steel. And in that dreary monotony of flame and dirt all day long, they seized the molten plate until at the end of the day shift or the night, they had transformed hundreds if not thousands of the heated slabs into finished pipes.

When Eddie Mooney's father complained, he complained to Sarah Heneghan Mooney, or passed it off to the children that it was a killing pace. Men in those days could not be banded together to talk it over with the boss. If Mooney did not like his job, he could leave and get another. To ask for better conditions was to imply a rebel in the plant. We can little wonder that those days of rigor left an indelible recess in the spirit of Eddie. He knew something of the labor problem.

A strike was called in the Dodge plant toward the end

of 1939. This was controlled by the U.A.W. Coughlin denounced the strike and said that the workers should return to work. This gratuitous interference which bounced back against labor was bound to bring some sort of reply from the Archbishop. He addressed a Catholic conference on trade unionists early in 1940.

"Organized labor under the protection of a federal statute which in its essential purpose is clearly in harmony with Catholic principles of social order," he declared, evidently referring to the Wagner Act, "has progressed with giant strides and challenges attention as a force to be reckoned with in industrial life. No voice that merits heeding has ever denied that the overwhelming majority of union members are sound American citizens who love their families and their homes, who seek only what they have the right to seek—economic security and a freeman's status in their working lives."

Now Mooney, more to learn what was going on than to make a show of it, had often held conferences with Philip Murray. It is an accepted fact that whenever "Phil" gets to Detroit he always stops in to see the Archbishop if the time fits in. Some others have met Mooney, too. They know he is on their side even though he does not come out to the big mass meetings like Bishop Sheil. He has said enough to give them confidence as well as pleasure. On one occasion General Motors paid for full-page ads in the Detroit newspapers to get over to the population that the strikers in the 1946 strike were all wrong. Mooney checked the ad and found that they had given a confusing slant on the issues. Immediately and with not a little fire, he denounced the statement as entirely misleading to the public.

Mooney works hard—long hours, tough problems, the parsimony of time—he has to work hard. But he plays, too. Long has he been a believer in the Latin proverb, *mens sana in corpore sano*. He played baseball in Youngstown and Cleveland. He played baseball as a student in Rome. When he became the spiritual director of the North American College, he turned to golf—not because it was more in keeping with the dignity of his office but because he only needed one companion, and if necessary not even one, in golf. We often met on the Rome course. His partner was usually Monsignor Godfrey of the Scotch College, who afterward became apostolic delegate to Great Britain. He played in India and in Japan, too.

Golf was his game when he went to the see of Detroit. He used to play on the municipal course. If a championship should ever take place among the prelates of the Catholic Church when Mooney is in form, he would run away with the cup. He gets an eighty quite often. His playmates were generally chosen for their wit first, and for their golf second. Mooney never had any second-rate quipsters about. They always had to be somebody with whom he could match his own wits. His secretary, Reverend John J. Donovan was one of these. Then by a golf acquaintanceship, he admitted Edgar A. Guest, the sage of Detroit, and just as good a golfer as Mooney. Quite equal to them all was the rector of the cathedral, Monsignor Babcock. Babcock stacks up as just about one of the most vivacious minds I have ever met. This would make a foursome; but Donovan was sent to Rome and his place was taken on the quartet by Bishop Murphy of Saginaw, another undoubted expert in the give-and-take of social parlance, and just as good at golf.

Jokes fly around the course as common as bad drives, though Mooney is always good on the drive. In fact he is good on all his long shots. The professionals say of him that if he would keep his head down, he could reduce his score by five or six strokes.

"I am a priest, not a track walker," he told one of them.

Mooney, Guest, Murphy, and Babcock were in a whirling finish on one occasion. Murphy was paired with Guest. They arrived at the sixteenth hole and were three down. If they lost that hole, the match would be over. Murphy was fifteen feet from the hole. Guest suggested that if he could call upon some heavenly patron of golf, either established or improvised, he might ask him to help put the ball in the hole. Murphy said it would require the saint of the impossible. Guest, who is better versed in poetry writing than in the powers of sanctification, suggested the saint was never more needed. Informally and without any commitment, the improvised patron of golf was invoked. The ball was struck. Evidently celestially propelled, it found its place in the cup. Mooney and Babcock lost the hole.

A similar situation occurred on number seventeen. This was too much for the Archbishop. The opponents were now only one down. The Archbishop claimed an illegal intercession, and though he would not make formal protest to the saint of the impossible, he did advise Murphy that he was taking advantage of episcopal prerogative and imposing on the patron's good nature. Despite the call-down, Murphy again is supposed to have used the same patron, and again on a long putt they won the hole. It was necessary to play a nineteenth. This they won, too, and the match.

"It's unfair," quipped the Archbishop, "to take advantage of a saint who couldn't say no."

In Rome, when he played, Mooney used to wear black trousers. This was usually the garb of members of the cloth who went out for physical upbuilding on the links. But in Detroit when he wore black, it attracted attention, and in time he was soon spotted by everybody. Some there were, no doubt, who thought that an archbishop on a golf course would be a curiosity. Those he would gladly relieve of their not-so-human misapprehensions. But he never liked attention, never courted it. Guest finally persuaded him to wear gray. Gray he wore, and now goes around the course just as any other player, except that he does a little better than most and without benefit of episcopal prerogative.

When he was tendered an elaborate banquet on his return as a cardinal from Rome, the special civic committee presented him with a new 1946 Cadillac car. The Ford Company, with the definite intention of also registering its attendance, awarded him a 1946 Lincoln car with a permanent exchange right, which meant that he could always turn in the old car for a new model, whenever he wished. Guest, who presided at the dinner, had to draft some of his wit. Following the presentation of the two cars, Detroit's sage held up a new golf ball.

"I guess," he said with a slight savor of satire, "I shall have to give the Cardinal something that I know His Eminence *can* drive."

He lifted the white little globe a little higher.

"This is my present," he chided.

The audience broke into hilarity which almost threw off all controls of archiepiscopal dignity. Nevertheless it was the place for hilarity, and Mooney was in it.

Soon afterward what was now a cardinalatial foursome informally dated a match for the Detroit course. Guest got there first. But just as he was getting out of his car, he noticed that a new Cadillac drove up. He was curious

about a new Cadillac in March of 1946. He turned to get
a look at the owner. There, seated at the wheel, was Edward Cardinal Mooney. He was driving his present. He
was probably the first cardinal in history to drive a car, at
that. He was certainly the first in gray. He caught sight
of Guest.

"I had to try out the new toy, Ned," he quipped. "I
had to try it out myself, that's the fun in it. Anyway, I
wanted you to know, too, that I can drive other things besides golf balls."

On the trip to Rome to receive his red hat, Mooney
held to a line of reserve in his publicity, or rather his
avoidance of publicity, which almost bordered on reclu-
sion. He traveled in the same plane as Cardinal Stritch.
Each had his own entourage of prelates and distinguished
laymen. But not a single newsman, newsreel man, or
radio reporter got a place on that plane. The Detroit
newspaper corps on the story hopped privately to New
York. Henry Hock for the *Detroit News,* John Manning
for the *Detroit Times,* and Clem Lane, of the *Chicago
Daily News* but covering for the *Detroit Free Press,* joined
us all and flew alongside the Spellman and Glennon plane
over Ireland, France, and then on to Rome.

At first I thought this voluntary retirement from the
public view was due to a latent shyness. He was shy in
that way, but this did not cover it all. I thought, too, that
he may have preferred to have the spotlight look for him
rather than that he should seek the spotlight. This was
not the case either. He adamantly did not want to be in
the newspapers and movies. It was as if he thought it van-
ity, serving no worthy purpose, to show him off in press
and screen. With his own special gift for weighing values,
social as well as spiritual, he had decided that it was not

the applause and cheering which made for sterling achievement but only the innate substance of the achievement.

During the consistory he took a villa on the outskirts of Rome, where he seemed to withdraw from all unnecessary public show. But with postwar transportation what it was, this made it difficult for the newsmen to reach him. Even if he had not taken the villa to get away from them, it served that purpose just the same. We all knew that he was sincere. There was no doubt in any of our minds. It was not a caprice.

Reverend Joseph M. Breitenbeck, his secretary, talked this sense of public withdrawal over with me. He knew that the newsmen had to get the news and tried to help them. He was just as sure that it was Mooney's expressed and deep-rooted conviction that he should try as best he could to make his earthly call a fulfillment. The showmanship of the new honor was of no consequence or value to him. He wanted to realize a mission. Usually newsmen have a hard time eschewing those who want to get into the press, the newsreels, and the radio, but here was one who eschewed them. To those who thought it a pose, Breitenbeck had the answer.

"I assure you," I heard him say, "that Cardinal Mooney does not want publicity. He strives to be a good archbishop and a worthy member of the Sacred College. He thinks that he best reaches these ends by working it out his own way."

All through the long succession of ceremonies he carried out his settled will. He prepared no speeches in advance to be given the news agencies but always spoke extemporaneously. Everywhere he said what the spirit moved him to say at the moment. He was ready and easy to talk to when we met him. I noticed how affable he was, especially with all the young seminarians, no matter what their nationality.

When he finally returned, his plane could not land in Detroit but was forced to proceed to Chicago on account of weather conditions. Monsignor Hickey was directing a reception for him at the Detroit airport. From Chicago, however, Mooney had to come by train. Hickey phoned him to ask what time he expected to arrive, as there were thousands waiting to welcome him. This was not what he wanted.

"Send the people home," he commanded. "Do not let them wait around in the cold. Why make them wait for me, anyway? After all, I'm no mannequin."

12. A Prince Was Not Denied

LOVABLE is not supposed to be such a manly word nowadays. To apply it to a man, at the moment when masculinity is supposed to be characterized by Bogarts and Beerys, implies an emotional softy. By the nature of our times, we have become accustomed to asking for the strong man more bull than sage. We raise him on our heroic altars in sports, in business, in politics, and in war. A cult for the mighty and decisive, be he ruthless or unscrupulous, has coursed through our mass mind. Our memories are short indeed if we do not recall how Mussolini was deified and Hitler lifted up as an idol by many of our own in business and politics, too. And though abstractly admired, there was no love. If there had been, it would have gone quite unrequited. Love was an unnecessary attribute.

For all the prowess of the mighty and the glory of the hero, I am risking nothing in true virtue by summing up the life of John Cardinal Glennon as lovable. He loved mankind and was beloved of it. And yet, he was indeed no softy. He possessed an abundant measure of most of man's diversified talents. He used those talents in the one direction where man himself reaches out to seek the highest in spirit on this earthly planet—the realm of religion. Had he chosen finance, he would have achieved financial

206

distinction. If his bent had turned to politics, he would have become a statesman among lesser statesmen. Were he to have embraced the arts, his artistic gifts would have elevated him to the honors of the great. Even as an industrialist, his genius for organization would have carried him to the administration of those colossal combinations which manufacture and fabricate our needs from pins to battleships. But he was called to religion, and there flowered the complexus of his gifts in a true purity and unselfishness of spirit. Strong, gifted, and tireless, he was lovable.

Glennon was learned, hard-working, sympathetic, interested; and, crowning the variety of his traits, he was blessed with a bubbly outpouring of humor. He had delved into the recesses of history—sacred and secular—and he could discourse on Turks and Tartars, Copts and Celts, Tao and Shinto, Aztec and Malayan. He knew the philosophies of the pagan as well as the Christian. The sciences became part of his general knowledge. Public affairs from an ecclesiastical viewpoint he embraced as one charged with the safeguarding of morals. He could write well. He could speak well.

Pedigree had endowed him with a sturdy and a handsome frame. Whether legend or fact, everyone affirmed that he had never suffered a single day of serious illness in his life until he died. He was six feet two in height. With no sign of superfluity, this tall straight figure commanded acquiescence in if not submission to his charm. His face had always borne a ruddy, robust tint as if he had been used to the out-of-doors, though this was perhaps more heredity than habit. His countenance radiated health even when he had become an octogenarian. When at rest, it emitted that aura of satisfaction which portrayed an inner spirit that was at peace with God and man. He smiled, and smiled often, because his soul was abundant with joy. When sober judgments were necessary, a just determination was readily detectable in his frown and stiffened jaw.

As to his humor, it had become a national achievement. It is certain that had his turn of life taken him to one of the professions of entertainment, he would have succeeded not only in amusing the public but in edifying it as well. His humor was ready, spontaneous, dry, sharp, and always pointed. It was not necessary for him to possess a large library of joke books or to catalogue the jokes of all time according to their place or time of application, as is done in the studios of our radio and movie comedians today. When we think of the battery of script writers which modern humorists recruit to toil on their fun, we can justly say that compared to Glennon they are not humorists at all but mechanics tinkering with the nuts and bolts of the language to make it work askew.

In Rome, I often saw how Glennon's periodic visits were welcomed by all the prelates around the papal throne. He had served under five popes, and under four of them as archbishop. The pontiffs were always captivated by the truly joyous manner in which he could recount the progress of the archdiocese of St. Louis. It was balm to their souls, because only an American archbishop could relate such growth. And he carried his humor with him to Rome, too.

On one occasion we were seeing him off on the train. He occupied a compartment at the end. We stood on the platform as he looked at us from the open window. At the front, near the engine, a large party of Italian nuns, some fifty or sixty, were seeing off an American bishop who had been most philanthropic with that particular order. The send-off to the bishop was not only numerically strong but submissively vociferous in tone. The contrast to the few prelates who had gathered about Glennon was emphatic.

"You do not have as many loyal friends in Rome as the bishop," offered a Vatican prelate as a softening touch.

"I don't belong to a sorority," quipped the St. Louis archbishop with a broad smile.

John Joseph Glennon was born in Kinnegad in the county of West Meath, Ireland, in 1862. His predilection for the church was early realized. He passed through all the religious experiences of the youthful. He was the eager one who was always ready to assist the priest in the early Mass. In his teens he had shown ability as an orator, which marked him as destined for a great future in the art of preaching. He finished his theological training before he was twenty-one, and thus was definitely set for his clerical career.

This was at a time when there were not enough priests in the United States to meet the spiritual needs of an increasing Catholic population. Highly recommended by the Bishop of Mullingar, in whose diocese he was born, and crowned with the prowess of his preaching and scholarship, he was invited by Bishop Hogan of Kansas City to risk his talents in the still untamed but developing regions of the Middle West. He accepted and as a young and stalwart youth in clerical garb set off to meet the call. Octogenarians now living who remember him say that he was always "a fine hulk of a man." With every gift of priestly requisition, Bishop Hogan appointed him his secretary.

Now, while he had completed his studies, he had not yet been ordained because of his youth. A special dispensation was granted him by Pope Leo XIII and he took holy orders at twenty-two. His brilliance had so impressed the

Bishop that he assigned him for further study in Europe to give a finishing touch to his learning. On his return he was assigned a parish. He distinguished himself so much that in 1896, at the age of thirty-four, he was called to be the coadjutor bishop of Kansas City.

But Glennon, even in those creative years when he was still charting his life's work, stood out. It does not mean alone that he possessed a keener intellect among other brilliant minds. He stood out to be thought of first, by all, as the outstanding priest among the rest. Many priests have to work hard as assistant pastors for years, and it is not until they reach forty, and in many cases fifty years of age that they are entrusted with the administration of a parish. But Glennon's gifts were commanding. There is little doubt that he was picked by his own superiors to be coached for head shepherd. It was as if he had been trained from youth to accept great tasks.

Long and detailed reports were made about him to the Sacred Consistorial Congregation in Rome. Much thought was put on his ability, and he received great notice from the advisers of Leo XIII. The more that was learned of him, the greater his fame became. Accordingly, and with not a little surprise to himself as well as to many in Kansas City, he was promoted from coadjutor to the bishop there to be coadjutor to the archbishop of St. Louis *cum jure successionis,* a circumstance so rare that it confirms more than anything else how his ability had impressed the Pope. It meant that the Pontiff had decided to entrust the future of the growing archdiocese to his skillful talents and youthful drive. This was in April 1903.

His arrival in St. Louis was awaited with a certain anxiety, not unexpected but natural, because of his youth. Once the tall, godlike figure had officiated at Mass in the old Cathedral along the Mississippi, which was the oldest church in those days, he had won St. Louis to him.

In October of that same year Archbishop Kain, the incumbent, died. At the age of forty-one, Glennon succeeded to the see, the youngest resident archbishop ever appointed in the United States. Long years of arduous endeavor filled his career. He became such a favorite that the people in his jurisdiction hoped over the years that the Pontiff in Rome would make him a favorite, too, and create him a cardinal. However, it was not until he was eighty-three, as we saw, and had served forty-two years as archbishop that Pius XII made him a cardinal. He wore his cardinal's robes but twenty days and died in Ireland on his way back to St. Louis from Rome.

From the beginning of his episcopal career he made a practice of preaching at least one sermon every month. He delivered numerous addresses in schools, at confirmations and other convocations. At first, strong Irish flourishes of the vowels and consonants enchanted his hearers. Then these, through contact with the Middle West, tapered to a more liquid discourse of cosmopolitan ease. His timbre was vibrant. His tones were rich. He modulated them to high and low, strong and sweet, depending on the drama or humor of the occasion. Men were seized by his eloquence. This eventually traveled very far. He was in great demand to deliver addresses all over the country at important Catholic gatherings, jubilees, consecrations, and congresses. Within a few years he was recognized as "the most eloquent Catholic orator in the United States."

And this oratory did not alone derive from his presence or from his pleasing voice. He made it a duty to be master of his subject. He conceived it also as a responsibility not to burden these great gatherings with efforts which were not his best. Great care was therefore taken by him to phrase and form his expressions so that they would carry the vividness and the depth that he held in his own mind. His prose was epigrammatic. He could coin phrases. Many of these have remained to this day and have become bywords in our own folklore. It was he who said of Prohibition, "It is better to take the man away from the drink than the drink away from the man."

Women clamored to hear him. He enjoyed a mystic adoration from them. This was quite natural since out of his commanding presence he spoke with such emotion and directness. On one occasion he was more than amused by overhearing a woman chide her sex for the fuss they made of him. She feared for the Archbishop.

"Why, the women of St. Louis will ruin him," she cried in desperation.

It was ten years afterward that the turns of fate brought him face to face with the same woman again. Endowed as he was with an almost unfailing memory, he greeted her by recalling the incident.

"It was ten years ago that you predicted that the women of St. Louis would ruin me," he said. "Why, bless them, they haven't done it yet."

As part of his preacher's stock-in-trade, he had learned with facile adroitness to make sayings and turn events to his own advantage. He was always ready to capitalize on an incident and oftentimes to change tragedy into comedy by the poignancy of his wit.

A Catholic day was being held in one of the small towns in St. Charles County, Missouri, and he was the chief speaker. Streamers of red, white, and blue with words of welcome to the Archbishop were stretched overhead across the streets. Public buildings and stores were decorated with bunting for the occasion. A brass band had been recruited and parades with colorful costumes whisked back and forth up and down the streets of the town. The time came for the great outdoor address of the Archbishop. Just as he was introduced and got up to speak, the band, proud of its clattering accomplishments but unmindful that there was a time for everything, started up a martial air as if in vicious opposition to the Archbishop. He stood there and smiled. Then he raised his voice above the din of the blaring brass, the thumping drums and clanging cymbals, and shouted:

"It looks as if I'm going to have to talk to beat the band."

He loved to travel, and oftentimes a simile on trains would occur to him in his figures of speech. Addressing a group of Catholic women on one occasion, he lamented their division into several different sodalities rather than one strong organization.

"When you want to pull a train," he said, "all the cars should be on the same track."

But he decided against trains when he was addressing an outdoor meeting in growing Arcadia, Missouri, on the opening of a hospital. A train was working hard to get up a hill, and it was well nigh impossible for him to get his voice over to the crowd because of the labored emissions of the engine. He paused and then said:

"I am waiting until that train gets up on the hill because I have found that it is hard to talk back to a railroad train, much less talk against it."

An example of his ease of expression before large audiences of women was brought out when he was the chief speaker at a Catholic women's convention in Detroit. Looking down from the platform, he was astounded to see so many of them, each representing some community in the United States.

"Why, this is a great symbol of your strength," he said. "There must be a thousand-odd women here today. Yes, a thousand at least, but very few odd."

On one occasion, a mayor of St. Louis had introduced him at a civic gathering with a certain amount of lament that he had not been made a cardinal. While he was speaking, Glennon recalled to himself that when the pallium of archbishop was imposed on him by the late Cardinal Gibbons in 1905, the Baltimore prelate referred to him in public as "the new Pontifex Maximus of the Rome of the West." When it came his turn to speak, Glennon decided to make it plain that he could not be cardinal and pontiff both.

"Our mayor would like me to wear the red robes," he said. "The great cardinal appointed me the Pope of the West and thus would design me in white robes. I have to wear something. I'll wear anything so long as it is all wool and a yard wide."

Many of his vast flock used to wonder why he did not take up some kind of recreation. Golf was suggested to him. He went out to the golf course and after three or four attempts found that his usual calm complacency was more than ordinarily flustered. More perplexed than recreated, he was disappointed with both golf and his own efforts. He gave it up.

"Yes," he said speaking to a friend about his personal lack of athletic prowess, "I once tried golf and so disfigured the scenery that I have never played again, in fear of public indignation."

Athletics in every form intended for the development of the physique received his hearty approval, however. He endorsed every sport as a builder of body. He encouraged all sorts of mass games and physical exercises.

"Athletics have a proper place for the physical development of the boy, and not for a few that parade on the ball field," he once said in a sermon. "Athletics have a place in training a boy—or a girl—ever to grow vigorous health with a sound body as a background for a sound mind."

And though he encouraged mass participation in sports rather than sport as a spectacle, he was quite enthusiastic nevertheless during the baseball and football seasons. Whether he was captured by a peculiar personal fancy, or subconsciously influenced by the popular swing of the day, remained an archiepiscopal secret; but he did choose his favorite team, even though he usually kept his choice pretty close to the archiepiscopal residence. He listened over the radio to the St. Louis games and quite demonstrably was a rooter for the Cardinals. Often he was momentarily disappointed when they came out on the wrong end. On opening day of one year, he threw out the first ball for the Cardinals.

He was also a great partisan of the football team of Notre Dame University, especially after he had learned that the players were reported to be very devout. When the knowledge of this fact came to him, he decided to mention it in a sermon, though he did not cite the Irish by name.

"We read a lot about football these days," he said. "I suppose some of you see the mauling and trampling, the racing and diving and piling up of the living. It looks as though they ought to be dead before the pile is unraveled. Well, even a football player can be a saint."

Then it was that, knowing his predilection for the South Bend team, his hearers took it for granted that he was referring to Notre Dame.

"I know one football team," he continued, "that always goes to Holy Communion on the morning they are going into action—and every other day as well, for some of them

—and strange to say, though their morning is with the saints, they are very many times victorious in the struggle; not that their winning is very much to their credit spiritually, but it shows that the spiritual and what might be called the material go hand in hand."

Once, however, a boy puzzled him slightly in choosing a college. He had suggested two or three institutions to which the boy might think of going. The lad vetoed each one of them on the ground that neither one could boast a good football team.

"Oh, I see," said the Archbishop, "you want to go to the kind of school which would educate the foot and not the head."

There were few subjects of public interest on which Glennon, during his long tenure, had not pronounced his own conviction. His sermons were invariably devoted to the discussion of some exacting civic problem.

In 1921 he had served twenty-five years in the episcopate and celebrated his silver jubilee. At that time he gave an over-all summation of his thoughts as they affected the social and political life of the nation. He had been doubtful of the success of giving women the vote even before that amendment to the Constitution was passed. He also held very decisive views on the relations between capital and labor, which it is well to consider today because of the great changes which have taken place since that time.

Of the woman suffrage amendment, he said:

"It will add, it is true, to the number of voters, but in very rare instances will there be any change of verdict. The women voters will eventually follow party lines. They may or may not improve the party. The women who hope by an independent movement to reform all things are doomed to disappointment."

The struggle between labor and management had already been launched with fierce bitterness at that time.

"Twenty-five years ago," he said, "we also had capital and labor. It is doubtful if the lines between them have changed much since then. Much of our legislation has been dedicated to the work of the diffusion of the world's goods amongst all the people; but the legislation is inadequate and probably never can be made to solve the great problems. It is certain today that the so-called laboring man lives better and fares better than he did twenty-five years ago. It is true, also, that the so-called wealthy either have not the opportunity or the desire to parade their wealth now as then. The big dinner party and the extensive menu have vanished. There is less pomp in modern life. Nor is there the pride in great fortunes. On the other hand, there are few homes of the great and unfortunately few homes at all. Not only are there few homes; but there is little home life or little desire to promote it. This I take to be the most discouraging symptom of the age, for when the home fails, the family must fail, and so must fail our civilization. Man is a social animal but he cannot remain civilized by being simply gregarious."

As a churchman, he followed very closely the line enunciated by the papal encyclicals on marriage and divorce.

"As a matter of fact," he once declared, "the modern marriage, based on carnal love and carnal love alone, is of its very nature passing and evanescent. They cannot contract reasonably an indissoluble marriage if there be that feature and that feature alone. It must be based on Divine Law, a knowledge of the sacredness of the union and its indissoluble character."

"Marriage is treated very lightly today, and unfortunately so," he said on another occasion. "To enter rashly into the marriage ceremony expecting, hoping that all would be right, but not at all certain that it will, men and women run their chances. Some say that marriage is only a lottery anyway. It is too bad that people enter a lottery on which they stake not only their fortune but their lives as well."

In accordance also with the pronouncements of the popes, he was a crusading apostle against birth control. In keeping with his ability to express his antagonism in colorful terms, he often launched an attack which while striking the subject in its vital spot carried with it the charm of his own homespun philosophy.

"Last week," he remarked in an address before the Vincentian Society of St. Louis, "a number of reverend gentlemen advocated the new fad euphonically called 'birth control'; and that form of birth control which would be obtained by the introduction of mechanical devices into the married state. They seek to legalize a practice which runs counter to Scriptural teaching and the Christian ethics; and one which in the opinion of most physicians is gravely deleterious to mental and physical health. Would it not be more fitting for these reverend gentlemen to cultivate a higher respect for the sanctity of the marriage bond and to advocate on the part of those who feel they cannot properly care for a large family the principle of abstention and self-control?"

Glennon fought the Federal child labor amendment on the basis that it deprived the family of its control and responsibility in the welfare of the children. He was not opposed to the principle of safeguarding the health of children by the state, but he condemned the practice of the state's interference in what he termed the jurisdiction of the family.

"None of us are opposed to the Child Labor Amendment of the Constitution because it prohibits child labor," he proclaimed from the pulpit. "We are opposed to it instead because it turns over to government supervision all the youth of the land up to eighteen years of age."

He then recounted how the youth of Italy under Mussolini and of Germany under Hitler had been regimented into military units from as early as ten years of age.

"They are marching and countermarching, ten, twelve, sixteen and eighteen years of age," he said. "We oppose the Child Labor Amendment on that account but there is not one of us who is not opposed also to the child labor which takes place in sweatshops, mills and so forth. Whatever our duty in opposing the Child Labor Amendment was and is, we should urge legislation which will cope with the evil of actual child labor."

Glennon was most emphatic in his condemnation of the organization of women's auxiliary corps in both the Army and the Navy. He had a presumption which was somewhat in error in that he thought that women would be inducted into combat units and take their places on the firing line. Though subsequent experience showed that their services were limited to auxiliary tasks and seldom were they called upon to be in the actual line of battle, he did not seem to waver in his first pronouncement.

"We have been told," he asserted in an address before the Archdiocesan Council of Catholic Women, "that it would be well if we would conscript the young women of the nation—train them in the army how best to kill, to murder and to slay. That is the plan being followed in Russia on a less honorable basis. It is the order today of nations that have turned communistic. They are very, very brutal—sending women out into the plains of Siberia to work in mud, ice and snow, building railroads that their fellows, whoever they are, can travel on these roads to slaughter. And in Finland, so the legend goes, they put the women before the men as targets for the soldiers to shoot at. In Germany, too, the women must do all the work on the farm, in the factories, and at the same time are authorized by the government to produce babies to grow up to be strong to conquer the world."

In less condemnatory vein, he lightly rapped the fingers of the career woman. He had watched women driving their cars to work and he likened the rush to get to work to a race.

"Take the women today," he observed from the pulpit. "They are in the race. Some of the women go downtown in the race and race beside the men—working, very honorable and very proper, that is, if they have to do so. It is regrettable that men have to let them, to be compelled to let them. Time was when the father of the house, the husband, cared for the home and sustained it in all its splendid unity, in all the homeliness of a home."

Whenever any Soviet move against religion appeared in the press, he was quick to announce his studied indignation. He fought communism with periodic utterances against its atheistic trends and rallied his flock to a realization that there was a danger to the faith in the tenets of Marxian philosophy.

"Over in Russia," he declared on one occasion, "the government with its Red army and drawn sword say no God, no united family, no homes. The children are taken from their homes as soon as they grow up. They are trained not by their parents but by the infidel state, trained to be soldiers and to fight to conquer not in God's name but in the name of infidelity."

"The leaders of the Soviet Republic declare," he asserted on another occasion, "that religion is the opiate of the people. It is not a new idea, this declaration of theirs. It was made by Rousseau, who in making these and similar declarations had not time to take care of his own children and abandoned them to orphan asylums. It was made also by Voltaire, who declared among other things that he was out to abolish Christianity and that as a man of genius—such as he was—was not bound by any moral law—he was above it.

"But," he concluded, "the superior men of history were they who knew how to bend the knee before the living God, acknowledge his power, his supremacy. He alone is omnipotent. He alone is great."

"Communism destroys," he fired in another blast. "Communism destroys all that God above and man below has established and places him in a groveling pit where each one is seizing whatever bone is there and clawing it as the wild animal does. Communism is the release of human passion and human craving and the destruction of brotherhood, of faith in man or of faith in God."

As a priest he conceived it his duty to acquire more than a general knowledge in new discoveries and of all man's research whether in the realm of the sciences or in the arts. He gave a thorough study to the theories of Einstein, and as was inevitable with the churchman he was, condemned them on the ground that they did not include the existence of God.

"Einstein tells you that everything is relative," he narrated in one of his monthly sermons. "Two trains pass one another. Well, they are passing, but who can tell how speedy they are? In this universe, everything is relative to something else. It is quite true, but Einstein forgets that everything is relative toward the One that is not relative— and that is God, Who made space and time and current events but Who is eternal, unchanged. Einstein forgot

Almighty God, and consequently his theory of relativity is only confusion."

Of the arts, music attracted his attention as much as any, though he was devoted to painting and especially to architecture, which, as we shall see, permitted him what is perhaps his greatest expression of an artistic nature when he superintended and built the new Cathedral of St. Louis. But to music he gave joyfully of his emotional propensities. It is not an exaggeration to say that he knew as much about the development of the art of music from its primitive beginnings as a learned professor of the history of music in a conservatory.

It was his custom to make an annual address before the St. Louis Organists Guild, which included the choirmasters of the churches of the archdiocese. What he had to say had the depth of scholarly research and studied reflection. On one occasion he traced the gradual development of choral singing, which, he said, came long after the Gregorian chant and was not altogether accepted at first by the doctors of the Church. It was not until the Council of Trent in the sixteenth century when the great composer of liturgical music, Palestrina, rendered one of his works before the learned delegates, that choral singing received the full approbation of the ritualistic authorities.

His pleasant expressions, so bountiful when he was in complete accord with a melody or a score, were completely lacking when he even thought of jazz with all its modern variations. If there was one human endeavor which received his disapproval more than any other, it was the effort of composers to syncopate the great masterpieces to a jazz score.

"Jazz," he told the organists on one occasion, "is like an old cloth unraveled to the wind. It has no beginning but it does have an end. The only good thing about it is the suddenness with which it stops. Jazz is nearing its end, and with the failure of jazz, the possibility is that people will return to truly great music. That means that we have to render church music well for those worldlings."

The Catholic crusade for moral movies received his most eager contribution. Often statements were issued, written by him, commenting on the worthiness of the good lessons or condemning the unworthiness of the bad lessons in them. Naturally he did not see all the films, but he relied on the reports furnished him by the Legion of Decency to which he had appointed an overseer in his complete confidence. When the film *Two-faced Woman* appeared, in which Greta Garbo and Melvyn Douglas were starred, he issued what was perhaps his most violent condemnation. To make the effort all the more impressive, he sent it to every parish priest to be read in the churches as a pastoral letter.

"We wish you to make known to your people," the letter addressed to the priests read, "the condemnation of this film which offends not only the moral law but which is an insult to the decent and fair-minded citizens of our city and which tends to the destruction and degradation of the sacred institutions of marriage and the family."

The film had been disapproved by the Legion of Decency because of a double-life motive throughout the plot. Scenes of compromise also brought forth the indignation of the organization.

Born in Ireland, his sentiments naturally were unequivocal for Irish independence after World War I. He followed the vicissitudes of the Irish struggle and was quite disposed to accept the formation of the Irish Free State as the final settlement of what had been known as the question of Ireland. After he returned from Ireland at the very outbreak of the war, he granted numerous interviews on what he found in his native land. These showed that he did not adhere to a narrow viewpoint on Irish aspirations but judged Ireland's modern problems in the light of her relation to her neighbors and the other powers.

"Almost all the young men in Ireland," he asserted in one interview, "are either in the British army or engaged in English defense work. The sympathy of the great majority is with England—first because they are nearer England and secondly because their greatest volume of trade is with England. The future of Ireland is largely dependent on the future of England, for if England would be defeated, Ireland would be at the mercy of the dictators."

Before Pearl Harbor, the hope was often expressed from his pulpit and before numerous gatherings that the United States would find a way to keep out of the war. In keeping with the pronouncements of the popes, Glennon kept to the line that peace rather than war stood unassailed as the hope and aim of the just man. But when we were attacked and had entered with our full weight into the conflict, Glennon summoned his talents and his organizational genius to the muster of the archdiocesan resources, moral and material, for the common aim.

"We are not a military nation," he declared in his first Sunday sermon after Pearl Harbor. "But we are at war. We are not a nation prepared to go to war—no democracy is—and yet we are at war. In a democracy, there has to be so much discussion, an opportunity given to every citizen —for that is the essence of democracy, to express his opinion and we cannot obtain the unity of purpose until the cogent reasons therefor are known. So, when a democracy declares war, it is only the end of much discussion and agitation.

"Churches have a duty in time of war not to promote hatred, racial or otherwise," he went on to say. "Churches should give their moral aid and their physical support to the nation. I am glad to say, yes, to rejoice that the Catholic Church has been and is doing its full duty. It stands in the nation at perhaps twenty per cent, or a little less, of the entire population, but in the ranks of the army, its ratio is thirty per cent of these brave young men who are facing the fortunes of war."

The establishment of the Catholic Church in St. Louis dates from the beginnings of a French colony in 1764, which settled on the east bank of the Mississippi. Swells and floods did far more damage on the east bank, so the colony moved to the west bank. A log church was built and the little colony placed under the patronage of St. Louis, the king. The community grew. The Louisiana Purchase brought it into the United States. It became a part of the vicissitudes of the history of the country in general. In 1826 it was large enough to form a diocese. In 1831 a cathedral was built along the banks of the river at what is now Third and Walnut Streets. By the turn of the century St. Louis had grown to a great metropolis, and the small, albeit historic cathedral was neither spacious enough to administer to the great throngs nor elaborate enough to do honor to the great city that St. Louis had become.

The cry for a new cathedral had arisen. The cry was heard for years. Finally the financial prospects of the archdiocese encouraged Glennon in his fourth year as archbishop to join with the flock for the construction of a new cathedral. This met with an immediate and enthusiastic response. Word went out to build the edifice. People were ready to contribute. Willing consent permeated willing donors. Glennon chose as his architect a St. Louisan, George D. Barnett, though there were contestants for the eagerly coveted job from all over the

United States and from some foreign countries as well. In giving out the simple formula of his specifications, Glennon announced that it was to be an undertaking which would do honor to the Church and the archdiocese.

"We want a million-dollar structure," he said, "that shall not be classic, Gothic, or Renaissance. We hope to have a very large and beautiful structure. Its seating capacity is estimated between four thousand and five thousand. We do not expect to go into debt. It is a bad thing to have a mortgage between you and the Almighty."

The cornerstone was laid on October 18, 1908. Building went on with regulated schedule. Glennon was often seen around the scaffolding in clerical garb and silk hat. At that time he always wore a silk hat. Avid in the great enterprise and anxious that it might meet the extravagant expectations of the most hopeful parishioner, he was insistent on one thing—that the funds for the cathedral should be gathered as the construction proceeded. The official date of completion was October 18, 1914, six years after the cornerstone was laid. Glennon, both in his countenance and his manner, displayed a soul full of satisfaction. What was more, and perhaps the very thing which crowned his happiness—when the Cathedral was opened, everything had been paid for.

"We opened without debt," reported Glennon in joyful mood in a sermon. "We have funds for every contract thus far signed. Today we see a cathedral finished as a building, though much still is left to be done."

Some were there who were critical that the Archbishop had chosen a Byzantine motive in the architectural line of the edifice. It was so foreign to St. Louis, they claimed. He explained his reasons in the same sermon.

"The Gothic spire," he said, "like the prayer offered, goes upward to the skies; the Byzantine, like unto a prayer answered, brings the dome of heaven down to earth. One is a prayer asked, the other a prayer answered. The Gothic tells of northern forests where stately pines go upward unchallenged until pine is joined to pine near the summit, and as you look through the vista as in a Gothic church, the vertical pine tree multiplies itself in every pillar, while up in the roof the branches unite as sure protection against the inclement sky. The Byzantine, on the other hand, takes its first line from the desert where the Baptist preached and the Saviour prayed, and brings to it no other covering save the sky above, under which the Saviour's life was lived and beneath which He agonized and died.

"The Gothic will bring all its light and color from without through its glasses that are stained with the colors of the rainbow and the sunset. The Byzantine will make of all these colors, her own, and set them upon her walls in all the mysticism of the Orient and the brilliant coloring of the southland.

"The Gothic is best when the gray monotone of the north rests upon her every arching line and stately column; but the Byzantine will not be complete until it has set on its walls the luster of every jewel, the bright plumage of every bird, the glow and glory of every metal, the iridescent gleam of every glass. If the diction of the Gothic be more stately, the working of the Byzantine is more varied.

"Its argument is that Christ came to men here on earth in His temple to dwell, and therefore the flowers of the field with fragrance, the birds of the air with their songs, and the children of men with their prayers, shall unite in making His home, in so far as they may, acceptable to Him. Hence the decoration of the Byzantine with its involuted capitals, its delicate arabesques, with its blending of the iris, acanthus and the fleur-de-lis with all the flowers that bloom in the valley or on the hillside, with all the blossoms of May and all the fruits of autumn, with the antlered stag and fabled pelican, with the dove that proclaims innocence, and the peacock, bird of immortality, will call them into being and set them in the splendor of mosaic unity, beckoning them to chant, with the servants of God, His praises and to live in His service, and in so far as possible, speak in their myriad tongues of the earth's subjection to its Lord and Creator.

"Are we not told in the Psalms that the heavens show forth the glory of God and the firmament showeth the work of his hands? And are not fire and snow and the mountains and the trees and the beasts and the cattle and the serpents and the fowls of the air invited to praise the Lord 'for he spoke, and they were made; he commanded, and they were created'? Therefore should not all creation proclaim His power, mercy and love?

"And it is this that Byzantine architecture tries to do when it covers the walls and spandrels and arches with all the color, form and life that nature around it is so prodigal of. Byzantine decoration levies on it all, and with all of them it makes in imperishable mosaic one grand psalm of praise to God."

But while the Cathedral was opened in 1914, the interior had only begun to show the richness that had been intended. When one visits the Cathedral today, it is not an exaggeration to say that its lavish color and form take the breath away. Gold mosaics in profusion enrich its ceilings and arches. Stained-glass windows abundant in color and generous in melodious harmony give a glowing aura to its religious setting. Pillars of rare marbles—red Verona, yellow Sienna, pink Fiori di Pesco, antique green, purple of Brescia, and the golden-black of Oporto intersperse the flowing scene. It is as if each strand of color had set out to outdo the other. Grandeur and abundance is everywhere present, so that one longs to dwell in each niche, chapel, and shrine.

The work of embellishment is still going on. And while Archbishop Glennon had set out to construct an edifice which would cost one million dollars, today its truly precious adornments have increased its present value to eight million dollars. Every cent of debt was paid when each of the multitude of artists had finished his work. Few cathedrals either in the Old World or the New can boast the riches of this Byzantine structure. The one cathedral it resembles most of all is St. Mark's in Venice. It is no idle fancy to conclude that Glennon had St. Mark's in mind when he chose the Byzantine style and adorned it in the manner of St. Mark's on the Venetian lagoons. Its arches, pillars, domes, towers, and mosaics bring to the New World what was unquestionably the best example of Byzantine art in the Old. To Glennon can be attributed the merit of it all.

And while the Cathedral remains as mute testimony to an archbishop's varied and abundant talents, it was not all. He did not neglect the construction of parish churches, of schools, of colleges, of hospitals and other institutions of mercy and charity. He built forty-seven new churches. The ordinary life of a bishop is considered fulfilled if he should consecrate four or five new churches. It was often observed, in and out of Rome, that Glennon in his long and fruitful career had done the work of ten bishops.

His building genius was carried into educational institutions as well. Kenrick Seminary, St. Louis University, St. Louis Preparatory School, Fontbonne College, Webster College, and Maryville College were the product of his organizing skill. When all his works of construction and organization were counted up, they reached a grand total of $30,000,000, which is an impressive figure for any man, whether churchman or philanthropist, to leave to posterity. Before he died, a project was already on his desk for the construction of six new Catholic high schools to cost over two million dollars.

The edifices standing as monuments in rare marbles, artistic friezes and frescoes, stained glass, and mosaics manifest the drive of his spiritual nature. But he left other monuments not of stone but of the virtuous currents he made to course through the civic life in his own midwestern metropolis. The arts and sciences engaged his genuine encouragement. St. Louis had to be made a worthy exemplification of this age. Though the feuds of wicked political manipulators raged about him, he remained impervious to their blandishments and stood boldly for rectitude in the exercise of political power.

St. Louis had become one of the notorious cities in the era of gangsterism. The nefarious schemes of the outlawed perpetrators often took shelter in ecclesiastical asylum. Often the sting of conscience would torture a gangster's soul. If of the faith, he would seek condonation through the church. Glennon openly condemned them and warned that they would suffer the remorse of their deeds without ecclesiastical mitigation. He instructed priests to refuse a Christian burial to those of them struck down in the cold-blooded orgies of which they were the authors. Gangsters regarded him an enemy, but a strangely annihilating spell fell over them when they realized that here was one enemy who could stand unassailable against them, condemning their traffic but impervious to their bullets.

He was gifted with an unusual sense of foreseeing the development of uncharted areas. The course of growth in St. Louis was adroitly divined by him. It is by no means an idle saying to declare that first he built the church and then the population clustered about it.

Monsignor Francis O'Connor, pastor of the Church of Our Lady of Lourdes, was priest in the St. Louis archdiocese before Glennon was transferred from Kansas City. They were about the same age. O'Connor was an assistant pastor in the Cathedral. They became intimate friends. In 1927 the Archbishop invited O'Connor to see him.

"Father," said Glennon when they met, "I am going to give you a parish which does not yet exist."

He took a map of St. Louis and its environs and showed the priest the boundaries of the new parish. It was then beyond the city limits. There were no streets. Only a house here and there may be found. O'Connor took up his new assignment. In the whole district he could collect but four Catholic families. Glennon advanced him $8,000 from archdiocesan building funds, with the instruction that he should first start a school. He found a retired teacher, and a school was organized from the children of the four families. It was after that, and long after, that they should think of building a church.

But they built the church, one of the most beautiful parish churches in St. Louis. Today that church stands in the midst of a wealthy residential section. The rolls of the parish include six hundred Catholic families, while a new school gives instruction to three hundred children. This and many others were examples where Glennon built a church and the people came after. O'Connor still rules the parish with the same laborious tenacity which brought it into being. At eighty-five, erect, wiry, enthusiastic, he displays an energy hardly found in men decades his junior. His speech is firm, his sermons a mark of clarity.

As a token of the love which the vast flock bore the Archbishop, they began naming their sons after him, as if to make "Glennon" both of the family and of the faith. The practice started some thirty-five years ago and showed how his soulful personality had already permeated the hearts of his spiritual wards. On New Year's Day of 1938 he invited all these Glennon namesakes to a party at his house. Eighty of them, ranging in age from mere infants in arms to a man of twenty-nine, came in as the first response. It might have been a problem to many to entertain the varying ages, but the Archbishop had had plenty of experience with humankind, old and young.

The party could not be crashed. Even though parents came with the younger children, they were not asked in. Tots were cared for by the Archbishop himself or by his housekeeper, Catherine Flynn. Besides, rigid exclusiveness required that a boy must have a first or second name "Glennon." And the party was unqualifiedly stag. Ecclesiastical form was set aside. Glennon helped serve the cake, the cookies, the pop, milk, chocolate, candies, and ice cream. An archiepiscopal dispensation condoned any overeating and ignored the intemperance of overdrinking.

He kept a record of all of these boys. They filled out cards telling what they intended to be. Those too young to talk were going to be invited in the later years and then they could make known their selected career. The number of careers was almost equal to the number of boys present. So diverse in station and social position were they that each one chose a different profession, ranging from priest to polo player. Glennon made an annual event out of the New Year's Day party. The last one was held in 1942. At that time a hundred and thirty-five came. From an examination of the cards with other years, the number of Glennon namesakes in the archdiocese had grown to five hundred. Though parents often name children after popular heroes, it is unlikely that any other popular personality ever enjoyed so much adoration expressed in the namesake formula in proportion to his limited territorial jurisdiction.

His keen introspection has been told in no more colorful language than by Miss Flynn, who also was Irish-born. We had a talk after the funeral in St. Louis. Serious, though not without her native wit, short and presently somewhat stocky but sunny just the same, gray but alert to training speed both in body and mind, she had been in service in the Archbishop's house for thirty-eight years, the last twenty-five of which she passed as head housekeeper. During this time her Irish ruggedness of diction had been delightfully blended with a Missouri drawl.

"He could see through a stone wall," declared Miss Flynn with unforgotten Irish imagery describing his shrewd and sagacious intuition. "He knew a man's character before he opened his mouth."

This estimate finds ready acquiescence in all the priests of the archdiocese. Realtors, contractors, architects, sculptors, painters, and businessmen knew this, too. He had always been able to beat them to the punch.

Of her admiration for his buoyant yet paradoxically monastic spirit, this domestic keeper of the keys and guardian of his welfare could not conceive of a better-lived life.

"He was with everybody and yet he was always alone," she recounted. "His life was spent more in solitude than society. It was certainly not because he did not enjoy company. His wit was always the brightest spark of the evening. He was pleasing to all, offensive to none. It was a lifetime's honor for me to serve him. His was a complete life."

Eager in her trust, the laborious matron of the house had waited on every need. She had prepared all the linens for his private chapel and arranged all his vestments for ceremonies both high and low. She had cooked all his meals.

"He ate sparingly," she narrated as she looked back over the years he had enjoyed such vibrant health. "He had a few likes and dislikes. Even at eighty-three he enjoyed a steak or a chop. He was not fond of elaborate desserts, though he ate candy quite often as a substitute."

With a sigh, she paused.

"He always read at night," she continued. "And that is why he knew so much. I doubt whether any man knew more than he. It was this study into the long hours which gave him such command. This is how he became such a master before the multitudes."

A mission had passed out from Miss Flynn's orbit. We can feel the shock, for shock it is. Mourning, truly mourning a soul for whom she held no other bond than to serve him well, it was her only career as she herself saw it.

In meditative mood, she gave her simple total of his life.

"God created him perfect," she claimed. "Only once in five hundred years do we see a perfect man. Archbishop Glennon was the one of our time."

St. Louis had despaired that their revered chief pastor would ever become a cardinal. In their minds they believed that the personality of the man should outweigh the bigness of New York, the importance of Chicago, or the rotarian claims of other large cities. They thought of

Glennon much in the same terms as Miss Flynn. There could be no archbishop like him. He had been an archbishop longer than any of the aspirants from larger cities. He had built up a strong archdiocese. He had become a national figure and a chief citizen in St. Louis itself.

Glennon himself cherished no vain ambition in desiring red robes. I talked with him when he was seventy-seven. At that age he was an active, vital worker taking on the management of the churches and institutions under his care with the same energy that he possessed ten or fifteen years earlier. More from the physical strength he enjoyed and the mental alertness he then displayed, he never envisaged giving up work. Strangely enough, we talked about a too early retirement and not about red robes. He never thought of them.

"I think men who retire at sixty or sixty-five are withdrawing when they could be of very useful service," he mused. "They have stored up a reservoir of rich experience and could use this experience for far greater good than ever before in their lives. I notice how many important persons write memoirs when they are forty or fifty. What memoirs have they got to write when they have only passed the halfway mark?"

Then, blossoming out in a smile, he barely uncovered what perhaps was the aim in his own life.

"The time to write memoirs," he said, "is when one has reached a hundred—at least."

Glennon expressed a similar thought to Monsignor O'Connor, his lifelong friend.

Late in 1945, when they had both reached their eighty-fourth year, they were complimenting each other on their common longevity and mutual state of enthusiastic activity.

"Father," said Glennon to O'Connor, "you and I have

worked together for a long time—forty-three years. We are now in our eighty-fourth year. There is no reason why both of us should not live for at least another twenty years."

It was on the morning of the day before Christmas, 1945, that James A. Farley telephoned to Archbishop Glennon that he had been nominated a cardinal. It was seven A.M. in St. Louis. Glennon was surprised and even taken aback, because now, in his mid-eighties, he did not expect the promotion. Joy coursed through his spirit. To be raised to the highest honor when that honor had seemed to be outside of his aspirations almost overcame him with both astonishment and gladness. Ruminating on his age in relation to a journey to Rome in midwinter, he played with the thought that he would send Monsignor John P. Cody, his closest ecclesiastical associate and chancellor of the archdiocese, to Rome to bring back the red hat for him. Friends persuaded him that he should go to Rome. He could stop in Ireland on the way, too, they said. He decided to fly there with Archbishop Spellman.

Cody he chose to accompany him. Cody was really an *alter ego*. He was only thirty-eight, but he had risen to his post through the merit of knowing what to do and how to do it. It is said that in choosing him for the chancellorship, the Archbishop knew what a live man he was. Cody was born in St. Louis. The archdiocese was home to him. He was educated in Rome and for a time was assistant to the rector of the North American College there. He had been another bright man who finished his theological training before the minimum age to be ordained, and he had obtained a dispensation from Pius XI. For a while, too, he worked in the Vatican secretariat of state.

When he returned to St. Louis, Glennon picked him to

be his secretary. Smiling, affable, and efficient, he made a trip to Europe with the Archbishop in 1939. The war broke out while they were in Dublin. Throughout he had shown how to travel with high ecclesiastical personages. He knew what they should wear, say, and do. The appointments they were required to make were all second nature to Cody. Now that he had been chosen by the Archbishop to accompany him to Rome, his knowledge fitted the occasion. The vestments were all ordered by Cody, even down to the last detail. The schedule was fixed by him. The visits the new cardinal was required to make were listed by this untiring chancellor. Glennon admitted that he never made a mistake.

Accompanied by this faithful factotum and Commodore MacMahon, his personal physician, Glennon reached New York on February 11, to join the cardinalatial coterie traveling in the two planes.

We traveled to Ireland. All the way, Glennon's buoyancy kept bubbling. His step was brisk. His eyes were bright, his spirit high. He was in perfect health. High honors were showered on him by the people of his native land. He was to have stayed there two days to complete the tokens of regard which the people and government were to bestow on him. But a change of plans required that he stay but one day and then drop in on his return trip for a state banquet which would be tendered him by the Irish government in Dublin after he had been created a cardinal. And so, with one day's stay, we continued on our trip to Rome.

As he boarded the plane at the Shannon airport, an unusually attractive stewardess, prim in her smartly designed uniform and beautified by both natural endowment and her own supplementary artifices, welcomed him and said how glad she was to see him back.

"And Archbishop Glennon," she smirked in an eager sense of accommodation, "I've saved your old seat for you."

The tall, smiling, ascetic prelate looked down upon her face, his eighty-three years giving dignity to his pose.

"Miss," he said in one of his light veins, "I presume that that is quite correct. I believe that that is what one should call it."

It took a moment. Then she burst into laughter.

Arriving in Paris, he looked out through a window of the plane. He turned immediately to announce to us all with great enthusiasm what he had seen.

"There are thousands waiting to see us," he said excitedly.

I happened to be right at his side. I bent down to look out of the window.

"Thousands?" I said almost as if I had been a certified public accountant.

He looked at me with some surprise, but he kept up the enthusiasm.

"One thousand anyway," he said in a that-will-do-for-you mood.

We arrived in Rome on February 14. He was tired but he was in good spirits. He ate with the rest of the party. The usual acts of courtesy on arrival in Rome he performed without any physical hardship. But on the following Saturday he caught a cold. Almost all of us caught colds—four out of five, as I said. That cold dogged him throughout the stay and gave him many unpleasant hours, fight it off as he would.

On February 18, Glennon was at his place in a row of four thrones in the elaborate medieval palace of the chancellery. Mooney, Stritch, and Spellman were at the others. He was arrayed in his archiepiscopal robes of purple. He sat there complacently. Batteries of press and motion-picture cameras were concentrated on the four neo-cardinals. He sat on the extreme right because he was senior to them, senior to them all because he had been forty-one years an archbishop while the next in rank was Mooney, who had been an archbishop but a scant sixteen years. Bishops, monsignors, priests, and laymen of distinction filled the room.

Presently a messenger arrived from the Vatican. He was admitted and walked directly to Glennon. He announced his name and official position.

"Excellency," he said, "His Excellency the Assistant Secretary of State has instructed me to carry to Your Excellency this *biglietto.*"

The *biglietto* was in an envelope. It was opened and its contents read. It was the usual brief formula:

"The Holy Father has been pleased to create you a cardinal in the Holy Roman Church."

Then the messenger, after the reading of the *biglietto,* was the first to address Glennon. He was the first to address him as a cardinal, adhering strictly to protocol.

"Your Eminence," he said, "I bring you the congratulations and felicitations of His Excellency the Assistant Secretary of State for the great honor which has been conferred upon you."

This was at eleven o'clock on a Monday morning. Glennon, who had built a huge cathedral, constructed forty-seven new churches, erected schools and colleges, and ordained 4,700 priests, finally at the age of eighty-three received the highest honor of the Church. The hopes of all the faithful in his charge had been fulfilled. At that moment he became a member of the Sacred College of Cardinals and from that moment on would sit in council as one of the chief advisers of the Pope.

The ceremonies and the heavy array of etiquette when a cardinal is created were surmounted quite masterfully. I watched him at each function. His erect figure performed the symbolic ritual with an air of dignity and of grace which would have done credit to men decades his junior. I was impressed with his steady step when he approached the papal throne. He genuflected three times and did it with the flourish of a young priest. Others far less aged than he needed assistance to complete the rite.

His humor was present whenever occasion bestowed an opening. He was standing beside Cardinal von Galen in the reception which the Pope had tendered the Sacred College. As the Pope approached him, he was ready to speak.

"Here we are, Holy Father," he said with his face alight with joy. "Von Galen and I are standing up for you like two cedars of Lebanon."

When he took possession of the church in Rome which he was by tradition to administer as part of his office, he wore his red robes for the first time. Seated on the throne behind the altar and viewed from the back of the church, he appeared like some benevolent though powerful patriarch. He spoke over the radio for his people in St. Louis. His voice was strong and reached all parts of the ancient edifice.

Meanwhile he conducted his own correspondence. He ate his meals in the public dining room of the hotel. But his cold dragged on. The weather was bleak. Seldom did the Mediterranean sun come out. The climate was not propitious for throwing off a cold. He attended receptions and held receptions himself. Many of these could have been dispensed with, but he felt in good enough health to carry on in his accustomed vitality. He did carry on.

When all the pomp and fuss was over, he still had that

rendezvous with the Irish Free State, since he had promised to be guest of honor at a state dinner on his return
trip. Accordingly he flew with his untiring Cody and
Commodore MacMahon to Ireland to fulfill the promise.
He arrived at the Shannon airport on Monday, March 4,
and continued by air to Dublin with Prime Minister De
Valera. He knew Ireland so well that he was able to point
out various landmarks to the Irish premier in his own
country. In Dublin he was the guest of the president of
the Irish Free State, Sean Te O'Kelley.

But on that very first day in Dublin, Cody noticed that
there was evident lack of spring and vitality in the actions
of the Cardinal. He consulted MacMahon. They decided
to ask him to slow down to save his strength. That evening was the state dinner. Cody, anxious to restore him to
his usual vim for the trip home, found a formula to keep
him seated while he addressed the dinner.

"Your Eminence," Cody pleaded with him privately,
"you should take it easy now. You don't have to stand up
to talk. It is correct protocol that you as a cardinal remain
seated."

"Oh," replied Glennon, "that is all very well, but these
Irish friends of mine, they don't know anything about
your protocol."

Undismayed, Cody then went to President O'Kelley, who
was to preside, and begged him when he introduced Glennon to insist that he enjoy the prerogative of his rank by
remaining seated during his address. Kelley agreed.

When the time came to introduce the Cardinal, O'Kelley
lavished a variety of generous sentences on the accomplishments of the Irish native son. But he did not forget
his promise to Cody. Concluding the presentation, he
rose to official heights while keeping a deferent mien to
say:

"As President of Eire, I insist that His Eminence remain seated while he talks to us."

Smiling, Glennon obeyed the presidential order.

"Friends," the Cardinal mused in a colloquial and easy manner, "we have just fought a war against dictators. Though we have won that war, we still have the dictators. Here I am told that I must sit down, even though I desire to stand up."

This brought great laughter from the assembled Irish officials and prelates. They were captivated by Glennon's flowing phrase.

"I am not going to say very much," he continued, "because I have a cold. It is a cold which has lasted a long time. It is like the Roman faith—deep-rooted."

This produced another wave of hilarious applause.

"Instead of making a speech," he went on in his graceful style, "I am going to introduce two young men who have been with me all along on the trip. The first is Monsignor Cody, who is supposed to be one of these experts in protocol. I will say that so far he has kept me out of trouble and perhaps can tell you, if he wishes, how he has done it."

The audience was joyous.

"And the second young man is Commodore Mac-Mahon," Glennon recounted. "He is my personal physician. Perhaps he can tell you how he has succeeded in making this cold last so long."

The audience applauded. Glennon rose and the banqueters rose with him. He bowed. Saluted by President O'Kelley and accompanied by Cody, he left the hall, to retire to his room. Cody returned to comply with the Cardinal's request for a speech. He thanked the Irish Free State on behalf of the Cardinal for the devotion they had shown him, and concluded by hoping that it would not be the last time. Commodore MacMahon also was brief and finished his address in a similar vein.

Cody was somewhat apprehensive about the Cardinal's obvious inability to throw off the cold. And though his spirit was down, his wit was up. The Monsignor suggested that since they did not have much to do, he stay in bed most of the time. There was a diplomatic reception Tuesday. He got up and attended the reception. In the evening his ecclesiastical *alter ego* again suggested that he stay in bed all day Wednesday and remain in Dublin for five days to take a rest.

Glennon looked at Cody in a benign way. He held great affection for Cody, but he just wondered whether this had some ulterior, albeit efficacious motive back of it. He had a slight suspicion that Cody was some kind of spokesman for the Irish government officials.

"Monsignor," said the Cardinal to Cody, "does this plan to stay five days mean a *motu proprio* of yours, or do you have any promoters back of you?"

President O'Kelley was in the room at the time. He spoke up and said that indeed Cody had "promoters" and that the whole of the Irish government wanted to give him a rest so that he could continue on to St. Louis in real high spirits. On that basis Glennon decided to take the rest.

On Wednesday, after all, Cody succeeded with gentle persuasion in keeping him in bed. But there was definitely no pickup in his condition. MacMahon still thought that he would throw off the cold. He prescribed some pills which Glennon only reluctantly took. And though not himself at all, the Cardinal still kept up his humor. This was an attribute which coursed through him even though his physical state was more than a little abused.

Two nuns were waiting on him. One of them suggested

that it would make everybody happy over there if he decided to remain in Ireland.

"I don't belong in Rome, nor to Dublin, nor to Ireland," he hastened to reply, lifting up his head and looking straight at the devoted sister who made the suggestion.

"I belong in St. Louis," he affirmed with a certain emphasis. "And back there I'll go, dead or alive."

That evening it was noticeable that uremia had set in. Cody knew that "anything could happen" now. He had carried a phial of holy oils. With heavy heart, but still with unrestrained hope, he anointed his beloved and revered superior. During the night, the great cardinal passed into a coma. Cody took his hand and spoke to him.

"Eminence," he said, "it is Monsignor Cody. Do you hear me? How are you?"

"All right," replied the Cardinal with labored breath but with a strength which he seemed to have mustered for the one final act. "All right, and how are you?"

These were his last words. He expired at nine o'clock on Saturday morning, March 9.

When the news reached St. Louis, the mourning was widespread and deep. He left a will with personal property valued only at $325.07. In trust, he left a monument —thirty million dollars' worth of property for the aims of worship, of charity and education. He left uncounted riches in the spirit and heart of St. Louis itself.

13. One out of Them

ONE cardinal in my experience has risen above them all. He is Eugenio Pacelli, born in Rome in 1876.

Providence prevised his life. The touch with humankind was so spaced that by the time he was called for his master role—that of setting right the present raveled miscellany of man's indiscretions—he was ready. He was born not of the well-to-do but of rigidly disciplined stock and respectably fixed. His childhood was lived in the atmosphere that surrounds those who must earn all that they have. He was not given any special rights but had to take his chances in the combative give-and-take of the other boys. His education was derived from no swank school. He went to college. Scholarship was one of his talents.

The priesthood beckoned to him. He accepted the call. Studies in the ecclesiastical knowledges absorbed his mental and spiritual propensities. He was good enough to become a professor. The Vatican Chancellery thought so well of him that he was assigned a duty reserved only for the intellectually skillful. Leo XIII asked him to become a diplomat. Pius X made it possible for him to meet kings and emperors while still in his youth. At forty he was assigned by Benedict XV to the task of making peace while World War I raged in its maddest fury—1917. The Germans thought his proposals pro-Ally; the Allies thought them pro-German. At fifty-three he became a cardinal. As we hinted, he went on from there. At sixty-two he became pope. He is Pius XII.

Surveying his ramiform career, we behold how he passed through the world's travail to learn about it first and at first hand, too. The tremendous climax in the world's course was in his youth and early manhood gathering its contrasting currents, which were to involve it in chaotic catastrophe. His post of duty placed him right in among the whirling winds of hostile omen. To none of the other statesmen of today was given the privileged lot of seeing and being in the midst of the forces which have brought the world to its present confusion.

His life divides itself into two concepts of duty. The first was when, in the long years of preparation for the gathering crescendo of human wrath, he had served and obeyed. The second found him in the post of command. When he served, he submitted with all his ready eagerness to accomplish what he was assigned. Work had been no deterrent to duty. Even when he became a cardinal, he still served and obeyed. Reaching the pontificate, he assumed the responsibility of direction with a strength of will inherent in a world navigator.

When all the schooling was done and he had answered the call to join the Vatican diplomatic service, his touch with the men who were charting the courses of nations began. He was but twenty-six when he was chosen by Merry del Val to accompany him as secretary to London. The lithe and agile cardinal with the aristocratic bearing was the Pope's legate to carry the papal condolences to King Edward VII on the death of his mother, Queen Victoria. All the kings of the world of those days were there. The great statesmen from East and West attended the funeral. Eugenio Pacelli saw the men and rulers who held the destiny of nations in their hands. With some he talked.

Returning to his working job in Rome, he mingled more in the currents. For one so young, the fortune of being able to get the feel of the controls which regulate the relations of peoples reinforced his youthful will to know and to understand the likes and dislikes which either bind or separate. What made one nation hate another he learned as if by rote. He acquired a mental catalogue of those who loved and those who detested. The state of animosity of the one for the other sowed the seeds of conflict. He learned this. He learned which ones would fight.

Then when he was thirty-two, "Merry" asked him to go again to London as secretary. This time the ravishing London-born Spaniard had been chosen by Pius X to be the papal legate to the Eucharistic Congress of Great Britain. He was the guest of the Duke of Norfolk, the highest ranking Catholic in England. He stayed in the Duke's mansion at St. James Square. And so did his secretary. Such entree put him on the fringe of the great.

And still a third time the welcome invitation came to go to London, and again it was on a great occasion. This was in 1910. On the recommendation of the amiable "Merry," he was chosen by Cardinal Granito Pignatelli di Belmonte, who, as we cited, is at ninety-five the present dean of the Sacred College of Cardinals, to be his secretary. The occasion was the coronation of King George V. If there were any rulers or statesmen he had not seen in his first and second visits to London, he certainly saw them now. This was the last great royal assemblage before World War I.

Studious as he was, Eugenio Pacelli sought deeply into

the history, traits, accomplishments, rule, and religion of
the British people. He learned to cast the diagram of
Britain's course through the centuries to its imperial apex.
He knew its military power. It was a study for one who
was concerned with the grand turns and twists of international life. What would they all do—Britain, France, Germany, Russia, Italy, and Austria? They were even then
choosing sides. It was fortuitous to have learned of Britain then. It was knowledge which was basic all of his life.

The not so strange line-up of powers for World War I,
as we see it with hindsight wisdom today, posed Germany
against England. The war was on. Now it was the turn
of Eugenio Pacelli to learn about Germany. He was entrusted with a mission usually assigned only to men of
long years of international dealing. Yes, he was sent by
Benedict XV at forty to make the peace of the world.
This was verily a touch of the controls. This was a close-
up in world relationships. He was the key man.

No record in youth was established when he went to
argue with the German chancellor about ending the war
and making the peace. We know of Napoleon, Thomas
Jefferson, and others who did world-shaking things when
they were younger. But that Eugenio Pacelli should try
to arrange the affairs of nations at forty spaced his life in
its relation to what was to come later on. Nothing could
have given him greater assurance of the part he was to
play in world affairs than having to persuade Count von
Bethman-Hollweg that the powerful German forces
should be withdrawn from the fight. And what is more
conclusive for his own self-confidence, he *did* convince this
German chancellor that the proposals he brought from
Pope Benedict were a firm basis for peace. He struck a
snag in the Kaiser, who was so fixed on victory regardless

of bloodshed that he refused to heed. He it was who called the proposals pro-Ally.

Now, Pacelli was to stay on in Germany as the Pope's representative. He saw the Germans at war. He learned the German avidity for war. Even then, they used to tell him of the superiority of the race. Their culture could impress him but not their cults—of battle, race mastery, and world subjugation. He was there early enough to witness them at the peak of their power. Their smashing offensive of March 1918, which seemed in its early crushing power to assure them conquest, impressed and shook him. Then he saw them after their black Friday in the following July preparing to ward off the haunting nightmare of collapse. In one year, he had seen them descend from the haughty pinnacle of pride to the dread gutter of ignominious defeat.

When the fell blow came, the ties which had held the vainglorious nation together snapped. Authority vanished, confusion set in and then exploded in chaos. In this dire degradation of a state endowed with potential greatness, Pacelli witnessed the abject calamity that greed and national expansion brought on. Anarchy, massacres, starvation, poverty, and disease were the returns of the massive national effort bent on vassalage for free peoples.

To say that he learned of it first hand would only imply that he was an interested or disinterested bystander. Instead, he was part of the hopeless disorder into which the German nation had been thrown. Subversives in military groupings actually attacked the legation of the Holy See.* They entered the building and commanded him to deliver all he had—food, money, jewels, everything. He stood his ground and refused. His life was threatened. Still he

* *The Listening Post*, G. P. Putnam's Sons, 1944.

held his ground. Dressed in his archiepiscopal robes, he ordered the marauders to withdraw by telling them they were on extraterritorial ground. His firmness combined with more than a modicum of tact forced the assailants to leave the building. He could not meet rifles with revolvers because he had none. He used the only weapon he had —skilled diplomacy. It was but one incident in the melee of disorder sweeping the German domain. But he won his. Closer to real lawlessness he could not come—and live.

Still as the representative of the Pope in Germany, Pacelli stayed on in that continuing period of unrest—of *Putsch* and riot, of rebellion incurred by poverty and defeat. The melancholy effect of chaotic inflation, the quarrel over reparations, and the final refusal to pay any at all were major events in the career which destiny was shaping for him. The melange of German trouble operating on a proud and defiant people gave him insight into how the nation was likely to react in almost any given circumstance.

That he had in his early years cultivated a touch with Britain and that now from 1917 to 1930 he had been steadily engrossed in the learning of what the Germans were like made him of effective value in the diplomatic service of the Holy See. They were the two powers on which the burden and hardship of another war would fall. They would be the leaders of the two sides. It was plain to many that the Germans silently and cunningly were seeking revenge. That revenge was meant for England. The weight of their destructive potential, if ever they could again muster it, would be thrown against the power which had been intent on keeping her in her place.

His career in Germany had evolved into a perfect mission so far as the Pope was concerned. Pius XI had got to know Pacelli through his thoroughness, his knowledge of international crosscurrents, his judgment, and his analysis. Promotion must be his reward. In 1930 the Pontiff called him to Rome to create him a cardinal. He also needed a new secretary of state because Gasparri was then over eighty and had asked to be relieved. With his knowledge of the latent hates and hopes in the international atmosphere, and out of the array of profound intellects which cluster about the Vatican chancellery, Pacelli stood above the rest. He was called to be secretary of state at fifty-four with an experience in the field that few Vatican diplomats ever achieved in their restricted spheres of diplomatic approach. He had truly been on the firing line. He knew the rebel as well as the king.

Finally, the muddled and complex combination of adverse forces in Germany exploded. Strong movements and organizations were scattered by the blow. The government itself was unable to resist the devouring convulsion. It fell, defeated. From the remnants, one single, compact, ruthless, and arrogant group remained intact. In the disintegration and confusion of all the rest, the tyrannical autocracy of Nazism emerged to take command. Hitler assumed the dictatorial rule of all the Germans. From Rome Pacelli recognized the phenomenon in all of its repressive terror. He knew its influence on the mass. He knew who the Nazis were and what they intended to do. Now and later, it would be his own task to tell them boldly their duty to humankind.

When Hitler came to power, men did not recognize the dark forebodings. Many regarded him as of passing duration. Germany had been isolated and, for that reason, very few indeed looked for a nation that could challenge the world. Subterfuges were found in arguments that what the Germans did about their internal affairs was their own business. The way German strength was built up stands now as an unbelievable accomplishment, but it was built up—from practically a deficit economy.

In religion, the Nazi regime was disposed at first to accept adherents from every faith. They welcomed pastors and priests if they would liken the words of Christ to the words of Hitler. But what is more, in their early days the Nazis needed the strength of religion. They rejoiced in approval because they were then but building up their own strength. Accordingly, they made a concordat with Pacelli whereby they would allow absolute freedom of worship and religious education for Catholics. This they did to obtain the support of the bishops and clergy.

But when they had gathered momentum in their own numbers, they defied the Church and repudiated the signed agreement. Pacelli urged all the bishops to hold fast and insist on the rights which Hitler had signed to bestow. But, as Nazi strength increased, respect for the signed word decreased. In the end, the Church was left without protection. Priests were thrown into concentration camps for performing the rites and for things they had said. The Church underwent a terror akin to that of pagan rulers. The Nazis attempted to set up a cult to destroy the faith in Christ.

In these gathering omens of gloom, it will redound to the acute vision of Pius XI, then nearing his eightieth year, that he was preparing for one to follow him. The Cardinal Secretary of State had lived his life in the midst of the forces which were then mustering their resources for a show of strength. It is now no secret that the aging Pontiff had picked Pacelli to be his successor. The times threatened the dread disaster. He wanted—not for his own sake but for the sake of the world and the Church—

one whom he regarded as worthy to be there to take his place.

It was not in his power to decree the succession to Pacelli. Nevertheless, he determined to present to the Sacred College of Cardinals a candidate for the throne of Peter who would lead the Church with directness and breadth through the clouded horizon of unhappy foreboding. He could only prepare his successor. He could not name him. The furthest he could go was to tell the members of the Sacred College that Pacelli was worthy. This he formally did from the throne, recommending him for his talents, his gifts of judgment, and his firm devotion to the faith. Then it was entirely in the hands of the cardinals after his death.

Accordingly, he sought to increase the world knowledge of this cardinal who had spent much time in England and still more time in Germany. He appointed him papal legate to the Eucharistic Congress of France so that he could feel the pulse of the French government, its clergy, and its people. When the International Eucharistic Congress was held in Budapest, Hungary, Pacelli was the legate. Here pilgrims from another world, as it were, attended. Here he saw many of the adherents of the faith from diverse cultures and territories.

Then in 1934 the grand tour of enrichment by contact with new peoples and customs came when he was chosen to be the Pope's personal representative in the congress at Buenos Aires. This grew to the proportions of a triumphal tour. The visit of a sovereign could not have been more elaborate. On the return journey he was received in Montevideo and then at Rio de Janeiro with the acclaim of a king. This gave him the feel of another continent.

The pontifical tutelage would not have been complete without a visit to North America, too. In 1936 the Pontiff gave him permission to make a trip to the United States. Accompanied by Cardinal Spellman, who was then a bishop, he traveled by plane from one end of the country to the other, visiting churches, colleges, and institutions and talking with professors, students, laymen, and their pastors. He had lunch with President Roosevelt at Hyde Park.

When Pius XI died in February 1939 the cardinals met. In the balloting for the next pope, Pacelli received the unanimous call of his colleagues. One vote had been registered against him and that was his own. He was elected. He was Pius XII.

And while he had scrupulously served his call in those formative years of secretary, diplomat, and cardinal, he had now become the master. Men there are who make of themselves ready subordinates, who know the joy of following the prescriptions laid down for them. It has often happened that those who take orders well are not able to give orders well. Sometimes the pupil rises beyond the achievements of his master. More often the master remains at the summit of his craft.

Pius XI had shown himself a supreme master. But, throughout his early life, command had never been a duty. He had been a librarian. No one knew that he *could* command. When he became pope this hidden talent emerged. He was able to bind the forces of the Church into one compact whole serving one common faith and obeying a common father. Strength in his authority coursed through the nerve centers in the complex network of hierarchical and lay relations.

Under such a strong master, the assertiveness of Pius XII might well have been diluted. But on the day that

he assumed the prerogatives of supreme pontiff he surveyed his field. He had caught the democratic spirit of
this age to an extent undreamed by any Roman prelate
even a decade ago, precedent notwithstanding.

Hardly had the tiara been placed upon his head than
the sounds of prebattle alertness began to disturb a world
of peace. And it *was* the year of war. He had only been
pontiff six months when Hitler invaded Poland. Now
that the catastrophe was upon mankind, the Pope who
had had his contact with high and low could but try to
stop its macabre effects from involving a world. But the
avarice of the conquerer extended beyond even Europe—
to Africa, to Asia, and to America. The conflict took its
awful course, and all the world was involved. The lines
of combat were strictly drawn between those who believed
in the rights of mankind and those who denied those
rights.

When Rome was eventually liberated, alone and without police escort the Pope stepped out to talk to the Roman crowd, whose language he knew even to the most
folksy phrases. This was an adventuresome step for a
Roman pontiff, whose person is cherished with divine
reverence. He received the crowds even in the Vatican
palaces and there stepped down from the throne to mingle
with them. He went among the Allied newsmen, allow-
ing them to take candid photo shots—a supreme test of
condoning patience as well as a democratic gesture.

I noticed how he circulated among the people in the
great gatherings in St. Peter's and other shrines. The
police charged with the safety of his person spend anxious
hours whenever he appears in public lest he descend
among the crowd and risk injury at the hands of an over-
expressive populace.

It is not without significance that it was during this

pontificate that the Pontifical Academy of Noble Ecclesiastics, which formerly recruited only students of noble birth to train for the diplomatic service of the Holy See, became open to students of all classes of society. The name has even been changed. The aristocratic tint is removed. Now it is just "the Pontifical Academy."

He revealed his own mastery of movements and events by his pronouncements on the democratic concept. It has always been the policy of the Roman Church never to interfere with a specific form of government. The Holy See has dealt with monarchies and republics on the same basis. But in his address to the Sacred College of Cardinals on Christmas of 1945 Pius XII established it as a Catholic principle that the rights of the people as the components of the state stand higher than the rights of rulers. This is the essence of the American form, which in the words of the Declaration of Independence says that "governments derive their just powers from the consent of the governed."

The issues on which this war was fought were strictly defined by the Western powers. Pius XII has come out unequivocally for the establishment of those issues. President Roosevelt had epigrammatically crystallized them in his Four Freedoms. The position of the papacy under Pius XII is more extensive in its application of the free principle. He has shown it in his person, by deed and word.

The long succession of ceremonies creating the cardinals in February 1946 exalted the Roman Pontiff high on his throne of apostolic authority. For me, while the event in its world-wide and historic significance surpassed all previous consistories, almost on an equal plane of impressive importance was the democratic bearing of Pius XII. He was abreast of the currents sweeping through the world. Never before had I witnessed such easy companionship as this pope exhibited in receiving his spiritual subjects.

This magnanimous openheartedness was poured out from the very first ceremony. He spontaneously left the throne and personally passed among the new cardinals to shake each by the hand and embrace him as an elder brother. Even more striking than this fraternal affection was the reception he offered for them with the diplomats. The United States was represented by Franklin Gowen in the absence of Myron Taylor, who was ill in America. The four new American cardinals were there.

Definitely parting company with rigid papal protocol, Pius XII eschewed the sitting posture. He stood up and mingled with cardinals and diplomats as a genial host. He went even further. He decided to give each one present a huge bronze medal commemorative of the occasion. These he handed out, passing from one to another, talking with each one, asking them about relatives and friends, as if it had been a human family reunion as well as a spiritual one.

This democratic propensity of Pius XII was brought to even more expansive expression when he received the New York pilgrimage which had accompanied Cardinal Spellman. Between sixty and seventy persons made up this entourage. The Pontiff received them all in his library, though the library had only been reserved for the most intimate conversations by preceding popes. Each New York visitor was presented by Spellman. The Pope stood up all the time. Never had I seen such facile munificence in the Pope's own living room.

Much to-do had been made about what should be worn. The women came in black high-necked dresses with black veils. The men, if they adhered to papal etiquette, should have worn full evening dress. Farley, Walker, Macdonald, Gillespie, Morissey, and others were impeccably outfitted. There were a score of newsmen and photographers. From us, one could expect the bizarre without intent of disrespect. A lone photographer appeared in a fuzzy tweed suit of vociferous gray. This was not so much to emphasize his incongruity as to enable him to run off early with his pictures. He could run better in tweed. For good measure, he had donned a dark blue shirt with vivid stripes. The Pope received him with at least as much warm generosity as those arrayed in sartorial impeccability.

And more impelling than the journalistic indiscretion was the patience which Pius XII exhibited in the welcome of the pilgrims. Though his tall presence and ascetic countenance created a spiritual aura, he talked with everybody. Everyone had brought quantities of religious objects to be blessed. Many were so overloaded that only with difficulty were they able to genuflect and kiss the ring. He counted this as a symbol of their devotion to the faith and to their loved ones. Again he gave everyone a present—either a rosary or a medal. Some of the newsmen were not Catholics. They profited by papal beneficence just the same.

Still further did these evidences of democratic largess appear in the general concept of how the great mass of people should share in the doings at Vatican City through the press, radio, and motion pictures. Not so long ago the press was a somewhat shunned institution at the papal court. Radio reporters and moviemen were not allowed at all. More openheartedness has been successively appearing under the more recent pontificates. Now the press is accorded honors which hitherto had only been reserved for kings and queens. And while this may seem pert on our part, it is one of those true words spoken in jest.

Two elaborate loges grace the Hall of Benedictions— one on the left side of the papal throne and the other on the right. On such occasions as the creation of cardinals I have seen nothing but royal personages and men of high estate occupying these loges, sometimes with their wives. I saw the late king of Spain there once. At another time I beheld the former king of Italy, Victor Emmanuel III. Men in elaborate uniforms and women with impressive black veils and gowns always filled these regal tribunes.

At this part of the consistory, it was as if royalty had been uninvited if not totally ignored. Indeed, occupying these royal boxes were the dashing, scribbling, fidgety, and cocksure newsmen with their colleagues, the photographers, moviemen, and radio reporters. Galaxies of machines stuck out indiscriminately in these former royal enclosures. During the ceremony bulbs exploded with somewhat carefree frequency. What a day, I thought, as I sat there where kings before had sat. Actually on the right hand was the Holy Father on his throne. What a day when the reporters took the place of kings! We had to tell the public everywhere all about it—in the press, on the newsreel, over the radio. That day we were truly the representatives of the great world public.

This was another symbol of the democratic soul of Pius XII. He is a democratic pope.

Index